PFS

Your key to financial success.

CONTROL

Your Personal Finances

A Practical Guide to Wealth Accumulation, Wise Use of Credit, and Investment Decision Making in Seven Easy Lessons

Elindoro S. Rodriguez II

PERSONAL FINANCE SOLUTIONS

PFS

Canadian Cataloguing in Publication Data

Rodriguez, Elindoro II S. (Elindoro II Suarez), 1954–
Control your personal finances: a practical guide to decision making in seven easy lessons

Includes bibliographical references and index.

ISBN 0-9684524-0-X

1. Finance, Personal. 2. Consumer credit. 3. Investments. I. Title

HG179.R627 1999 332.024 C98-932963-1

PFS

Published by:
Personal Finance Solutions
2025 Guelph Line, Suite 236
Burlington, Ontario L7P 4X4
Canada

Phone No. (905) 331-0200
Fax No. (905) 331-0244

Cover and interior design by Gilda Mekler
Edited by Gilda Mekler
Cover Film by SE Graphics
Printing by Transcontinental Printing Inc.

This book is dedicated to my wife, Letty, and my children, Angie and Leo (Elindoro M. Rodriguez IV), to Nanay Adeling, and in memory of Tatay Leony (Elindoro J. Rodriguez). As well, this book is for every group of young people entering the workforce each year that they may understand the importance of learning the fundamentals of personal finance as they start to take responsibility for their financial future. And finally, to you, the reader. You have taken the first step towards controlling your personal finances. Continue the journey, and good luck.

AUTHOR'S FOREWORD

Like many people, I've recently come to realize how important a secure financial future is to me. I set out to keep track of my retirement fund, using a scientific calculator and mathematical equations readily available from standard business textbooks. Well, I managed to perform this task, but it was cumbersome working with the scientific calculator.

Luck came to me one day when I chanced upon a financial calculator. It became so much easier to do my retirement fund calculations ... as well as for loans and mortgages and other applications. This experience convinced me that anyone with the interest could be guided to understand the fundamentals of personal finance. The financial calculator will be an indispensable tool in speeding up the learning process.

Since I've been in the process control field for almost twenty years, it was only natural to extend the controls methodology to personal finance. In any field, you can exercise effective control only when you fully understand your process. Thus, when you know the fundamentals of personal finance, you can make intelligent decisions, thereby creating a finer financial future for yourself. This belief was my starting point in writing this book. It's taken more than three years to produce.

Now I would like to share with you, in an easily understood format, the fundamentals of personal finance and its very important applications: implementing a savings plan, loans and mortgages, planning for the children's education, planning for retirement, and investment decision making.

E. S. Rodriguez II

ACKNOWLEDGEMENT

The topics covered here have been covered before in several textbooks. My contribution with this book is that I compiled, organized and presented them in an easy-to-understand format. As Sir Isaac Newton once said in a letter to Robert Hooke (February 5, 1675), "If I have seen farther it is by standing upon the shoulders of giants." Thus, I would like to thank all the practitioners in the field of personal finance who have come before me, who have contributed so much to the field and have made my work easier.

Thank you to Gilda Mekler of Mekler & Deahl, Publishers for editing the manuscript and for the page and cover design.

WARNING — DISCLAIMER

This book provides information on the fundamentals of personal finance. Every effort has been made to make it comprehensive and accurate. There could, however, be mistakes, both typographical and in content. Thus, this book should be used only as a guide and not as the ultimate source on personal finance. It should complement, augment, and amplify the numerous textbooks already available in this field. The services of a competent expert or professional should be sought when making personal finance decisions.

The author and Personal Finance Solutions shall have neither liability nor responsibility to any person or entity in regards to any loss or damage caused, or alleged to be caused, directly or indirectly by the information contained in this book.

If you do not wish to be bound by the above, you may return this book to the publisher for a full refund.

TRADEMARKS

The TI BA-35 Solar, TI BA II Plus, Constant Memory™, and Automatic Power Down (APD™) are trademarks of Texas Instruments.

The HP 10B, HP 19B II Business Consultant, HP 17B II Financial Calculator, and HP 12C Financial Calculator are trademarks of Hewlett-Packard.

The Sharp EL-733A and EL-735 are trademarks of Sharp Corporation.

The Casio FC-100 is a trademark of Casio Computer Co., Ltd.

Table of Contents

Part 3: Supporting Materials

PREFACE

Imagine that you recently entered a lucky draw. A week later, you receive a phone call at home "You have been chosen as the top prize winner," says the voice at the other end. "However, in order to receive the prize, you have to answer a skill-testing question."

"I've never won anything in my life," you say. "I'll sure do my best." The caller continues:

Assume you are asked to work for 30 days. You are given two choices for your wages. The first is that you will receive $10,000 at the end of each day. The other choice is that you will receive 1 cent at the end of each day, but each day's payment will earn interest at the rate of 100% per day for the succeeding days. First, which payment method will provide you with the larger salary amount at the end of 30 days? What will the total wages be at the end of 30 days? If you compute the right answer, your prize is the amount of money you have just calculated. If you don't, your consolation prize is $100.

Numbers start popping in your head. For the first payment method, the total salary at the end of 30 days is $10,000 multiplied by 30. Even without using a calculator, you know the answer is $300,000. You wonder about the second method of payment. You don't understand the implications of earning interest at the rate of 100% per day and you don't know how to calculate the correct answer. But 1¢ is just no comparison to $10,000. You make up your mind.

You reply to the caller that you are choosing the first payment method and that the total payment at the end of 30 days is $300,000. The caller hesitates for a moment, then says that the correct answer is the second payment method. It will generate total earnings after 30 days of **$10,737,418.23**. (See Section 2.2, Interest, Annuity, and Inflation, Table 2.2.30 for more details on this calculation.)

You can hardly believe it! One cent a day! "I knew it was a trick question," you mutter.

We can all relate to this experience. Most of us would have made the same choice. The point I am making here is that all too often, when making important decisions concerning our personal finances, we fail to make the best ones. I believe the basic problem is that most of us do not understand the fundamentals involved in personal finances. Most of us finished high school, college, or university to become skilled workers, technologists, doctors, lawyers, engineers, scientists, teachers, etc., without ever taking a simple course on personal finance. If the fundamentals are understood, it does not take great effort to apply it to personal finance problems. In fact, it does not take a math wizard to answer correctly such questions as our hypothetical example above.

Personal finance is a universal subject, applicable anywhere; in Canada, US, Germany, Brazil, China, Africa, etc. The topics covered in this book are so down-to-earth that anybody with the interest will be able to understand and apply the concepts learned. This is a self-help book that will show the reader, step by step, how to tackle the five basic personal finance problems: implementing a savings plan, loans and mortgages, planning for the children's education, planning for retirement, and investment decision making. Money is as important to most of us as an exciting career or good health. In various stages of our lives, we are faced with important decisions involving money. How many times have we eventually closed deals — for example, buying a new home or a new car — and said to ourselves, "I would have felt better making those decisions had I understood how the monthly payment or the loan amount was calculated." This book will do exactly that for you and more. All that is required is an understanding of the basic concepts and a modest investment in an inexpensive financial calculator (not to be confused with scientific calculators). You will not even need a pencil and paper to learn how to solve financial problems. This is a self-help book filled with practical examples. Several tables and figures are used to emphasize the concepts being discussed. Solutions to selected examples are covered. To make the book more interesting, interspersed within its pages are items of financial trivia. You should not buy this book if you are expecting tips on how to invest your money. This book will *not* teach you whether you should buy stocks, bonds, or mutual funds, which ones, or at what ratios.

Have you noticed, at your local bookstore and advertised in the paper, how many seminars, self-help books, and short courses are being offered on financial investing and on taking charge of one's financial future? One such book has sold more than 1 million paperback copies. Why have these topics become so popular these days? Because we are being driven to take more responsibility for our financial future.

Industries have taken drastic measures such as "right-sizing, or re-engineering," to survive and make a profit. National and even local governments, forced to operate on a balanced budget, have resorted to similar measures. The prospect of an assured future through lifetime employment in the same company is definitely gone. Job security is becoming a thing of the past. The world of work is rapidly changing as our society moves toward the service industries and self-employment. More and more, our financial future is being forced onto our own shoulders.

This book will teach the new skills we need to take control of our personal finances. We owe it to ourselves to become aware and to participate actively in managing our hard-earned money. The fact that you purchased this book shows your commitment to a better financial future. Read on and you will not be disappointed.

This book is a reference to the seminar, *Applications of Personal Finance*. Refer to page 348 for more details.

INTRODUCTION

To achieve the maximum benefits, it is important to read this entire section before proceeding to any other part of the book.

The book has three basic parts. The first part starts with a short quiz to check your literacy on important facets of personal finance, Chapter 1, A Short Quiz on Personal Finance Literacy. You invested in this book and, very likely, in a financial calculator. The quiz provides a feedback mechanism to measure how much you have absorbed the important concepts being taught in this book. To accomplish this, you will need to take the quiz twice. First, take it after reading this section. Use a separate sheet for your answers and keep it for later comparison. Take the quiz again after reading the book in its entirety. Compare the answers from the two quizzes with the correct ones, which are available in Section 7.3, Answers to Short Quiz on Personal Finance Literacy.

Chapter 2, The Seven Lessons to Control Your Personal Finances, is the heart of the book. It will lead you from the very basics of solving personal finance problems to their important applications. Several examples will be covered and you will be given the opportunity to use the financial calculator to solve these sample problems.

The second part of the book consists of Chapter 3, Hands-on Exercises Using the Financial Calculator. The objective here is to reinforce the concepts explained in the first part of the book. All examples in Chapter 2 are solved, but only the important ones are selected for a complete demonstration of the solutions. This is where the book will differ from all others. Representative example problems in Chapter 2 indicated by a key symbol [🔑] will be covered in detail in Sections 3.3 to 3.6. Here, the calculator keystrokes to solve the problems will be shown step by step, using the six financial calculators covered in this book. It is very important, when learning new skills, to develop confidence in the concepts being learned. The best way of doing this is by performing hands-on exercises. Once you have this confidence, you can start using the financial calculator to solve personal finance problems unique to your situation.

The third part of the book provides supporting materials to assist in acquiring the new skills. There is a chapter on short-cut financial estimation techniques that can be used even without financial calculators. Amaze your friends and associates with the rules that will be covered in Chapter 4, Rules of Thumb. The Glossary in Chapter 5 clarifies the specialized terms covered in the book. The Bibliography in Chapter 6 lists the reference books and materials used, which the reader may want to access for further reading. Finally, Chapter 7 starts with an appendix on the importance of revisiting the personal finance calculations at least once a year. Useful worksheet templates follow to assist in charting your financial future. The next appendix gives the answers to the quiz in Chapter 1. Finally, the symbols and characters used in this book are explained.

What really started me writing this book was my concern regarding my own retirement. I wanted to know whether I was saving enough for a comfortable retirement. If not, I wanted to know how much more I should save annually. In performing the financial calculations I had to make certain assumptions — such as that interest and inflation rates would remain constant over the calculation period. As we all know, in reality, these numbers fluctuate not only every year but every day. My strategy, therefore, is to make the best assumptions I can today and then repeat my calculations every year to make adjustments as necessary. In this way, the numbers I calculate are more accurate, as the assumptions are closer to current reality. The beauty of it all is that I have this set of skills I can call upon to confidently analyze my unique situation any time and anywhere.

WHICH FINANCIAL CALCULATOR TO BUY?

To acquire the greatest benefit from this book, you will need to purchase a financial calculator. After reading this entire section and taking the personal finance literacy test, read Section 3.1, Introduction to Hands-on Exercises, to understand the difference between financial and scientific calculators. Sample financial problems are discussed to show that financial calculators permit easy and straightforward analysis of personal finance problems. Section 3.2, Comparative Tables on Financial Calculators, shows the functions of the six financial calculators which represent most of the inexpensive financial calculators available in the market today. As you will see in Table 3.2.1, these six calculator models are all under $50 (1996 CDN retail price). Other available models are not covered in this book simply because they are more expensive: more than $100 (1996 CDN retail price) each. This table shows that not all financial calculators have equal capabilities. I hope the information in the table will be able to assist you in purchasing the brand and model best suited for your use.

If after reading Sections 3.1 and 3.2, you are still not sure what financial calculator to buy, reading Chapter 2 will give you further insight into which personal finance application problems you will most commonly be faced with. This additional information should help you decide which financial calculator will best suit your needs. Depending on the calculator you purchase, you can check out the appropriate sections of Chapter 3 for hands-on exercises to reinforce the concepts of how to control your personal finances.

TO MAXIMIZE THE LEARNING PROCESS

Chapter 2, The Seven Lessons to Control Your Personal Finances, should be read in the order presented. It is suggested that as each example problem with the key symbol [] is encountered, the reader should follow its solution using the financial calculator in the appropriate section of Chapter 3. Repeated exercises like these will build confidence. Test this confidence on other examples that do not have the key symbol and compare your answer with those provided in the book.

I will have achieved success in teaching how to control your personal finances if, after reading and following the example problems, you can start taking your own unique situations and begin the process of making intelligent personal finance decisions with confidence.

PART 1
THEORY

1

A SHORT QUIZ ON PERSONAL FINANCE LITERACY

Never too late to learn.

Proverb

As mentioned in the Introduction, I suggest you take this quiz twice. Your answers to the questions below will provide a snapshot of how familiar you are with important concepts involving personal finance before you actually read the book. Take the quiz again after reading the entire book, except of course for Section 7.3, Answers to Short Quiz on Personal Finance Literacy. You should have more correct answers the second time!

1. Money is an invention of man. It has taken several varieties, including shell beads, stones, cattle, fur, gold and silver coins, paper money, and several others. What is the single most important quality that makes any item function as money?
2. Today, currencies of most countries are still backed by gold reserves. True or false?
3. What are the five basic parameters involved in analyzing financial problems?
4. What are the four basic types of financial problems?
5. Money has time value. What are the two time mileposts used in time value of money problems?
6. Interest is always compounded at the same interval as the schedule of loan payments. True or false?
7. Interest compounding on Canadian mortgages is calculated monthly. True or false?

8. The interest rate is the real rate of return that the borrower is expecting for lending you money. True or false?
9. The value of the effective interest rate is generally higher than the nominal value of interest. True or false?
10. For time value of money (TVM) and discounted cash flow (DCF) applications, annuity payments refer to annual payments only. True or false?
11. For TVM applications, annuity payments cannot be made at irregular periods. True or false?
12. The last Great Inflation occurred in the 1920s. True or false?
13. There are two measures of inflation. One is how much the price of goods increases over time. What is the other measure?
14. Generating an amortization table involves complex calculations and requires a powerful computer and sophisticated software. True or false?
15. You are 25 years old and have just won a $5,000 lottery. You have a choice of investing it now towards your retirement or spending it now and waiting until you are 35 years old before you invest $5,000 for your retirement. Assume that the interest rate is 8% per year compounded yearly and that you plan to retire at age 65. How much money will you lose if you delay the investment?
16. Financial calculators and scientific calculators can solve the same financial problems with the same ease. True or false?
17. Not all financial calculators are the same. True or false?
18. The rule of 72 states that to estimate how long it will take to double your initial investment, you divide 72 by the annual interest rate. Describe how this rule came about.
19. Use a rule of thumb to estimate the monthly payment per $10,000 borrowed on a 20-year mortgage at 10% interest.
20. What is the difference between time value of money (TVM) problems and discounted cash flow (DCF) problems?
21. DCF analysis is used to appraise investment alternatives. What are the two types of investment appraisal used to see whether an investment alternative meets profit objectives?
22. What are the four basic methods of implementing a savings plan?

Probably the most productive painter of all time was Pablo Diego Jose Francisco de Paula Juan Nepomuceno Crispin Crispiano de la Santisima Trinidad Ruiz y Picasso. In Picasso's 78-year career, he produced about 13,500 paintings, 34,000 book illustrations, 100,000 prints, and 300 sculptures. In total, these works are valued at about $800 million US in 1996.

23. Of the four methods to implement a savings plan, which method provides the best return on the money considering the total money outlay?
24. Which combination of the following variations of the second method to implement a savings plan (by annuity payment method) provides the best return on the money: end-of-period payment, beginning-of-period payment, less frequent payments, and more frequent payments?
25. What is the tough policy, which the US government implemented as sure cure for inflation?
26. Is DCF a specialized application of TVM? Putting it another way, can DCF problems be solved by using TVM analysis methods?
27. In DCF problems involving various cash flow sign changes, is there always one solution for IRR? How about for NPV?
28. With the exception of the Texas Instruments BA-35 financial calculator, when solving TVM and DCF problems using the other five financial calculators covered in this book, it is not important to enter the signs of the cash flow values. True or false?
29. You are 43 years old and have been saving up for retirement. The retirement fund is currently worth $150,000. If you would like to retire at age 55, what monthly payment should you make into your retirement fund if you expect this fund to provide you with $3,000 per month retirement income (in today's dollars) for 25 years? Assume inflation is at 2% per year compounded monthly and that money earns interest at the rate of 8% per year compounded monthly. Use beginning-of-period for the annuity payments.
30. You have an existing $95,000 mortgage on your home. The mortgage is amortized over 20 years and your current monthly payment is $844.73. The interest rate is 9% compounded semi-annually, as this is a Canadian mortgage. You have just completed the first five-year term on the mortgage and it is up for renewal. What is the mortgage principal balance?

    The new term is for 15 years amortization with 10% interest. What is the new monthly payment?

    If you increase the monthly payments by $50, how much interest will you save?

    Another option to reduce the interest is by reducing the amortization period. What is the new monthly payment for 10-year amortization? How much interest is saved compared to the regular 15-year amortization?

    Investigate the effect of reducing the principal mortgage balance by $5,000 at 15-year amortization and 10% interest rate. What is the new monthly payment? How much interest is saved compared to the regular 15-year amortization?

According to surveys released in September 1998 by the global central banks, Britain is the world's center for foreign exchange trading. Average daily volume is $637 billion US compared to $351 billion in the US.

31. You have a nine-year old daughter and you would like to set up an education fund that she can use to finance her four-year university education, starting at age 18. Assume that today, it costs $13,000 per year to put a student through university, including tuition, books, board and lodging, and miscellaneous expenses. What monthly payments should you be making now in order to have an education fund ready for your child when she begins university? Assume 8% interest rate per year compounded monthly and 3% inflation rate compounded monthly. A savings fund has already been started and its present value is $4,500. Use beginning-of-period for the annuity payments.

    What is the new monthly savings payment if the education fund is delayed by five years and all other parameters are the same?

32. TVM and DCF analyses methods will always provide the absolute correct answers to your personal finance problems. True or False?

33. In managing your personal finances, how can you get the most from the TVM and DCF analyses methods?

Alfred Bernhard Nobel, a Swedish chemist and engineer who invented dynamite, left his fortune in trust to establish the annual Nobel prizes in chemistry, physics, medicine, literature, economics, and world peace. The average value of each prize in 1901, the year it began, was $30,000 US. In 1994, the average prize value was $930,000 US.

2

THE SEVEN LESSONS TO CONTROL YOUR PERSONAL FINANCES

2.1
Lesson 1:
BASICS OF TIME VALUE OF MONEY (TVM) ANALYSIS

Procrastination is the thief of time.

Edward Young

Money has *time value*, whether you keep your money idle (leaving it under the bed, perhaps, or in your cupboard or wallet) or make it work for you by, for example, putting it into an interest-bearing account in your bank. In the first case, the amount of money will remain constant, as long as you do not add or remove any. Over time, however, it will lose its purchasing power because of inflation. (Inflation will be discussed in more detail in Section 2.2). In the second case, assume that a single lump-sum payment is made to a savings account in the bank. Over time, the amount will grow as the bank pays you interest for the use of your money. As long as the interest rate offered by the bank is higher than the rate of inflation, the purchasing power of your money will increase, keeping ahead of inflation.

Time value of money (TVM) analysis is a technique used to solve financial problems. It assumes that money has time value, which depends upon the length of time that money is held and the interest rate quoted for that time period. TVM is useful in calculating appropriate payments into a personal savings plan for the children's education, retirement, major purchases, etc. Another type of TVM problem is the payments made to a financial or lending institution to pay off a mortgage, car loan, student loan, etc. All types and classes of financial problems that can be solved using TVM will be covered in this chapter. As will be seen later, all financial problems will require the ***period*** and ***interest rate*** as problem parameters. They can both be known values or one of them can be the unknown parameter in a given problem. Three other parameters used in financial problems include ***present value***, ***future value***, and ***annuity payment***.

There are four types of financial problems, depending on how payments are made. **Type I** problems are those that involve a single lump-sum payment. **Type II** problems consist of a single series of equal payments made at equal intervals of time. **Type III** problems are those that include both a single lump-sum payment and annuity payments.

Type IV problems are commonly referred to as cash flow problems. In this type of problem, there can be more than one lump-sum payment and several series of annuity payments. Each payment period in cash flow problems need not involve a lump-sum or annuity payment. In other words, there might be periods in which no payments are made. The only requirement is that the payments occur exactly at the beginning or end of a payment period. Cash flow problems, used in making personal investment decisions, will be discussed in more detail in Section 2.7.

The lump-sum payment problem (Type I) involves four parameters; period, interest rate, present value, and future value. In series-of-payment problems (Type II), also called annuity problems, we are concerned with four parameters. These are interest rate, period, annuity payment, and either present value or future value. (Present value and future value are not considered simultaneously.) Type III problems consider all five parameters simultaneously. Examples of Type III problems are car lease calculations with option to buy at the end of the term and mortgage problems with a balloon payment. Refer to Table 2.1.5 for an overview of the types and classes of financial problems.

CASH FLOW DIAGRAMS

Before discussing each of the five parameters in detail, let me explain a very useful type of diagram used in this book. *Cash flow diagrams* provide a powerful method to visually represent a financial problem.

A *cash flow diagram* shows the time line drawn horizontally, with time increasing from left to right. The time line is divided into equal payment periods. It will show the entire period, the amount of money received and money paid out. Money received is assigned a positive value and is represented by an arrow pointing upwards. Money paid out is assigned a negative value and is represented by an arrow pointing down. The occurrence of the cash inflow or outflow along the time line is indicated by a line with an arrow pointing upward or downward at the appropriate payment period. These arrows are shown either at the beginning or at the end of the payment period.

Keep the direction of the arrows in mind, too, as you look at the numbers in the tables in this book. It may not seem obvious that $1,000 in a savings account should be a negative number. After all, the money is there, and belongs to you. But, as the cash flow diagram shows, for the purposes of financial calculations, this money is paid *out* by you to the savings plan, and must be shown as a negative number. When you look at future value, you will be considering the amount as if you were then withdrawing it from the savings account, so that it is a positive value coming *in* to you.

Columbus was paid 2,000 maravedis (a small silver coin — the Spanish unit of currency in Columbus's time) a month for discovering the New World. In the two months it took to discover the New World, Columbus was paid the equivalent of $85 US in today's currency. If this money had been invested at 2.5%, today the investor would have an account worth more than $20 million US.

For example, consider the following:

Assume you opened a savings account and you put down $5,000. At the end of each year for the next 25 years, you are planning to put $2,000 into the account. Assuming a nominal interest rate of 8% compounded annually, what is the future value of the savings account at the end of 25 years?

Two types of cash flow diagrams can be constructed, depending on the point of view. The cash flow diagram for this example is drawn from **your point of view** as the saver.

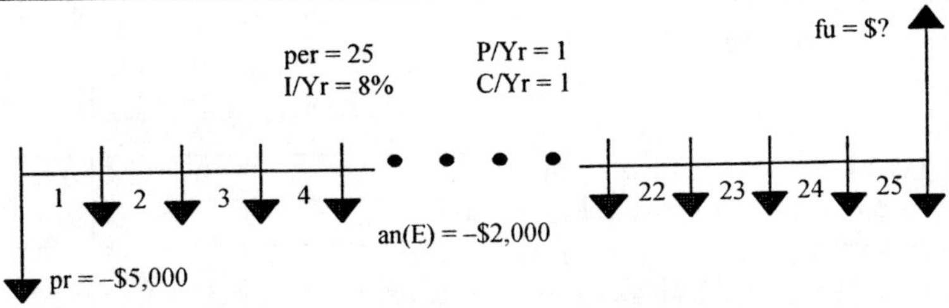

Figure 2.1.1 Cash flow diagram from your point of view

The following cash flow diagram for the same example is drawn from the **bank's point of view.**

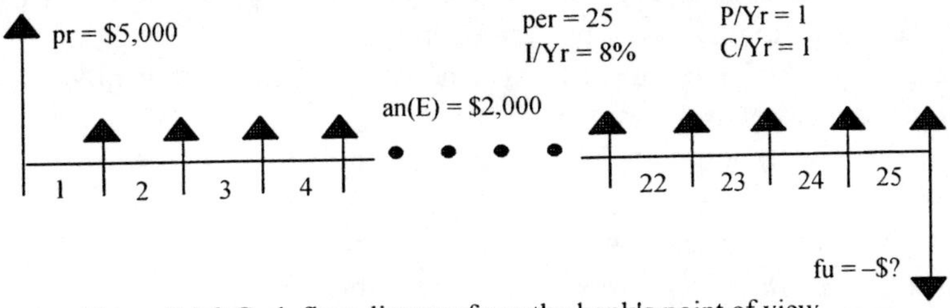

Figure 2.1.2 Cash flow diagram from the bank's point of view

For both figures, the $2,000 payments were made at the end of each period and are indicated by an(E). We will be using the cash flow diagram in several examples throughout the book. Let us now proceed to discuss in more detail the five parameters involved in TVM analysis.

In 1997, it has been estimated that the cost of 10 years of music education from age 5 to 15 is about $10,000.

THE PARAMETERS OF TVM ANALYSIS

Period (per)

The first parameter is period (per). It is used to express the time element in the analysis. Period (per) is calculated from the number of payments per year (P/Yr) which is a function of the given payment frequency multiplied by the given number of years (Yr). The equation is as follows:

$$\text{per} = (\text{P/Yr}) \times (\text{Yr}) \qquad \textit{equation (2.1.1)}$$

There is nothing complicated about equation 2.1.1. It just states that if you know the number of payments per year (P/Yr) and if this is multiplied by the number of years, the result is the total number of payment periods, per. Payment frequency can be daily, weekly, bi-weekly, semi-monthly, monthly, quarterly, semi-annually or annually. Table 2.1.1 shows the relationship between payment frequency and payment per year (P/Yr).

For Type I lump-sum payment problems, P/Yr is usually set to 1.0.

Table 2.1.1 Relationship between payment frequency and (P/Yr).

Payment Frequency	P/Yr
daily	365
weekly	52
bi-weekly	26
semi-monthly	24
monthly	12
quarterly	4
semi-annually	2
annually	1

For Type II and III financial problems, which involve annuity or series of payments, (P/Yr) refers to the total annuity payment periods *in one year.*

As mentioned at the beginning of this chapter, all financial problems require the parameter period (per), either as a known value or as the unknown variable.

To illustrate the use of equation 2.1.1, let us consider a Type I problem.

Assume you have extra cash and you would like to invest this money for four years, (Yr = 4). Table 2.1.2 shows the calculation for the period (per).

Disney World in Orlando, Florida, has three theme parks; Magic Kingdom, Epcot, and Disney-MGM Studio. A fourth theme park called Animal Kingdom opened on May 6, 1998 at a cost of $800 million US. The park's mission is not only to entertain but also to change attitudes toward wildlife and to promote conservation.

Table 2.1.2 Examples of how to use equation 2.1.1.

payment frequency	P/Yr	(P/Yr) × (Yr) = per
daily	365	365 × 4 = 1460
weekly	52	52 × 4 = 208
bi–weekly	26	26 × 4 = 104
semi–monthly	24	24 × 4 = 96
monthly	12	12 × 4 = 48
quarterly	4	4 × 4 = 16
semi–annually	2	2 × 4 = 8
annually	1	1 × 4 = 4

Depending on the payment frequency that applies to the financial problem, the value shown in the last column of Table 2.1.2 is the value to be entered in the financial calculator for period (per).

What do you do if the investment period is not in integer multiples of years; example, 100 months? Converting 100 months to years, Yr = 100/12. Table 2.1.3 shows the calculation of period (per) for various values of P/Yr.

Table 2.1.3 Calculating period (per) for non–integer years.

payment frequency	P/Yr	(P/Yr) × (Yr) = per
daily	365	365 × (100/12) = 3,041.67
weekly	52	52 × (100/12) = 433.33
bi–weekly	26	26 × (100/12) = 216.67
semi–monthly	24	24 × (100/12) = 200.00
monthly	12	12 × (100/12) = 100.00
quarterly	4	4 × (100/12) = 33.33
semi–annually	2	2 × (100/12) = 16.67
annually	1	1 × (100/12) = 8.33

The Whitbread Round the World Race is a nine–leg round–the–world boat race that starts in England in the fall and returns six or more months later. Global companies sponsor these boats at a cost of millions of dollars. Sailing these boats, a sailor can earn as much as $12,000 US a month.

Interest Rate Per Year (I/Yr)

There are two types of interest calculations: simple interest and compound interest. Section 2.2 discusses interest in more detail. For TVM analysis, we are more concerned with compound interest.

The annual interest rate is the time value attached to money. It is usually quoted as a nominal rate of interest per year (I/Yr). It is the rate at which banks or financial institutions will pay you for the use of your money or the rate at which you have to pay financial institutions for a loan. For simple interest, it is expressed as a percentage of the original principal, regardless of how long money is held. For compound interest, for savings applications, the interest rate is applied to the accumulated interest and principal per interest compounding period. For loan applications, compound interest is calculated per compounding period on the remaining outstanding balance and accumulated interest. Note that how often compound interest is calculated depends on the interest compounding frequency, C/Yr. It could be different from the payment frequency, P/Yr.

For compound interest applications, interest is usually calculated at the same frequency as the payment frequency. Not always, though. An excellent example is Canadian mortgages, where the frequency of payment is monthly (P/Yr = 12) but the frequency of interest calculation is semi-annually (C/Yr = 2). Canadian mortgages will be covered in more detail in Section 2.4.

Note that some financial calculators accept interest rate per year (I/Yr) as input while others require periodic interest rate (in%). Refer to Table 3.2.4 for interest rate data entry for the six financial calculators covered in this book. For financial problems where P/Yr = C/Yr, periodic interest rate (in) is calculated as follows:

$$in = \frac{(I/Yr)}{100 \times (P/Yr)} \qquad \textit{equation (2.1.2)}$$

where (I/Yr) is the nominal interest per year in percent (%) and (P/Yr) is the frequency of payment per year. Financial calculators that use periodic interest rate use periodic interest as a percentage, which is calculated as follows:

$$in\% = in \times 100 \qquad \textit{equation (2.1.3)}$$

For financial problems where P/Yr is not equal to C/Yr, the periodic interest rate (in) is calculated as follows:

$$in = \frac{(I/Yr)_{adj}}{100 \times (P/Yr)} \qquad \textit{equation (2.1.4)}$$

where $(I/Yr)_{adj}$ is the adjusted nominal interest per year in percent (%). This takes into account the compounding per year, C/Yr; (P/Yr) is the frequency of payment per year. For more on $(I/Yr)_{adj}$, see pages 63-66.

To illustrate the use of the periodic interest rate (in) from equation 2.1.2, let us continue the previous example. Assume the four-year term loan has an annual interest rate of 8% (I/Yr = 8). The periodic interest rate (in) is calculated as follows, depending on the payment frequency:

Table 2.1.4 Calculating periodic interest (equations 2.1.2 and 2.1.3.).

payment frequency	P/Yr	(I/Yr)/(100 × P/Yr) = in	in × 100 = in%
daily	365	8/(100 × 365)= 0.0002	0.02%
weekly	52	8/(100 × 52)= 0.0015	0.15%
bi–weekly	26	8/(100 × 26)= 0.0031	0.31%
semi–monthly	24	8/(100 × 24)= 0.0033	0.33%
monthly	12	8/(100 × 12)= 0.0067	0.67%
quarterly	4	8/(100 × 4)= 0.0200	2.00%
semi–annually	2	8/(100 × 2)= 0.0400	4.00%
annually	1	8/(100 × 1)= 0.0800	8.00%

Periodic interest rate (in, in%) is therefore determined from the quoted annual interest rate (I/Yr) and the number of payments per year (P/Yr). It is important to note that the calculated periodic interest rate is applied to each payment period regardless of the period (per) of the financial problem. That is, whether the period is four years, eight years, or 25 years, the periodic interest rate does not change.

As mentioned earlier, some financial calculators use interest per year (I/Yr) and payment per year (P/Yr) as inputs. For these calculators, the above calculation for (in) is performed internally. For others, the user has to calculate the periodic interest rate (in%) from the given interest per year (I/Yr) and payment per year (P/Yr). The resulting value is then entered into the financial calculator. For more on interest, see Section 2.2.

Present Value (pr)

As money has time value, there have to be mileposts along the timeline from which the value of money can be calculated. For financial calculations, money is assigned only two time reference points: *the present* and *the future*. This does not mean, however, that one can only calculate present and future money problems relative to the current time. In this context, "present" and "future" should be viewed merely as reference points from which the various financial calculations can be applied. Thus, one can solve time value of money problems where the reference points are both in the future, relative to the current time, both in the past, one in the present and one in the future, or any other combination.

The present value of money (pr), is one of the mileposts from which the time value of money can be calculated. In TVM analysis, present value (pr) represents the value at the present point of an investment, or of a loan or mortgage.

A first-class ticket on the Titanic was $4,700 US, which would be about $50,000 US in 1998.

Future Value (fu)

The future value of money (fu), is the other milepost from which the time value of money can be calculated. In savings applications, the future value (fu) is the total amount of money including the accumulated interest at the end of the period (per).

Annuity Payment (an(E), an(B))

Annuity payments are series of equal payments made at regular intervals in time. In TVM problems, annuity payments can be made daily, weekly, monthly, yearly, or at any other regular interval. A regular or ordinary annuity is payment paid at the *end* of each payment period, an(E). Payments made towards a loan or mortgage fall under this category. However, there are payments that are made at the *beginning* of each payment period, an(B). Rents, leases and payment to a savings plan are typical examples. (More on annuity in Section 2.2.)

Other Parameters (P/Yr) and (C/Yr)

Aside from the five basic parameters discussed above, there are two other parameters. These parameters are payment per year (P/Yr) and interest compounding per year (C/Yr). Values for these parameters are always known and should be a value greater than zero (0).

Payment per year, (P/Yr) is a function of the payment frequency, discussed above. Every financial problem requires knowledge of how often payments are made. For Type I, lump-sum payment problems, (P/Yr) is determined from the units used for the period (per). For example, if months are used, from Table 2.1.1, P/Yr is 12. If days, P/Yr is 365, etc.. If the period is the unknown parameter, the calculated value will have units depending on the value used for P/Yr. (See Table 2.1.1.)

For Type II and III financial problems that involve annuity or series of payments, (P/Yr) refers to the total payment periods *in one year*. For example, if payments are made quarterly, there will be 4 payments in one year, thus, P/Yr = 4. If the payments are made monthly, there will be 12 payments in one year, thus, P/Yr = 12, etc.. When calculating for period, the calculated value will also have units depending on the value of P/Yr. Thus, if P/Yr = 52, the calculated period will have units in weeks. (See Table 2.1.1.)

For Type IV financial problems, P/Yr is used to calculate the data entry for interest required for NPV calculation. See Table 3.2.5.

Using payments per year, P/Yr, one can convert the period to years. From equation 2.1.1, Yr is calculated as:

$$\text{Yr} = \frac{\text{per}}{(\text{P/Yr})} \qquad \textit{equation (2.1.5)}$$

Interest compounding per year, (C/Yr) defines how often interest accrues. Remember that interest is like the rent paid for the use of money. The interest is payable to *you* if, for example, you have a savings account in a bank. You pay the interest to a financial institution if, for example, you have a loan or a mortgage. If you have an interest-bearing savings account, do you know how often the bank compounds interest? Canadian mortgages are on a semi-annual interest compounding, that is, (C/Yr) = 2. Most loans have monthly interest compounding, (C/Yr = 12).

When P/Yr is not equal to C/Yr, they are used to calculate effective interest (Section 2.2) and adjusted nominal interest rate (equation 2.1.4).

The five basic parameters **per, I/Yr, pr, fu** and **an**, plus payment per year, **P/Yr** and interest compounding per year, **C/Yr** are used for TVM analysis to solve Type I to III financial problems. Type IV problems are analyzed using the DCF method. Type IV problems require cash flow values (**CF_i**), frequency of the cash flow (**N_i**), interest rate per period (**in% = (I/Yr)/(P/Yr)** or (I/Yr); see Table 3.2.5), P/Yr and C/Yr. The DCF method calculates NPV and IRR to evaluate if investment objectives are met.

TYPES AND CLASSES OF FINANCIAL PROBLEMS

As mentioned in the first part of this chapter, there are four types of financial problems. The first three are those financial problems in which the TVM method can be applied. The last type is for financial problems in which the DCF (discounted cash flow) method can be used. The DCF method calculates net present value (NPV) and internal rate of return (IRR) in evaluating investment options. This section will concentrate on the TVM method. The DCF method will be covered in Section 2.3 as one method that can be employed to implement a savings plan. A detailed treatment of DCF for investment decision making will be covered in Section 2.7. Table 2.1.5 shows an overview of the types and classes of financial problems.

Table 2.1.5 Overview of types and classes of financial problems.

Type/Class	per	I/Yr	pr	fu	an
Type I Class A	✓	✓	✓	✓	░
Type II Class B	✓	✓	✓	░	✓
Type II Class C	✓	✓	░	✓	✓
Type III Class D	✓	✓	✓	✓	✓
Type IV	use DCF (Discounted Cash Flow) method calculates NPV and IRR for investment decision making				

✓ = parameter required; one has to be unknown

░ = parameter not required

Financial problems relating to lump-sum payments (Type I problem) or annuity payments (Type II problem) require only four parameters. Financial problems that combine lump-sum payments and annuity payments (Type III problem) require all five parameters.

Tables 2.1.6 - 2.1.9 show the combination of financial problems within each class.

Table 2.1.6 Classes of Type I financial problems that use the TVM method.

Class	per	I/Yr	pr	fu
Class A.1	unknown	given	given	given
Class A.2	given	unknown	given	given
Class A.3	given	given	unknown	given
Class A.4	given	given	given	unknown

Table 2.1.7 Type II Class B financial problems that use the TVM method.

Class	per	I/Yr	pr	an
Class B.1	unknown	given	given	given
Class B.2	given	unknown	given	given
Class B.3	given	given	unknown	given
Class B.4	given	given	given	unknown

Table 2.1.8 Type II Class C financial problems that use the TVM method.

Class	per	I/Yr	fu	an
Class C.1	unknown	given	given	given
Class C.2	given	unknown	given	given
Class C.3	given	given	unknown	given
Class C.4	given	given	given	unknown

Table 2.1.9 Classes of Type III financial problems that use the TVM method.

Class	per	I/Yr	pr	fu	an
Class D.1	unknown	given	given	given	given
Class D.2	given	unknown	given	given	given
Class D.3	given	given	unknown	given	given
Class D.4	given	given	given	unknown	given
Class D.5	given	given	given	given	unknown

The following are example problems that will cover each type and class of financial problems.

Lump-Sum Payment Problems (Type I Class A)

Class A.1. Period (per) is unknown and interest rate (I/Yr), present value (pr), and future value (fu) are given.

How many months will it take for $5,000 today to have a future value of $10,000 if the annual interest rate is 8% compounded monthly?

Periodic interest rate (in%) = 8/12. The cash flow diagram is shown on the right.

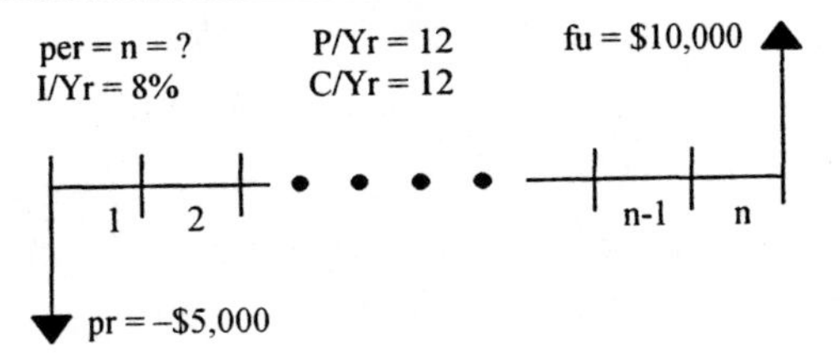

Figure 2.1.3 Type I Class A.1 problem

Table 2.1.10 Type I, Class A.1 financial problem. (P/Yr = C/Yr = 12).

per	I/Yr	pr	fu
104.32	8.00	-5,000.00	10,000.00

Answer: per = 104.32 months

Class A.2. Period (per) is given, interest rate (I/Yr) is unknown, present value (pr), and future value (fu) are given.

What is the annual interest rate so that a $5,000 investment today will be worth $10,000 after 100 months? Interest is compounded monthly.

The cash flow diagram is shown on the right.

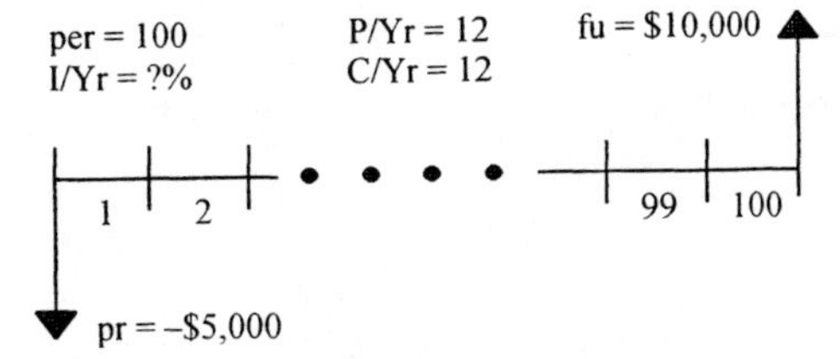

Figure 2.1.4 Type I Class A.2 problem

In 1982/83, tuition at Canadian universities was 8 percent of total operating revenue. In 1995/96 it was 14.5 percent.

Table 2.1.11 Type I, Class A.2 financial problem. (P/Yr = C/Yr = 12).

per	I/Yr	pr	fu
100.00	8.35	-5,000.00	10,000.00

Answer: annual rate (I/Yr) of 8.35% or (in%) = 8.35/12

Class A.3. Period (per) and interest rate (I/Yr) are given, present value (pr) is unknown, and future value (fu) is given.

How much should I invest today at an annual interest of 8% compounded monthly so that after 100 months, the investment will be worth $10,000?

Periodic interest rate (in%) = 8/12. The cash flow diagram is shown on the right.

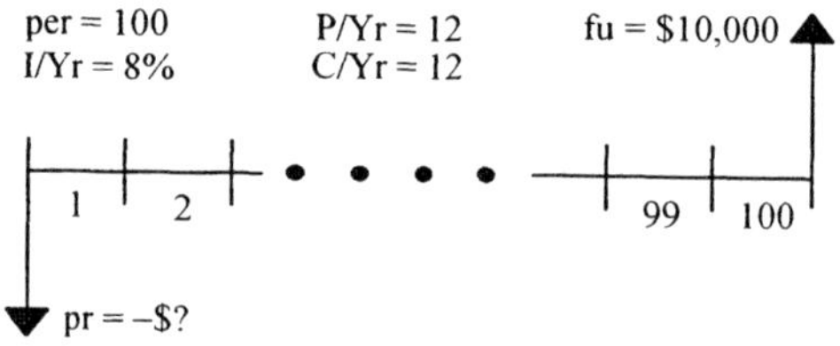

Figure 2.1.5 Type I Class A.3 problem

Table 2.1.12 Type I, Class A.3 financial problem. (P/Yr = C/Yr = 12).

per	I/Yr	pr	fu
100.00	8.00	-5,145.54	10,000.00

Answer: pr = $5,145.54

Lillehammer, Norway was chosen as the site for the XVII Olympic Winter Games in 1994. For the event, the Norwegian government spent more than $370 million US to prepare the site and stage the games, turning Lillehammer into a complete Olympic city. Most of the $300 million US that CBS-TV paid for Olympic broadcasting rights helped cover the costs.

Class A.4. Period (per), interest rate (I/Yr), and present value (pr) are given and future value (fu) is unknown.

If I make a $5,000 investment today at an annual rate of 8% compounded monthly, what is its future value after 100 months?

Periodic interest rate (in%) = 8/12. The cash flow diagram is shown on the right.

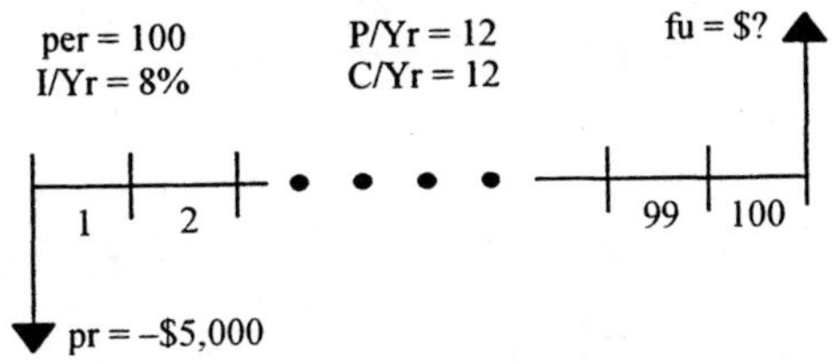

Figure 2.1.6 Type I Class A.4 problem

Table 2.1.13 Type I, Class A.4 financial problem. (P/Yr = C/Yr = 12).

per	I/Yr	pr	fu
100.00	8.00	-5,000.00	9,717.15

Answer: fu = $9,717.15

To summarize the results for Class A problems:

Table 2.1.14 Summary of results for Type I Class A financial problems. (P/Yr = C/Yr = 12).

Class	per	I/Yr	pr	fu
A.1	104.32	8.00	-5,000.00	10,000.00
A.2	100.00	8.35	-5,000.00	10,000.00
A.3	100.00	8.00	-5,145.54	10,000.00
A.4	100.00	8.00	-5,000.00	9,717.15

Chrysler engineers developed new V-6 aluminum engines in 98 weeks at a cost of $625 million US. Using typical design and testing technologies, this engine would have taken 2½ years (135 weeks) and $1 billion US.

Series of Payment Problems (Type II Class B)

Class B.1. Period (per) is unknown, interest rate (I/Yr), present value (pr), and annuity payment (an) are given.

If I have a loan for $5,000 and I can afford to make monthly payments of $100, how long will it take to retire the loan if the annual interest rate is 8% compounded monthly? Calculate both for annuity payments made at the end (E) of each payment period and for annuity payments made at the beginning (B) of each payment period.

Periodic interest rate (in%) = 8/12. The cash flow diagram for annuity payments at the end of each payment period is shown below on the left. The diagram on the right is for annuity payments at the beginning of each payment period.

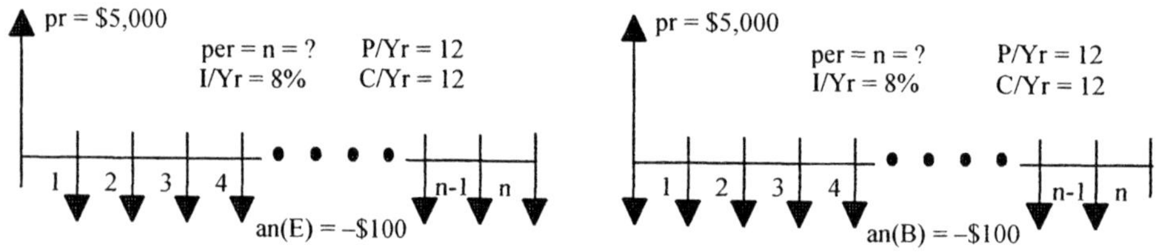

Figure 2.1.7 Type II Class B.1 problem.

Table 2.1.15 Type II, Class B.1 financial problem.

(P/Yr = C/Yr = 12).

per E	per B	I/Yr	pr	an
61.02	60.52	8.00	5,000.00	-100.00

Answer: per = 61.02 months if the payments are made at the end of each month.
per = 60.52 months if the payments are made at the beginning of each month.

American financier J. Paul Getty was worth $3 billion US by the time of his death. In his 16th-century Tudor mansion in Surrey, England, he had coin-operated telephones installed in the guest bedrooms.

Class B.2. Period is given, interest rate (I/Yr) is unknown, present value (pr) and annuity payment (an) are given.

If I have a loan for $5,000 and I can afford to make monthly payments of $150, what will be the annual interest rate (I/Yr) in order to retire the loan in 36 months? Calculate both for annuity payments made at the end (E) and at the beginning (B) of each payment period. Interest is compounded monthly.

The cash flow diagram for annuity payments at the end of each payment period is shown below on the left. The diagram on the right is for annuity payments at the beginning of each payment period.

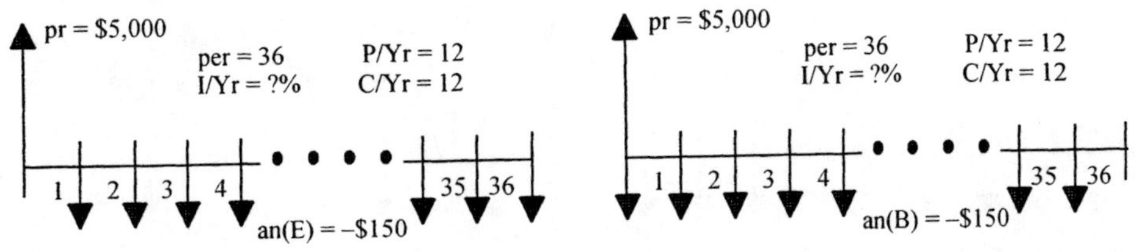

Figure 2.1.8 Type II Class B.2 problem.

Table 2.1.16 Type II, Class B.2 financial problem.

(P/Yr = C/Yr = 12).

per	I/Yr E	I/Yr B	pr	an
36.00	5.06	5.36	5,000.00	-150.00

Answer: Annual rate of 5.06% or (in%) = 5.06/12 if the payments are made at the end of each month.

Annual rate of 5.36% or (in%) = 5.36/12 if the payments are made at the beginning of each month.

Admission to the first cinema, the Vitascope Hall in New Orleans, was 10 cents on June 26, 1896. For another 10 cents, patrons were given the privilege of viewing Edison's Vitascope projector.

Class B.3. Period (per) and interest rate (I/Yr) are given, present value (pr) is unknown and annuity payment (an) is given.

If I can make a monthly payment of $350 for 36 months at an annual interest rate of 8% compounded monthly, what is the loan amount I can afford? Calculate both for annuity payments made at the end (E) and at the beginning (B) of each payment period.

Periodic interest rate (in%) = 8/12. The cash flow diagram for annuity payments at the end of each payment period is shown below on the left. The diagram on the right is for annuity payments at the beginning of each payment period.

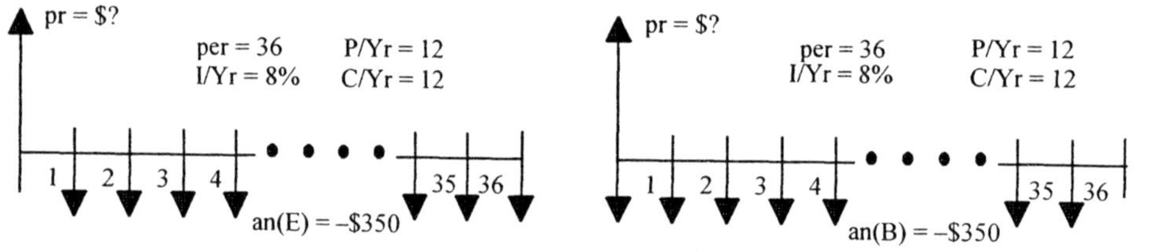

Figure 2.1.9 Type II Class B.3 problem.

Table 2.1.17 Type II, Class B.3 financial problem. (P/Yr = C/Yr = 12).

per	I/Yr	pr E	pr B	an
36.00	8.00	11,169.13	11,243.59	-350.00

Answer: pr = $11,169.13 if monthly payments made at the end of each month.
pr = $11,243.59 if monthly payments made at the beginning of each month.

In 1977, Paul MacCready's team won the $87,000 US Kremer prize for the first human-powered plane to fly a figure eight around two pylons half a mile apart and clear a 10-foot-high obstacle at the start and finish. Bryan Allen piloted the plane, the Gossamer Condor. In 1979, the team won again when their Gossamer Albatross crossed the English Channel.

Class B.4. Period (per), interest rate (I/Yr), and present value (pr) are given and annuity payment (an) is unknown.

If I have a loan for $5,000, what is my monthly payment if the annual interest rate is 8% compounded monthly and I would like to retire the loan in 36 months? Calculate both for annuity payments made at the end (E) and at the beginning (B) of each payment period.

Periodic interest rate (in%) = 8/12. The cash flow diagram for annuity payments at the end of each payment period is shown on the left. The diagram on the right is for annuity payments at the beginning of each payment period.

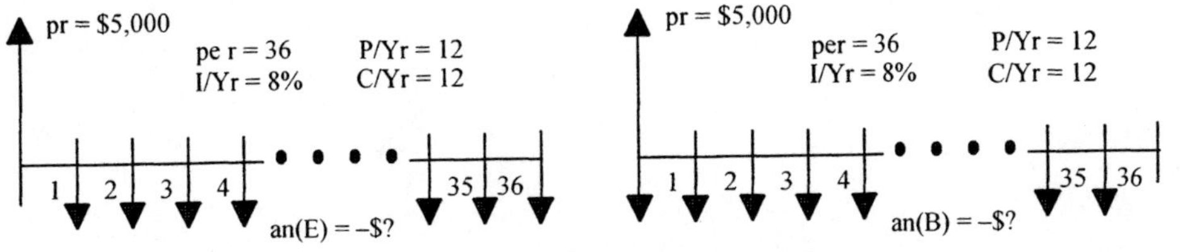

Figure 2.1.10 Type II Class B.4 problem.

Table 2.1.18 Type II, Class B.4 financial problem.

(P/Yr = C/Yr = 12).

per	I/Yr	pr	an(E)	an(B)
			E	B
36.00	8.00	5,000.00	-156.68	-155.64

Answer: an(E) = $156.68 paid monthly at the end of each month.
an(B) = $155.64 paid monthly at the beginning of each month.

Before the release of the movie, Titanic *in early 1998, the highest grossing movie in North America was* Star Wars *at $460 million (including the 1997 re-release). If older movies' box office sales were corrected for inflation, the all-time highest grossing movie according to* Daily Variety *is* Gone with the Wind, *at $1.2 billion US in box-office receipts.*

To summarize the results for Class B problems:

Table 2.1.19 Summary of results for Type II Class B financial problems.

Class	per		I/Yr		pr		an	
	E	B	E	B	E	B	E	B
B.1	61.02	60.52	8.00		5,000.00		−100.00	
B.2	36.00		5.06	5.36	5,000.00		−150.00	
B.3	36.00		8.00		11,169.13	11,243.59	−350.00	
B.4	36.00		8.00		5,000.00		−156.68	−155.64

E = monthly payments made at the end of each month.
B = monthly payments made at the beginning of each month.

The budget to send a Canadian team to Mount Everest in 1986 was about $300,000 CDN. On May 25, 1986, Sharon Wood and Dwayne Congdon reached the summit of Everest. Ms. Wood is the first North American woman to reach the top of the world's tallest mountain at 29,028 feet high.

Series of Payment Problems (Type II Class C)

Class C.1. Period (per) is unknown and interest rate (I/Yr), future value (fu), and annuity payment (an) are given.

If I can afford to set aside $200 per month, how long will it take until the accumulated future value of these monthly payments is $20,000? Assume 8% annual interest rate compounded monthly. Calculate both for annuity payments made at the end (E) and at the beginning (B) of each payment period.

Periodic interest rate (in%) = 8/12. The cash flow diagram for annuity payments at the end of each payment period is shown below on the left. The diagram on the right is for annuity payments at the beginning of each payment period.

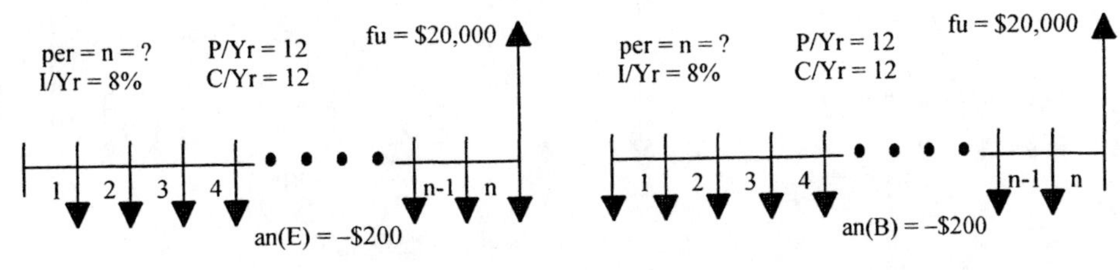

Figure 2.1.11 Type II Class C.1 problem.

Table 2.1.20 Type II, Class C.1 financial problem.

(P/Yr = C/Yr = 12).

per E	per B	I/Yr	fu	an
76.88	76.48	8.00	20,000.00	-200.00

Answer: per = 76.88 months if monthly payments made at the end of each month.
per = 76.48 months if monthly payments made at the beginning of each month.

Jerry Yang and Dan Filo, two electrical engineering students from Stanford University, dropped out just three months before completing their doctorates. They launched Yahoo! ("Yet Another Hierarchical Officious Oracle"), the Internet search engine. In 1997, they held stocks worth $140 million US.

Class C.2. Period (per) is given, interest rate (I/Yr) is unknown, future value (fu) and annuity payment (an) are given.

If I can afford to set aside $200 per month, what is the annual interest rate so that the accumulated future value of these monthly payments is $20,000 after 60 months? Calculate both for annuity payments made at the end (E) and at the beginning (B) of each payment period. Interest is compounded monthly.

The cash flow diagram for annuity payments at the end of each payment period is shown below on the left. The diagram on the right is for annuity payments at the beginning of each payment period.

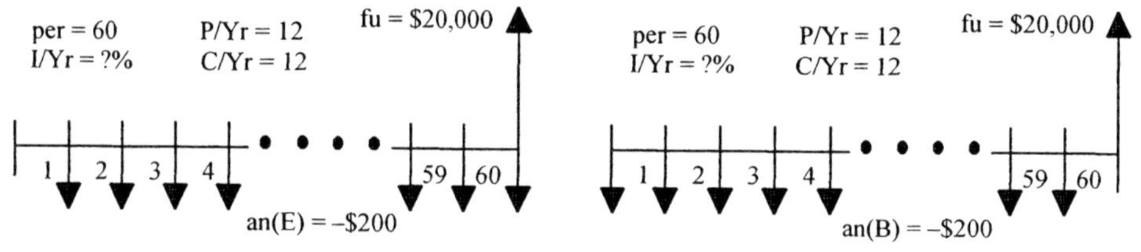

Figure 2.1.12 Type II Class C.2 problem.

Table 2.1.21 Type II, Class C.2 financial problem. (P/Yr = C/Yr = 12).

per	I/Yr E	I/Yr B	fu	an
60.00	19.38	18.82	20,000.00	-200.00

Answer: Annual rate of 19.38% or (in%) = 19.38/12 if monthly payments made at the end of each month.
Annual rate of 18.82% or (in%) = 18.82/12 if monthly payments made at the beginning of each month.

Agatha Christie wrote 78 crime novels, which were translated into 44 languages; over two billion copies were sold altogether. Annual royalty earnings from these novels amount to more than $4 million US per year.

Class C.3. Period (per) and interest rate (I/Yr) are given, future value (fu) is unknown and annuity payment (an) is given.

What is the future value of the accumulated savings after 50 months if I can afford to set aside $300 per month, and the annual interest rate is 8% compounded monthly? Calculate for both cases of annuity payments made at the end (E) and beginning (B) of each payment period.

Periodic interest rate (in%) = 8/12. The cash flow diagram for annuity payments at the end of each payment period is shown below on the left. The diagram on the right is for annuity payments at the beginning of each payment period.

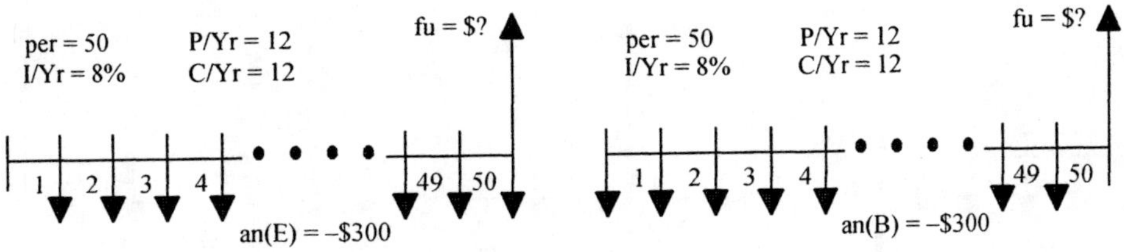

Figure 2.1.13 Type II Class C.3 problem.

Table 2.1.22 Type II, Class C.3 financial problem. (P/Yr = C/Yr = 12).

per	I/Yr	fu E	fu B	an
50.00	8.00	17,733.13	17,851.35	-300.00

Answer: fu = $17,733.13 if monthly payments made at the end of each month.
fu = $17,851.35 if monthly payments made at the beginning of each month.

In 1996, commerce via the Internet was worth $73 million US in the consumer market and $12 million US in the business-to-business market. By the year 2000, it is estimated that consumers will spend $10 billion US and business $134 billion US.

Class C.4. Period (per), interest rate (I/Yr), and future value (fu) are given and annuity payment (an) is unknown.

How much should I set aside every month so that after 50 months, the future value of the accumulated savings will be $20,000? Assume an annual interest rate of 8% compounded monthly. Calculate both for annuity payments made at the end (E) and at the beginning (B) of each payment period.

Periodic interest rate (in%) = 8/12. The cash flow diagram for annuity payments at the end of the payment period is shown below on the left. The diagram on the right is for annuity payments at the beginning of the payment period.

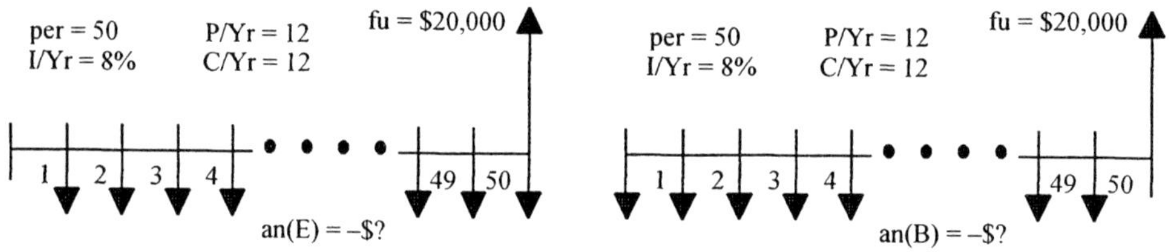

Figure 2.1.14 Type II Class C.4 problem.

Table 2.1.23 Type II, Class C.4 financial problem.
(P/Yr = C/Yr = 12).

per	I/Yr	fu	an(E)	an(B)
			E	B
50.00	8.00	20,000.00	–338.35	–336.11

Answer: an(E) = $338.35 if monthly payments made at the end of each month.
an(B) = $336.11 if monthly payments made at the beginning of each month.

As of early 1999, the leader in Internet book selling is Amazon.com Inc. However, new competitors are setting up shop such as Barnes & Noble Inc., Borders group Inc., Chapters Inc. and Bertelsmann AG. Analysts estimate that the on-line book business could be a $2.5 billion to $3 billion US industry by the year 2002.

To summarize the results for Class C problems:

Table 2.1.24 Summary of results for Type II Class C financial problems.

Class	per		I/Yr		fu		an	
	E	B	E	B	E	B	E	B
C.1	76.88	76.48	8.00		20,000.00		-200.00	
C.2	60.00		19.38	18.82	20,000.00		-200.00	
C.3	50.00		8.00		17,733.13	17,851.35	-300.00	
C.4	50.00		8.00		20,000.00		-338.35	-336.11

E = monthly payments made at the end of each month.
B = monthly payments made at the beginning of each month.

In January 26, 1998, Compaq Computer Corporation, the world's largest supplier of PCs announced a $9.6 billion US merger with Digital Equipment Corporation (DEC), the largest merger in the computer industry. This merger went ahead in June 1998.

Combined Lump-Sum Payment and Series of Payment Problems (Type III Class D)

Type III Class D problems require all the five parameters; period (per), interest rate (I/Yr), present value (pr), future value (fu), and annuity payment (an).

Class D.1. Period (per) is unknown and interest rate (I/Yr), present value (pr), future value (fu), and annuity payment (an) are given.

I would like to set up a retirement savings account. I am putting down $50,000 initially and every year I can put down $10,000. How many years will it take to accumulate a total of $1 M if the annual interest rate is 8% compounded annually? Calculate both for annuity payments made at the end (E) and at the beginning (B) of each payment period.

Periodic interest rate (in%) = 8/1. The cash flow diagram for annuity payments at the end of each payment period is shown below on the left. The diagram on the right is for annuity payments at the beginning of each payment period.

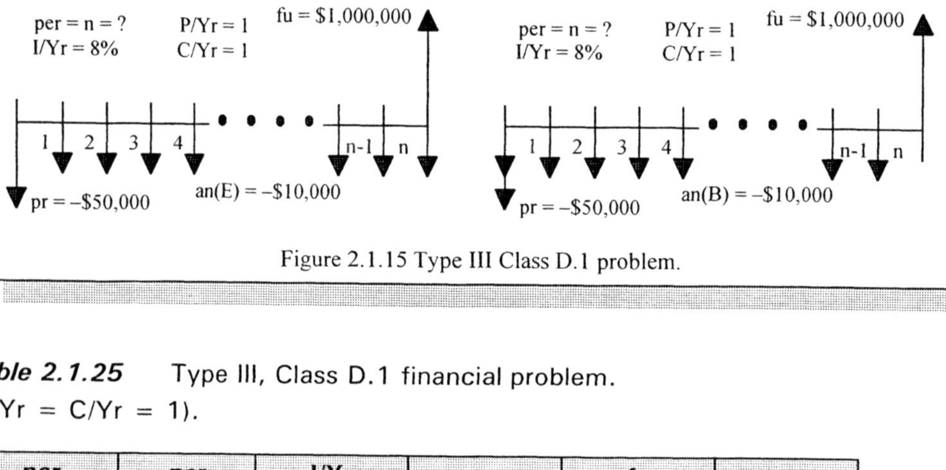

Figure 2.1.15 Type III Class D.1 problem.

Table 2.1.25 Type III, Class D.1 financial problem. (P/Yr = C/Yr = 1).

per E	per B	I/Yr	pr	fu	an
24.18	23.57	8.00	-50,000.00	1,000,000.00	-10,000.00

Answer: N = 24.18 years if annual payments made at the end of each year.
N = 23.57 years if annual payments made at the beginning of each year.

In 1948, Motorola first entered the television business with their $179 Golden View Model VT71.

Class D.2. Period (per) is given, interest rate (I/Yr) is unknown, present value (pr), future value (fu), and annuity payment (an) are given.

If I have twenty years available before I start my retirement, what is the interest rate that my money should earn in order to accumulate $1 M? I am starting my retirement savings plan now by putting down $50,000 and setting aside $10,000 every year. Calculate both for annuity payments made at the end (E) and at the beginning (B) of each payment period. Interest is compounded annually.

The cash flow diagram for annuity payments at the end of each payment period is shown below on the left. The diagram on the right is for annuity payments at the beginning of each payment period.

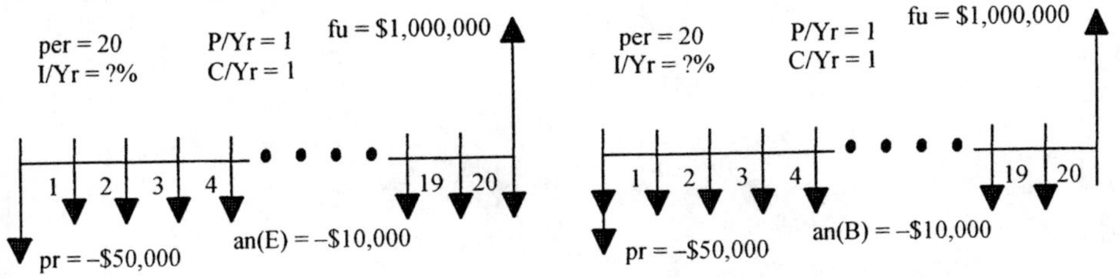

Figure 2.1.16 Type III Class D.2 problem.

Table 2.1.26 Type III, Class D.2 financial problem. (P/Yr = C/Yr = 1).

per	I/Yr E	I/Yr B	pr	fu	an
20.00	10.68	10.24	-50,000.00	1,000,000.00	-10,000.00

Answer: Annual rate of 10.68% or (in%) = 10.68/1 if monthly payments made at the end of each month.
Annual rate of 10.24% or (in%) = 10.24/1 if monthly payments made at the beginning of each month.

At midnight of December 31, 1999 the world's computers will be attacked by a non-malicious bug called the Y2K, or the "millenium bug," unless companies can find and fix it. Estimates on the amount of money required to fix this bug vary between $600 billion US and $3.6 trillion US.

Class D.3. Period (per) and interest rate (I/Yr) are given, present value (pr) is unknown and future value (fu), and annuity payment (an) are given.

I am starting a retirement savings plan now although I have twenty years to go before I start my retirement. I will put $10,000 annually into this account. How much should I put down now so that the account will accumulate $1 M if the rate of interest is 8% compounded annually? Calculate both for annuity payments made at the end (E) and at the beginning (B) of each payment period.

Periodic interest rate (in%) = 8/1. The cash flow diagram for annuity payments at the end of the payment period is shown below on the left. The diagram on the right is for annuity payments at the beginning of the payment period.

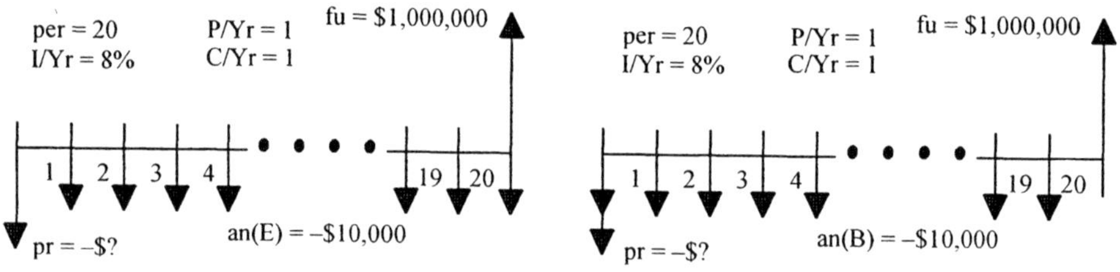

Figure 2.1.17 Type III Class D.3 problem.

Table 2.1.27 Type III, Class D.3 financial problem.
(P/Yr = C/Yr = 1).

per	I/Yr	pr E	pr B	fu	an
20.00	8.00	–116,366.73	–108,512.22	1,000,000.00	–10,000.00

Answer: pr = $116,366.73 if annual payments made at the end of each year.
pr = $108,512.22 if annual payments made at the beginning of each year.

F. A. Porsche, the grandson of the legendary German auto maker, is keeping alive the Porsche name beyond the autobahn by developing luxury products like titanium cameras for $2,500 US and mountain bikes for $4,500 US. His Austrian firm, Porsche Design, a sister company of the auto maker, markets these products.

Class D.4. Period (per), interest rate (I/Yr), and present value (pr) are given, future value (fu) is unknown, and annuity payment (an) is given.

I am starting a retirement savings plan now and plan to retire in 20 years. I will put $10,000 annually into this account. If I put down $50,000 now how much is the accumulated value of the account if the rate of interest is 8% compounded annually? Calculate both for annuity payments made at the end (E) and at the beginning (B) of each payment period.

Periodic interest rate (in%) = 8/1. The cash flow diagram for annuity payments at the end of each payment period is shown below on the left. The diagram on the right is for annuity payments at the beginning of each payment period.

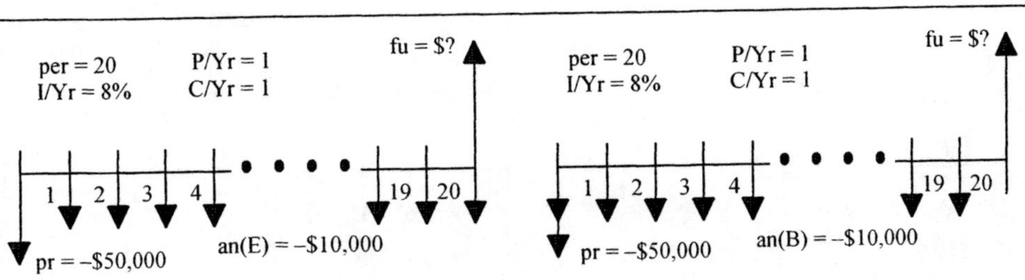

Figure 2.1.18 Type III Class D.4 problem.

Table 2.1.28 Type III, Class D.4 financial problem. (P/Yr = C/Yr = 1).

per	I/Yr	pr	fu E	fu B	an
20.00	8.00	-50,000.00	690,667.50	727,277.07	-10,000.00

Answer: fu = $690,667.50 if annual payments made at the end of each year.
fu = $727,277.07 if annual payments made at the beginning of each year.

Metals, especially gold and silver, have been used as money for at least 4,000 years. The first coins were made of electrum, a natural mixture of gold and silver. The bean-shaped ingots were crude and bore a primitive punchmark providing certification for weight, fineness, or both.

Class D.5. Period (per), interest rate, (I/Yr), present value (pr), and future value (fu) are given and annuity payment (an) is unknown.

I plan to retire in 20 years. I am starting a retirement savings plan now by putting down $50,000. How much should I set aside annually so that the account will accumulate $1 M if the rate of interest is 8% compounded annually? Calculate both for annuity payments made at the end (E) and at the beginning (B) of each payment period.

Periodic interest rate (in%) = 8/1. The cash flow diagram for annuity payments at the end of each payment period is shown below on the left. The diagram on the right is for annuity payments at the beginning of each payment period.

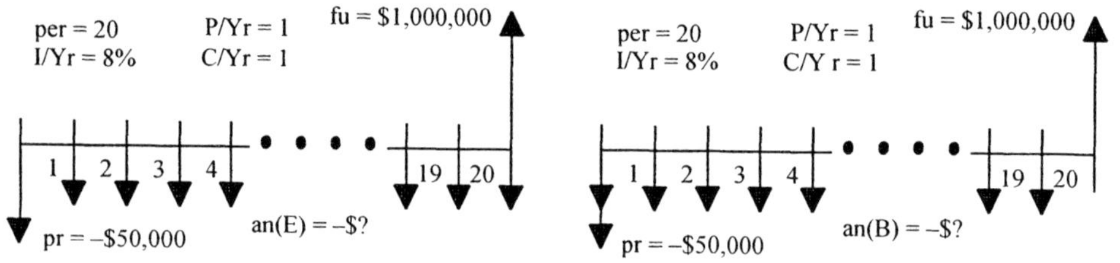

Figure 2.1.19 Type III Class D.5 problem.

Table 2.1.29 Type III, Class D.5 financial problem.
(P/Yr = C/Yr = 1).

per	I/Yr	pr	fu	an(E) E	an(B) B
20.00	8.00	-50,000.00	1,000,000.00	-16,759.60	-15,518.15

Answer: an(E) = $16,759.60 if annual payments made at the end of each year.
an(B) = $15,518.15 if annual payments made at the beginning of each year.

Counterfeit money is not a new phenomenon. Counterfeit wampum shells were circulated during the American colonial days, forcing the US government to stop their use for trading. Wampum shells are used by American Indians to record important events in the tribe.

To summarize the results for Class D problems:

Table 2.1.30 Summary of results for Type III Class D financial problems.

Class	per		I/Yr		pr		fu	
	E	B	E	B	E	B	E	B
D.1	24.18	23.57	8.00		-50,000.00		1,000,000.00	
D.2	20.00		10.68	10.24	-50,000.00		1,000,000.00	
D.3	20.00		8.00		-116,366.73	-108,512.22	1,000,000.00	
D.4	20.00		8.00		-50,000.00		690,667.50	727,277.07
D.5	20.00		8.00		-50,000.00		1,000,000.00	

Class	an	
	E	B
D.1	-10,000.00	
D.2	-10,000.00	
D.3	-10,000.00	
D.4	-10,000.00	
D.5	-16,759.60	-15,518.15

E = annual payments made at the end of each year.
B = annual payments made at the beginning of each year.

The world's largest laser is the NIF, National Ignition Facility. It is a stadium-sized $1.2 billion US, 192-beam laser complex currently under construction at the Department of Energy Lawrence Livermore National Laboratory. It is expected to be operational in 2003. The facility is expected to create brief bursts of self-sustaining fusion reactions similar to those occurring in the sun and stars.

2.2
Lesson 2: INTEREST, ANNUITY, AND INFLATION

The mattress doesn't pay interest.

Carlos Menem, President of Argentina, imploring people to "keep money in their banks rather than in their bed."

INTEREST

At one point or another, each of us has been both a lender and borrower of money. If you have a savings deposit account, you are actually lending money to the bank. In return for the use of your money, the banks pay you interest. It is usually paid monthly, based on the minimum monthly balance in your account at the quoted interest rate.

You are also a borrower of money if you take out a loan for a new car or a new home. Similarly, in return for using the money you borrowed, you pay interest to the financial institution. Loan contracts specify the amount borrowed, the *term* or length of time of the loan, the interest rate during the term, and the frequency and amount of the loan repayment. At the end of the term, the lender will have recovered the original loan amount, also called the *principal*, plus the accumulated interest.

Interest, therefore, is the *rental fee* for the use of money. Every dollar borrowed today is worth more than a dollar in the future by virtue of the interest that will have been paid when the entire principal is returned. This is the meaning of **time value of money**.

It is interesting to note that the concept of *time value of money* is not a modern one. In fact, in his excellent book, *A History of Interest Rates 2000 BC to the Present*, Sidney Homer notes that interest was generally applied on loans in ancient times by the Babylonians, Greeks, and Romans and in medieval times in Europe. For example, the dealings between lender and borrower were regulated in the Code of Hammurabi (a king of the first dynasty in ancient Babylon circa 1800 BC), the earliest record of formal laws. The maximum rate of interest was set at $33^1/_3$% per year for loans of grain payable in kind and 20% per year for loans of silver by weight. Pledges for debt were allowed, including personal slavery — but only up to three years. The penalty for collecting interest higher than the legal rate was cancellation of the principal loan. When, around 600 BC, Solon codified the laws of classical Greece, which survived for centuries, hypothecation or pledges for debt were permitted except for personal slavery. In 450 BC, the Romans also started their legal history with laws regulating credit. Interest on loans was limited to $8^1/_3$% per year and the penalty for collecting interest higher than the legal rate was fourfold damages. Personal slavery for debt was allowed; however, the laws protected the well-being of the slave.

During the Middle Ages, personal loans in England were made at interest rates of 52 to 120% per year depending on collateral. Dutch merchants borrowed at the rate of $1^3/_4$% and Italian merchants borrowed at 5 to 10%.

Aren't you glad that we live in these modern times when slavery for debt has been relegated to ancient history? Yet folks like us still have something in common with a debtor in ancient Babylonia: all debtors would like to have an idea of how much interest they will end up paying. Let us take a simple example.

Assume that you borrowed $10,000 for a period of one year. The quoted annual interest rate is 10% compounded annually (C/Yr = 1) and your payment, including principal and interest, is due at the end of the term, P/Yr = 1.

The table below indicates that your total payment at the end of the term, under the 'fu' or future value column, is $11,000. The interest therefore is $1,000, or 10% of $10,000.

Table 2.2.1 Type I Class A.4 financial problem.
(P/Yr = C/Yr = 1)

per	I/Yr	pr	fu
1.00	10.00	10,000.00	-11,000.00

Suppose, however, that the term of the loan changes from one year to six months. Although the interest *rate* is still quoted at 10% per year, the interest amount is prorated for the shorter term. Note that interest payment is still made only once, at the end of the term. From equation 2.1.1, period (per) = (P/Yr) x (Yr) = (1) x (6/12) = 0.5. From the table below, the total interest paid is $488.09 ($10,488.09 – $10,000).

Table 2.2.2 Type I Class A.4 financial problem.
(P/Yr = C/Yr = 1)

per	I/Yr	pr	fu
0.50	10.00	10,000.00	-10,488.09

We will cover more financial calculation examples involving interest later in this section and in other sections of this book.

Simple Interest

The future value of money by application of simple interest depends solely on the value of the principal and the agreed-upon interest rate. Regardless of the length of time that money is held, the calculated future value of money does not change. For example, whether the term length is one, two, three, four or five years, the future value of a $1,000 principal at 8% simple interest is $1,080 ($1,000 x 1.08). Would it not be good if financial lending institutions charge their customers using simple interest? Unfortunately, they use **compound interest** to calculate the rental fees for loans.

The first attempt to improve upon the time value of money using simple interest calculations is by increasing the rate of interest based on the length of the loan period. It just makes sense that as the borrowed money is held longer, the lender will expect more interest from his investment. For example, for a one-year loan, the simple interest charged could be 8%; for a two-year loan, the simple interest could be 9%; for a three-year loan, 10%; for four years, 11% interest and five years, 12% interest. The future values of a $1,000 principal will therefore be $1,080, $1,090, $1,100, $1,110 and $1,120 respectively.

The calculations therefore involving simple interest are as follows:

simple interest = (interest rate/100) x principal *equation (2.2.1)*

future value = principal + simple interest , or
= principal x (1 + (interest rate/100)) *equation (2.2.2)*

Compound Interest

The next step in improving upon the time value of money is by using interest rate quoted as a nominal rate on an annual basis, I/Yr.

For compound interest calculations, the quoted annual interest rate is converted to a periodic interest rate. For savings applications, at every interest compounding period, the periodic interest is applied to the accumulated interest and principal from the previous period. For loan applications, the periodic interest is calculated per interest compounding period on the remaining outstanding balance and accumulated interest. Note that how often compound interest is calculated depends on the interest compounding frequency, C/Yr, usually quoted on an annual basis. Therefore, as the period increases, for savings applications, the interest calculated increases, while for loan applications, the interest decreases. To illustrate, let us take a savings application.

Assume you are investing $1,000 to an account that pays 6% interest per year compounded annually. What is the future value of the account at the end of 5 years?

Compounded annually means that the interest calculation is done once at the end of each year. Since the term is for five years, there will be five interest payment periods. The table below shows the calculation results from using equations 2.2.1 and 2.2.2 at each interest payment period.

Table 2.2.3 Savings applications example of interest compounding calculation.

period	principal	simple interest equation 2.2.1	future value = principal + simple interest equation 2.2.2
1	1,000.00	60.00	1,060.00
2	1,060.00	63.60	1,123.60
3	1,123.60	67.42	1,191.02
4	1,191.02	71.46	1,262.48
5	1,262.48	75.75	1,338.23

Thus, compound interest is in fact the application of simple interest calculations repeated at the end of each interest payment period with the current principal coming from the sum of the principal and interest of the previous period.

Recall the problem types in Section 2.1. The problem above is a Type I, Class A.4 problem where period (per), interest rate (I/Yr), and present value (pr) are given and future value (fu) is unknown.

Using TVM analysis, Table 2.2.3 therefore is performed in one operation as shown in Table 2.2.4. The cash flow diagram for this problem is shown on the right.

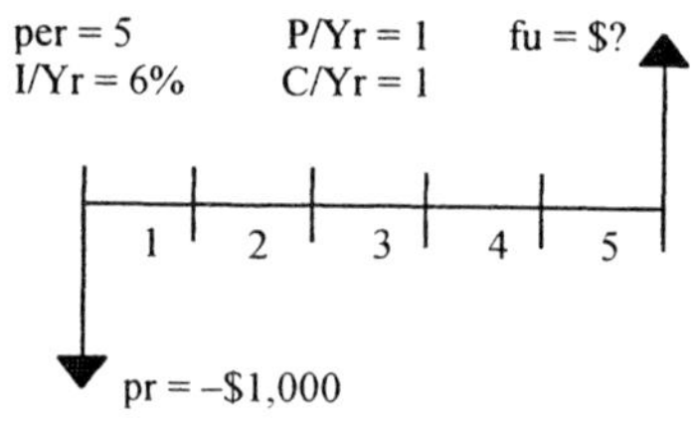

Figure 2.2.1 Type I Class A.4 problem

Table 2.2.4 Type I, Class A.4 financial problem.
(P/Yr = C/Yr = 1)

per	I/Yr	pr	fu
5.00	6.00	-1,000.00	1,338.23

Thus, using compound interest calculations, future value is $1,338.23 – the same as the final value in Table 2.2.3 and quite different from the $1,060 calculated using simple interest (6% for the entire 5 years).

Zegrahm Expeditions, a Seattle-based company, is accepting reservations for rocket-powered trips flying at 100 km above the earth. At this altitude, weightlessness is achieved. The 15 confirmed passengers made an initial deposit of $5,000 for the $98,000 US trip. Voyages will begin in 2001.

Effect of Different Compounding Periods

As shown in the previous example, the difference between simple interest and compound interest is that for simple interest the calculation is done only once for the entire investment period. However, for compound interest, the calculation is done several times within the investment period. In that particular example, it was done five times, from per x C/Yr = 5 x 1 = 5. It would then follow that the more often interest is calculated, the more money will be accumulated. Let us see how increasing frequency of compounding affects future value.

Assume a lump-sum payment with a present value of $1,000 invested at an annual interest rate of 8%. Let us calculate the future value of the investment after one year, using simple interest and compound interest with daily, weekly, bi-weekly, monthly, quarterly, semi-annual, and yearly compounding. Period (per) = 1, (I/Yr) = 8% and (C/Yr) = 365, 52, 26, 12, 4, 2, and 1 for daily, weekly, bi-weekly, monthly, quarterly, semi-annual and yearly compounding respectively.

Table 2.2.5 Type I Class A.4 financial problem.
per = 1 and I/Yr = 8%, (P/Yr = 1 and C/Yr = various values).

	C/Yr	per	I/Yr	pr	fu
Simple Interest	n/a	1.0	8.00	–1,000.00	1,080.00
daily compounding	365.00	1.0	8.00	–1,000.00	1,083.28
weekly compounding	52.00	1.0	8.00	–1,000.00	1,083.22
bi–weekly compounding	26.00	1.0	8.00	–1,000.00	1,083.15
monthly compounding	12.00	1.0	8.00	–1,000.00	1,083.00
quarterly compounding	4.00	1.0	8.00	–1,000.00	1,082.43
semi–annual compounding	2.00	1.0	8.00	–1,000.00	1,081.60
yearly compounding	1.00	1.0	8.00	–1,000.00	1,080.00

n/a = not applicable

As you can see from the above table, for the same interest rate, the more frequent the compounding is the greater the interest earned. Of course a higher interest rate would also increase the amount of interest earned.

With the same example, let us assume an investment period of five years instead of one year. Let us follow the future value of money at the end of each year for annual interest rates of 6% with yearly compounding.

The great painter Vincent Van Gogh lived in poverty, as he was able to sell only one painting in his lifetime – for about $30 US. Today, however, many of his paintings are sold for millions of dollars.

Table 2.2.6 Future values of $1,000 for periods 1, 2, 3, 4, and 5 at 6% interest rate and annual compounding.
(P/Yr = C/Yr = 1).

Annual interest rate	end of first year	end of second year	end of third year	end of fourth year	end of fifth year
6.00%	1,060.00	1,123.60	1,191.02	1,262.48	1,338.23

Let us redo the same example, but this time use daily compounding instead of annual compounding.

Table 2.2.7 Future values of $1,000 for periods 1, 2, 3, 4 and 5 at 6% interest rate and daily compounding.
(P/Yr = 1, C/Yr = 365).

Annual interest rate	end of first year	end of second year	end of third year	end of fourth year	end of fifth year
6.00%	1,061.83	1,127.49	1,197.20	1,271.22	1,349.83

The summary table below shows the future values of the $1,000 investment at different interest rates for daily and annual interest compounding.

Table 2.2.8 Comparison of annual and daily interest compounding for $1,000 at the end of each year for five years at 6%, 8% and 10% interest rates.

per	6%		8%		10%	
	Annual Comp.	Daily Comp.	Annual Comp.	Daily Comp.	Annual Comp.	Daily Comp.
end of 1st yr	1,060.00	1,061.83	1,080.00	1,083.28	1,100.00	1,105.16
end of 2nd yr	1,123.60	1,127.49	1,166.40	1,173.49	1,210.00	1,221.37
end of 3rd yr	1,191.02	1,197.20	1,259.71	1,271.22	1,331.00	1,349.80
end of 4th yr	1,262.48	1,271.22	1,360.49	1,377.08	1,464.10	1,491.74
end of 5th yr	1,338.23	1,349.83	1,469.33	1,491.76	1,610.51	1,648.61

It is estimated that having a movie in the Best Picture category for the annual Oscar awards can mean as much as $10 million US in North American ticket sales.

Table 2.2.9 % Increase of money from annual to daily compounding at the end of each period for 6%, 8% and 10% compounding interest rate.

per	6%	8%	10%
end of 1st yr	0.17%	0.30%	0.47%
end of 2nd yr	0.35%	0.61%	0.94%
end of 3rd yr	0.52%	0.91%	1.41%
end of 4th yr	0.69%	1.22%	1.89%
end of 5th yr	0.87%	1.53%	2.37%

Nominal Interest and Effective Interest

So far, the interest calculations we have discussed were for Type I lump-sum payment problems. These problems involve a single payment. The interest payment period is determined by the interest compounding period (C/Yr). For each interest compounding period within the term of the investment, interest payment is calculated. The frequency of interest calculation could be daily, weekly, bi-weekly, semi-monthly, monthly, quarterly, semi-annually or annually. We have already seen that for the same interest rate, money earns interest faster when the interest is compounded more frequently.

Types II and III problems deal with annuity or series of payments. These payments occur at regular intervals. When the frequency of the annuity payment (P/Yr) is equal to the frequency of interest calculation (C/Yr), the nominal interest is used for TVM calculations. Car loans are a good example; usually, both payment and compounding periods are monthly. At each period, therefore, two things are happening: the annuity payment occurs and the interest payment calculation is performed. However, if the frequency of the annuity payment does not coincide with the frequency of interest calculation, it will be erroneous to simply use nominal interest for TVM calculations. One will need to convert the nominal interest (I/Yr) to effective interest (Eff/Yr) and then calculate the adjusted nominal interest $(I/Yr)_{adj}$. An example is Canadian mortgages. Mortgage payments are made monthly. However, the interest is compounded semi-annually.

Five of the six financial calculators covered in this book have separate keys to calculate APR (Annual Percentage Rate or nominal interest rate) and EFF (Effective interest rate). The Texas Instruments BA II Plus financial calculator does not have these keys. Instead it has a separate interest conversion worksheet where the user can calculate these values. For TVM calculations, however, the TI BA II Plus uses compounding per year (C/Yr) and payment per year (P/Yr) and calculates internally the correct interest rate (adjusted nominal interest rate). Tables 2.2.10 - 2.2.12 show several examples of calculations involving (Eff/Yr) and $(I/Yr)_{adj}$.

Over the next 10 years from 1998, new infrastructure projects planned throughout the world, from Seoul to Bombay to Mexico City, are budgeted at about $1 trillion US total.

Table 2.2.10 Effective rate of interest (Eff/Yr) and adjusted nominal interest rate ($(I/Yr)_{adj}$) for various compounding periods at (P/Yr) = 1.

(I/Yr)	C/Yr	(Eff/Yr)	(P/Yr)	$(I/Yr)_{adj}$
6.00	1.00	6.00	1.00	6.00
6.00	2.00	6.09	1.00	6.09
6.00	12.00	6.17	1.00	6.17
6.00	365.00	6.18	1.00	6.18

Table 2.2.11 Effective rate of interest and adjusted nominal interest rate for various compounding periods at (P/Yr) = 2.

(I/Yr)	C/Yr	(Eff/Yr)	(P/Yr)	$(I/Yr)_{adj}$
6.00	1.00	6.00	2.00	5.91
6.00	2.00	6.09	2.00	6.00
6.00	12.00	6.17	2.00	6.08
6.00	365.00	6.18	2.00	6.09

Table 2.2.12 Effective rate of interest and adjusted nominal interest rate for various compounding periods at (P/Yr) = 12.

(I/Yr)	C/Yr	(Eff/Yr)	(P/Yr)	$(I/Yr)_{adj}$
6.00	1.00	6.00	12.00	5.84
6.00	2.00	6.09	12.00	5.93
6.00	12.00	6.17	12.00	6.00
6.00	365.00	6.18	12.00	6.01

From the above three tables; (C/Yr) = 1, 2, 12, 365 represents interest compounding on an annual, semi-annual, monthly, and daily basis respectively. Note the following:

- (Eff/Yr) is a function of C/Yr and not P/Yr
- when (C/Yr) = (P/Yr) = 1, (I/Yr) = (Eff/Yr) = $(I/Yr)_{adj}$
- when (C/Yr) = (P/Yr), (I/Yr) = $(I/Yr)_{adj}$
- for the same (P/Yr), as (C/Yr) increases, (Eff/Yr) increases as well as $(I/Yr)_{adj}$
- for (P/Yr) = 1, at each (C/Yr), (Eff/Yr) = $(I/Yr)_{adj}$

One of the more confusing things about financial institutions is that they only announce nominal interest rates. However, if two institutions list the same nominal interest but the compounding periods (C/Yr) differ, one will be offering a better deal or better return to the customer than the other. It is the *effective* interest rate that matters. Knowing the difference between nominal and effective interest rates should help when you shop around for the best deal whether for a savings account or a loan or mortgage.

For example, let us look at a Type I financial problem.

Assume you would like to open a savings account. Which of the four banks shown in Table 2.2.13 below offers the best return to your money? Assume P/Yr = 1.

Table 2.2.13 Investment problem: Interest Rates for Banks A, B, C, and D.

Bank	Nominal interest rate (I/Yr)	compounding (C/Yr)
A	8.05	1.00
B	8.35	4.00
C	8.40	2.00
D	8.25	365.00

Table 2.2.14 Effective rate of interest calculations for Banks A, B, C, and D.

Bank	(I/Yr)	(C/Yr)	(Eff/Yr)
A	8.05	1.00	8.05
B	8.35	4.00	8.62
C	8.40	2.00	8.58
D	8.25	365.00	8.60

Therefore, bank B with an interest rate of 8.35% compounded quarterly, offers the highest effective interest rate at 8.62%.

Let us now consider a different problem.

Assume you would like to apply for a car loan. Which of the four banks shown in Table 2.2.15 below will you take out the loan from?

In this problem, you want to choose the bank that provides the *lowest* interest rate.

In 1803, President Thomas Jefferson bought from France, for $15 million US, all the land between the Mississippi and the Rocky Mountains. It covered more than 2 million sq. km., doubling the area of the US.

Table 2.2.15 Loan interest rate problem: Interest Rates for Banks A, B, C, and D.

Bank	(I/Yr)	(C/Yr)
A	9.15	52.00
B	9.25	6.00
C	9.20	4.00
D	9.50	2.00

Table 2.2.16 Effective rate of interest calculations for Banks A, B, C, and D.

Bank	I/Yr	(C/Yr)	(Eff/Yr)
A	9.15	52.00	9.57
B	9.25	6.00	9.61
C	9.20	4.00	9.52
D	9.50	2.00	9.73

Bank C, with an interest rate of 9.20% compounded quarterly, offers the lowest effective interest rate at 9.52%.

Most financial calculators have built-in functions to calculate the effective interest rate given the (I/Yr), (P/Yr), and (C/Yr). They can calculate (Eff/Yr) from (I/Yr) or $(I/Yr)_{adj}$ from (Eff/Yr). The TI BA II Plus uses (I/Yr) and (C/Yr) as inputs and calculates (Eff/Yr) and $(I/Yr)_{adj}$ internally. In order to view these values, there is a separate interest rate conversion worksheet that will perform the calculations and thus will display the values.

Data Entry of Interest Rates

As mentioned in the Introduction, not all financial calculators are the same. One difference is the interest rate entered for TVM calculations. Some calculators require entry of periodic interest in percent (in%) while others require entry of nominal interest rate (I/Yr). The differences will be evident in Chapter 3, where solutions to the sample calculations will be shown for each of the six calculator models.

Another point to be noted is the entry of rounded-off values for periodic interest (in%). To illustrate this point, let us look at an example.

Assume you have $5,000 and you would like to put it in a savings account for 100 months, earning 8% interest compounded monthly. What is the value of your money at the end of 100 months?

> *The use of coins for money was most likely invented in ancient China, where gold cubes were used as early as 2100 BC.*

Table 2.2.17 Periodic interest has been rounded off to 0.67.
(P/Yr) = 12, Yr = 100/12.

per	in%	pr	fu
100.00	0.67	-5,000.00	9,749.38

Table 2.2.18 Periodic interest not rounded off.
(P/Yr) = 12, Yr = 100/12.

per	in%	pr	fu
100.00	8/12	-5,000.00	9,717.15

Tables 2.2.17 and 2.2.18 apply only to financial calculators that use in% as input for interest rate. (See Table 3.2.4 for a comparison of calculators). Rounding off the value used for periodic interest gave a final result ($9,749.38) that was higher by $32.23 than the correct value of $9,717.15. The difference is in the value used for periodic interest. Most likely the financial calculator you are using has been set to display 2 decimal places; 8/12 will thus show a calculated value of 0.67. However, internally, the calculator uses the value 0.6666666.... Therefore, when calculating periodic interest, divide the nominal interest rate by the period per year and then store it to the periodic interest register or memory. Do not re-enter 0.67 and store it to the periodic interest register or memory.

America's Mount Rushmore National Memorial is the world's most colossal sculpture. It features the faces of Washington, Jefferson, Roosevelt, and Lincoln sculpted on the face of a mountain. The four granite faces are so huge that from brow to chin, each is as tall as the Great Sphinx of Egypt. It took 14 years to complete, some 360 workers and less than $1 million US.

ANNUITY

To review, annuity payments are series of equal payments made at equal intervals in time. These payments can be made daily, weekly, bi-weekly, monthly, semi-monthly, annually, or at any other payment frequency. In TVM analysis, it is important to note that the chosen annuity payment frequency is applied for the entire period (per). Annuity payments are never made in the middle of each payment period. There are two types of annuity payments: ordinary annuities involve equal payments made at the end of each period. In some cases, annuity payments are instead made at the beginning of each period. The two types of payment are never mixed; if you start with end-of-period payments, you will continue that way throughout the entire period.

Ordinary Annuity or End-of-Period Annuity Payment

Examples of this type of annuity payment are loan and mortgage payments. To understand the concept and implications of annuity payments, let us consider the simplest example.

What is the future value of an annuity payment of $1 made at the end of one year if the interest per year (I/Yr) is 6%, compounded annually, (C/Yr) = 1?

From equation 2.1.1, (P/Yr) = per/Yr = 1/1 = 1. The cash flow diagram is shown on the right.

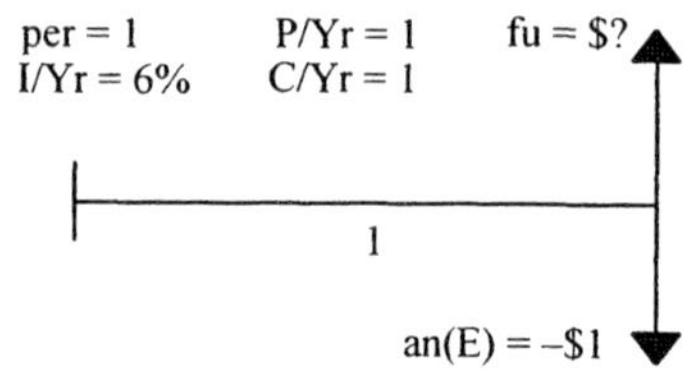

Figure 2.2.2 Ordinary annuity problem with future value unknown

Table 2.2.19 Future value of end-of-period annuity payment of $1. Type II, Class C.3 financial problem, (P/Yr = C/Yr = 1).

per	(I/Yr)	fu	an(E)
1.00	6.00	1.00	-1.00

It makes perfect sense that the future value is also $1 as there is only one period. The $1 annuity payment did not have the opportunity to earn interest. (Remember the time value of money?)

Volkswagen, Europe's largest car manufacturer, paid the equivalent of $870 million US to purchase Rolls-Royce Motor Cars Ltd. from Vickers PLC. Rival BMW had offered $554 million US. The deal was closed on July 3, 1998.

Instead of calculating the future value of $1, let us calculate the present value with all other parameters the same. The cash flow diagram is shown on the right.

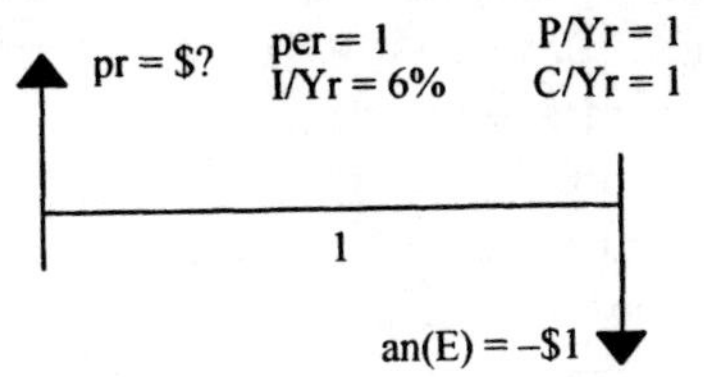

Figure 2.2.3 Ordinary annuity problem with present value unknown

Table 2.2.20 Present value of end-of-period annuity payment of $1. Type II, Class B.3 financial problem, (P/Yr = C/Yr = 1).

per	(I/Yr)	pr	an(E)
1.00	6.00	0.94	-1.00

In this problem, the present value has to be lower than $1. If the calculated $0.94 is invested at 6% annual interest rate, it will equal $1 at the end of one year. We can see therefore how the time value of money works.

Instead of one period, let us repeat the last two calculations but this time consider a period of 2.

The cash flow diagram for the future value problem is shown on the right.

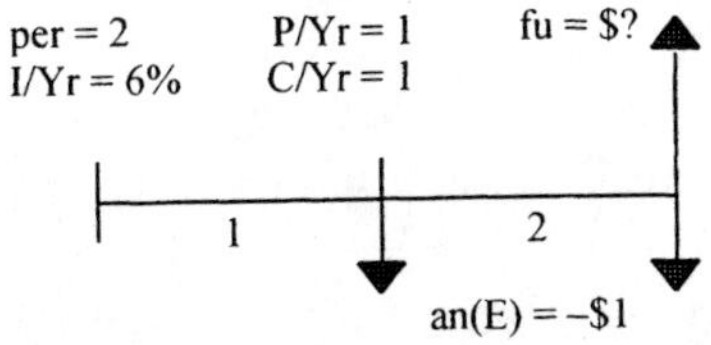

Figure 2.2.4 Ordinary annuity problem with 2 periods and future value unknown

Table 2.2.21 Future value of end-of-period annuity payment of $1. Type II, Class C.3 financial problem, (P/Yr = C/Yr = 1).

per	(I/Yr)	fu	an(E)
2.00	6.00	2.06	-1.00

As of 1997, Microsoft has sold 150 million copies of Windows worldwide, representing 90% of all operating systems sales.

The future value of two $1 payments made at the end of each period has to be more than the simple sum of $1 + $1. The $0.06 earned is interest from the first $1 payment, at the stated 6% interest rate. The second $1 payment did not have opportunity to earn interest.

The present value problem cash flow diagram with 2 periods is shown on the right.

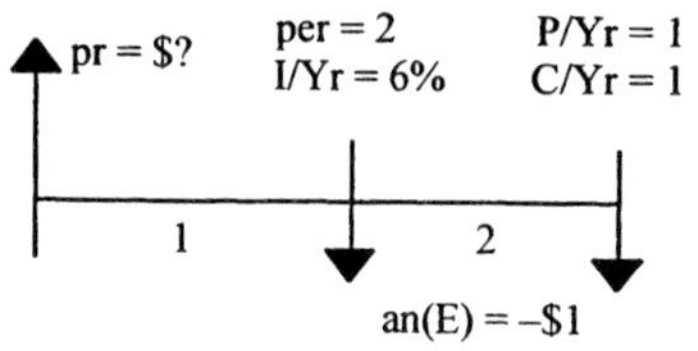

Figure 2.2.5 Ordinary annuity problem for 2 periods with unknown present value

Table 2.2.22 Present value of end-of-period annuity payment of $1. Type II, Class B.3 financial problem, (P/Yr = C/Yr = 1).

per	(I/Yr)	pr	an(E)
2.00	6.00	1.83	-1.00

The present value of two $1 payments made at the end of each period has to be less than the simple sum of $0.94 + $0.94 (see Table 2.2.20). The second $1 payment has twice the period as the first payment and therefore, its present value should be lower than $0.94. It is lower than the present value of the first payment as it has more time to accumulate interest. It is actually $0.89. Thus, 0.89 + 0.94 = 1.83, the calculated present value.

The same principles apply to any period and any annuity payment value.

Beginning-of-Period Annuity Payment

The other type of annuity payments is one where the equal payments are made at the beginning of each payment period. Examples are rent and lease payments.

Let us repeat the series of calculations we performed for ordinary annuity.

What is the future value of an annuity payment of $1 made at the beginning of the year if the interest per year (I/Yr) is 6%, compounded annually, (C/Yr) = 1?

From equation 2.1.1, (P/Yr) = per/Yr = 1/1 =1. The cash flow diagram is shown on the right.

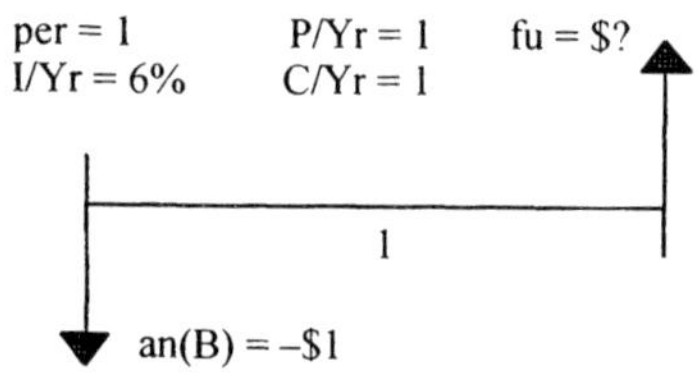

Figure 2.2.6 Beginning-of-period annuity problem with future value unknown

In 1997, the sneakers business, dominated by Nike, is a $9.5 billion US industry.

Table 2.2.23 Future value of beginning-of-period annuity payment of $1. Type II Class C.3 financial problem, (P/Yr = C/Yr = 1).

per	(I/Yr)	fu	an(B)
1.00	6.00	1.06	-1.00

By looking at the above cash flow diagram, one can see that it makes sense that the future value of $1 is $1.06, as the original $1 had the opportunity to earn interest.

Instead of calculating the future value of $1, let us calculate the present value with all other parameters the same. The cash flow diagram is shown on the right.

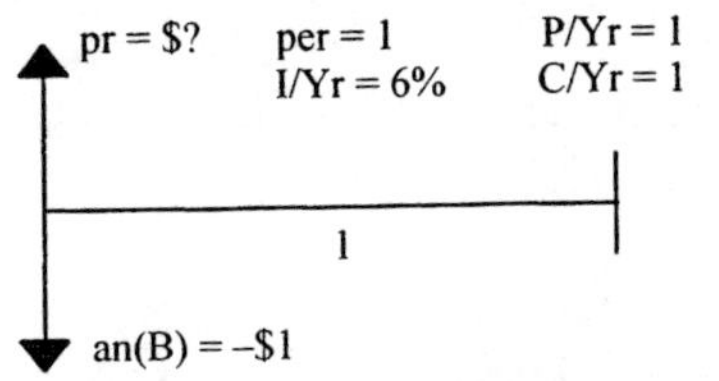

Figure 2.2.7 Beginning-of-period annuity problem with present value unknown

Table 2.2.24 Present value of beginning-of-period annuity payment of $1. Type II Class B.3 financial problem. (P/Yr = C/Yr = 1).

per	(I/Yr)	pr	an(B)
1.00	6.00	1.00	-1.00

From the cash flow diagram again, it makes perfect sense that the present value of $1 is also $1 as it did not have the opportunity to earn interest.

Let us repeat the last two calculations, but setting the period at 2 instead of 1.

The cash flow diagram is shown on the right.

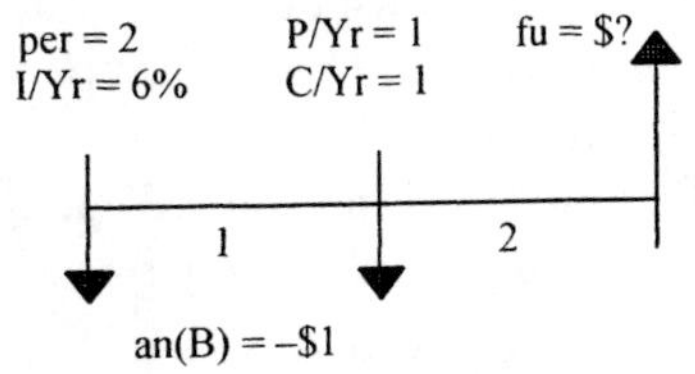

Figure 2.2.8 Beginning-of-period annuity problem for 2 periods with future value unknown

Most millionaires did not inherit their fortunes from their parents; 80% amassed their fortune through hard work.

Table 2.2.25 Future value of beginning-of-period annuity payment of $1. Type II Class C.3 financial problem, (P/Yr = C/Yr = 1).

per	(I/Yr)	fu	an(B)
2.00	6.00	2.18	-1.00

The future value of two $1 payments made at the beginning of each period has to be more than the simple sum of $1.06 + $1.06 (see Table 2.2.23). The first $1 payment had two periods in which to accumulate interest and the second $1 payment had one period to accumulate interest. The first payment accumulated a total of $0.12 in interest and the second payment earned $0.06 for a grand total of $2.18 including the principal of $2.

The cash flow diagram for the present value problem with 2 periods is shown on the right.

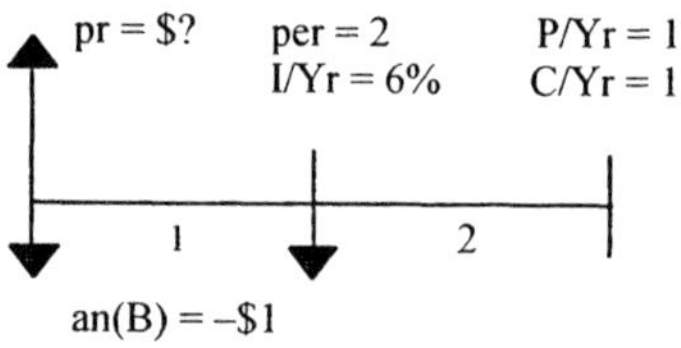

Figure 2.2.9 Beginning-of-period annuity problem for 2 periods with unknown present value

Table 2.2.26 Present value of beginning-of-period annuity payment of $1. Type II Class B.3 financial problem, (P/Yr = C/Yr = 1).

per	(I/Yr)	pr	an(B)
2.00	6.00	1.94	-1.00

From the cash flow diagram, it is obvious that the first payment will not have the opportunity to earn interest. The second payment, however, had one period from which to earn interest. This $1, when brought to the present, is actually $0.94. It had one period to accumulate $0.06 in interest, making it $1 after one period.

The same principles apply to any period and any annuity payment values.

Summary

The future value of a series of payments has a higher value when the payments are made at the beginning rather than at the end of the period. This value increases as period increases and as the interest rate increases. Table 2.2.27 summarizes the future values of $1,000 annuity payments made at the end and at the beginning of each year for various periods and interest rates.

The present value of a series of payments has a lower value when the payments are made at the end rather than at the beginning of the period. This value increases as period increases but decreases as the interest rate increases. Table 2.2.28 summarizes the present values of $1,000 annuity payments made at the end and at the beginning of each year for various periods and interest rates.

Table 2.2.27 Future values (fu) of $1,000 annuity payments made annually at the end (E) and beginning (B) of each year for 5, 10, 15, and 20 years at interest rates of 6%, 8%, and 10%. Type III Class C.3 problem, (P/Yr = C/Yr = 1).

per	Future Values (fu)					
	6.00%		8.00%		10.00%	
	E	B	E	B	E	B
5.00	5,637.09	5,975.32	5,866.60	6,335.93	6,105.10	6,715.61
10.00	13,180.79	13,971.64	14,486.56	15,645.49	15,937.42	17,531.17
15.00	23,275.97	24,672.53	27,152.11	29,324.28	31,772.48	34,949.73
20.00	36,785.59	38,992.73	45,761.96	49,422.92	57,275.00	63,002.50

Table 2.2.28 Present values (pr) of $1,000 annuity payments made annually at the end (E) and beginning (B) of each year for 5, 10, 15, and 20 years at interest rates of 6%, 8%, and 10%. Type II Class B.3 problem, (P/Yr = C/Yr = 1).

per	Present Values (pr)					
	6.00%		8.00%		10.00%	
	E	B	E	B	E	B
5.00	4,212.36	4,465.11	3,992.71	4,312.13	3,790.79	4,169.87
10.00	7,360.09	7,801.69	6,710.08	7,246.89	6,144.57	6,759.02
15.00	9,712.25	10,294.98	8,559.48	9,244.24	7,606.08	8,366.69
20.00	11,469.92	12,158.12	9,818.15	10,603.60	8,513.56	9,364.92

The last problem we will discuss is the hypothetical situation described in the Preface. If you will recall, the hypothetical worker was offered two choices of payment. It is the second we are interested in here:

Assume you are asked to work for 30 days. At the end of each day, you will receive 1 cent but each day's payment will earn interest at the rate of 100% per day for the succeeding days.

This is an annuity problem that consists of $0.01 paid at the end of each day for 30 days. The interest is 100% per day compounded daily (C/Yr = 365). Therefore, the interest per year (I/Yr) = 365 x 100 = 36,500%, (P/Yr) = 365 days, Yr = 30/365.

Table 2.2.29 Accumulated value at the end of the day for 1 cent a day at 100% per day compounded daily for 30 days.

end of day	accumulated value	end of day	accumulated value	end of day	accumulated value
1	0.01	11	20.47	21	20,971.51
2	0.03	12	40.95	22	41,943.03
3	0.07	13	81.91	23	83,886.07
4	0.15	14	163.83	24	167,772.15
5	0.31	15	327.67	25	335,544.31
6	0.63	16	655.35	26	671,088.63
7	1.27	17	1,310.71	27	1,342,177.27
8	2.55	18	2,621.43	28	2,684,354.55
9	5.11	19	5,242.87	29	5,368,709.11
10	10.23	20	10,485.75	30	10,737,418.23

The accumulated value in the table above is calculated as follows. At the end of the first day the annuity payment is 1 cent ($0.01). The accumulated value at the end of the next or any succeeding day is calculated by doubling the amount from the previous day (implementation of the 100% interest per day) and then adding 1 cent. For example, at the end of the 10th day, the accumulated value is equal to double the amount at the end of the 9th day ($5.11 + $5.11 = $10.22) and then adding 1 cent to give a total of $10.22 + $0.01 = $10.23. At the end of the 30th day, the accumulated value is $10,737,418.23.

The simpler way of calculating the same answer is by using the time value of money analysis and using a financial calculator.

To visualize the problem, the cash flow diagram is shown on the right.

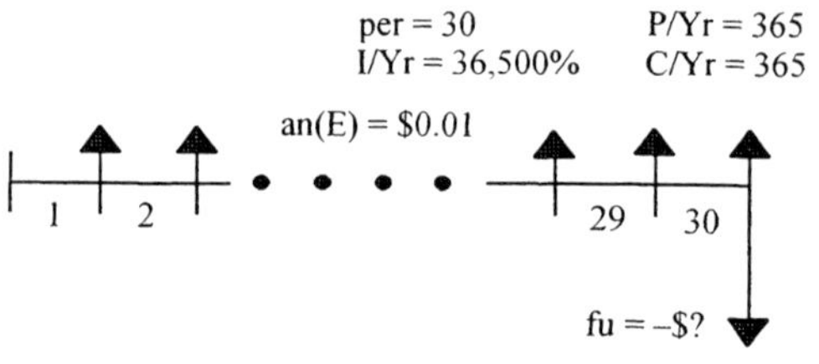

Figure 2.2.10 Wage Compounding

In July 1998, Claude Monet's painting Water Lily Pond was sold in London at a record price of £18 million ($44 million US).

Table 2.2.30 Future value of $0.01 annuity payment made at the end of each day for 30 days, at interest rate of 100% per day.
Type II Class C.3 financial problem, (P/Yr = C/Yr = 365).

per	I/Yr	fu	an(E)
30.00	36,500.00	-10,737,418.23	0.01

The graph below shows that most of the gains due to compounding interest accrue in the last five or six days.

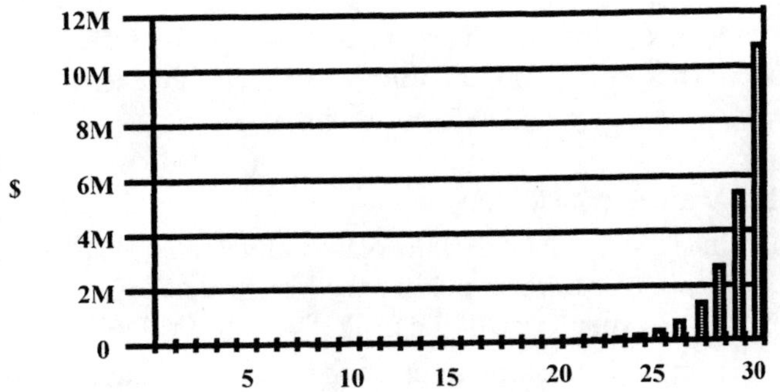

Figure 2.2.11 Future value of $0.01 per day after 30 days and daily compounding at 100% per day.

On July 4, 1997, JPL's (Jet Propulsion Lab's) Pathfinder landed on Mars, seven months from the day of its launch. It took three years to build, with a total budget of $280 million US. The last time NASA put a lander on Mars was in 1970s with the Viking mission, which cost $1.5 billion US (about $3 billion US in today's dollars).

INFLATION

Inflation is such an important subject that it deserves a separate sub-section. In personal finance, one needs to take inflation into account, especially when saving money towards a long-term goal (such as children's education or retirement) or determining the real rate of return of personal investments.

Inflation is a process whereby average prices increase substantially over a considerable period of time. In other words, more money is required to buy the same goods and services. A measure of the rate of inflation is either the *decrease* in the value of money or an annual percentage rate of *increase* in the cost of a typical "shopping basket" of goods and services.

Although the general tendency today is for prices to go up, there are products that have come down in price. I remembered buying a 12" colour TV in 1977 for about $250. In 1995, I bought a similar size colour TV for about $200. If you scan newspaper ads, you can see that the prices of personal computers have gone down more dramatically. Falling prices are common for popular electronic gadgets such as video cameras, VCRs, cellular phones, and fax machines. On the other hand, the things that have increased in prices include food, clothing, gasoline, and university and college tuition fees.

Decrease in the Value of Money

Statistics show that since 1900, $1 US has decreased in value so that $1 US in 1900 is worth only as much as $0.06 in 1993. Let us calculate the rate of decrease in value of the US dollar (negative value for I/Yr) from 1900 to 1993. (P/Yr) = 1, (C/Yr) = 1.

Note that, in the calculations, the signs of the numbers may not always seem to make sense. Of course the value of the dollar will never be negative. However, financial calculators are set up to consider present and future values in terms of cash inflow and outflow. To adapt these calculations to inflation, we have to work as though the money were being paid into a "savings plan," at negative interest.

Table 2.2.31 Rate of decrease in value of $1 from 1900 to 1993.
Type I, Class A.2 financial problem. (P/Yr) = 1, (C/Yr) = 1.

per	(I/Yr)	pr	fu
93.00	-2.98	1.00	-0.06

Thus, the decrease in value of the US dollar is at the rate of about 3% per year for the past 93 years. Statistics show that this rate was 5% for the past 30 years, 6% for the past 20 years and 4% for the past 10 years.

The Canadian dollar, too, has decreased in value over time. Let us do some simple analysis to get a feel for inflation as defined by a decrease in the value of money. Consider the problem from a slightly different angle. How long does it take for a dollar to lose half of its value? Let us calculate what the rate of decrease in the value of money (I/Yr) would be if a dollar decreased in value to 50 cents over five years; over 10 years; over 15 years; or over 20 years.

Table 2.2.32 Rate of decrease of $1 CDN to $0.50 in 5, 10, 15, and 20 years. Type I, Class A.2 financial problem. (P/Yr) = 1, (C/Yr) = 1.

per	(I/Yr)	pr	fu
5.00	-12.94	1.00	-0.50
10.00	-6.70	1.00	-0.50
15.00	-4.52	1.00	-0.50
20.00	-3.41	1.00	-0.50

Assuming a rate of change in the value of money (I/Yr) of -3%, what is the future value of $1 CDN for different periods (per) = 5, 10, 15, 20, 25, 30, 40, and 50 years.

Table 2.2.33 At (I/Yr) = -3%, future value of $1 CDN at the end of various periods. Type I, Class A.4 financial problem. (P/Yr = C/Yr = 1).

per	(I/Yr)	pr	fu
5.00	-3.00	1.00	-0.86
10.00	-3.00	1.00	-0.74
15.00	-3.00	1.00	-0.63
20.00	-3.00	1.00	-0.54
25.00	-3.00	1.00	-0.47
30.00	-3.00	1.00	-0.40
40.00	-3.00	1.00	-0.30
50.00	-3.00	1.00	-0.22

Every dollar is worth less in terms of what it can buy in the future. Even at a low inflation rate of 3%, every dollar you invest will lose 26 cents of its value in 10 years, 53 cents of its value in 25 years and 78 cents of its value in 50 years.

Increase in the Average Price Level

The other measure of inflation is the annual rate of increase of the average price of goods and services. This is the most commonly used measure of inflation.

Bookings from the growing cruise industry have been strong due to the release of the movie Titanic *by James Cameron. Thirty-five ships, ranging in capacity from about 400 to 3,000 passengers, have been ordered for delivery by the year 2002 at a total cost of $10.5 billion US.*

Economists use price indexes to measure the rise in prices. Price indexes provide a method to compare today's prices with those in a selected year, called the *base year*. Although there are several indexes that can be used to measure inflation, the one most commonly used by economists is the Consumer Price Index (CPI). The CPI expresses the cost of a basket of goods today as a percentage of the basket's cost in the base year. It is a measure of the consumer price changes as experienced by the target population within a reference period. The consumer price index for the base year is always 100. Thus, if the CPI is 120%, prices have increased 20% since the base year. That is, the basket of goods that cost $10,000 in the base year costs $12,000 today.

It is standard practice in most countries to measure the current month's level of inflation by using the percent change from the previous month's CPI. Although the CPI is compiled monthly, economists employ "smoothing" or "filtering" techniques to convert monthly indexes into an annual number. However, such attempts to improve the smoothness and reliability of the annual CPI also make the data less timely. In short, Marc Prud'homme concludes in his excellent article for Statistics Canada that "*there is no single and definite answer to the question 'What is the "current" annual rate of inflation?'*"

Table 2.2.34 Canadian and US rates of inflation 1962–1994.

Year (19__)	Inflation rate (%) in Canada	Year (19__)	Inflation rate (%) in the US
62	1.3	62	1.0
63	1.7	63	1.2
64	2.0	64	1.3
65	2.4	65	1.5
66	3.5	66	2.7
67	3.8	67	2.9
68	4.0	68	4.0
69	4.5	69	5.2
70	3.3	70	5.6
71	2.9	71	4.2
72	4.7	72	3.3
73	7.8	73	5.8
74	10.8	74	10.9
75	10.8	75	8.9
76	7.8	76	5.8
77	8.0	77	6.4
78	9.0	78	7.7
79	9.1	79	11.0
80	10.2	80	13.0
81	12.4	81	10.0
82	10.9	82	5.9
83	5.7	83	3.1
84	4.4	84	4.2
85	3.9	85	3.4
86	4.2	86	1.9
87	4.4	87	3.7
88	4.0	88	4.2
89	5.0	89	4.8
90	4.8	90	5.3
91	5.6	91	4.1
92	1.5	92	3.0
93	1.8	93	2.9
94	0.2	94	

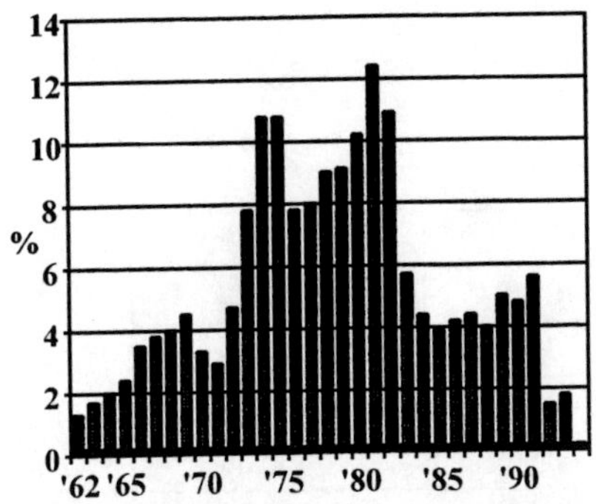

Figure 2.2.12 Inflation Rates in Canada, 1962-1994

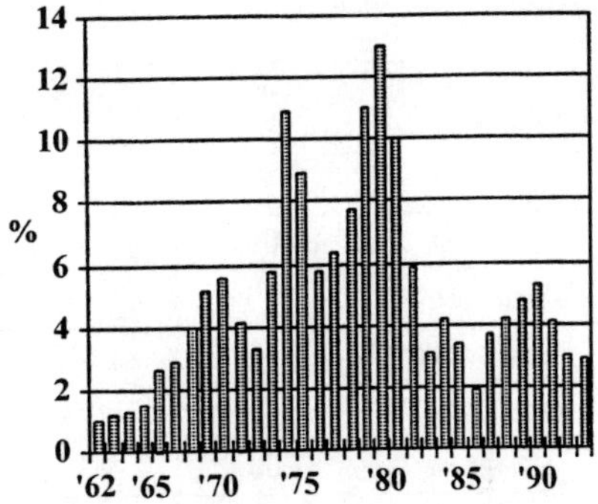

Figure 2.2.13 Inflation Rates in the US, 1962-1993

Let us look at several common items and see by how much their prices have increased through passage of time. The table below shows the price of various items in 1915, 1955 and in 1996.

Table 2.2.35 Price of various items in 1915, 1955 and 1996.

Items	1915	1955	1996
weekly newspaper	– –	$0.05	$0.75
dozen eggs	$0.32	$0.60	$1.79
lb of butter	$0.38	$0.62	$2.79
lb of coffee	$0.40	$1.00	$2.00
women's winter coat	$8.00	$40.00	$80.00
men's suit	$8.00	$65.00	$150.00
car	$850.00	$1,800.00	$20,000.00

For each item in the above Table 2.2.35, we can determine the rate of increase of price (I/Yr) using TVM analysis. In Table 2.2.36, the present values (pr) are the values under the column 1915 in Table 2.2.35. The future values (fu) are the values under the column 1996 also in Table 2.2.35. Table 2.2.36 shows the rate of increase in price (I/Yr) over the 81-year period. As explained earlier, the signs represent the conventions used by a financial calculator. Of course, the price of a dozen eggs was always a positive amount, but the calculator needs the input as a negative amount, as if that original price had been "paid out" to an interest-bearing account.

Table 2.2.36 Rate of increase in price for various items, with present values (pr) in 1915 and future values (fu) in 1996.
Type I, Class A.2 financial problem. (P/Yr) = 1, (C/Yr) = 1.

item	per	(I/Yr)	pr (yr = 1915)	fu (yr = 1996)
doz eggs	81.00	2.15	-0.32	1.79
lb of butter	81.00	2.49	-0.38	2.79
lb of coffee	81.00	2.01	-0.40	2.00
women's winter coat	81.00	2.88	-8.00	80.00
men's suit	81.00	3.69	-8.00	150.00
car	81.00	3.98	-850.00	20,000.00

Repeating the same procedure as in Table 2.2.36 but this time setting present values at 1955 prices, the results are shown in Table 2.2.37.

Table 2.2.37 Rate of increase in price for various items, with present values (pr) in 1955 and future values in 1996.
Type I, Class A.2 financial problem. (P/Yr) = 1, (C/Yr) = 1.

item	per	(I/Yr)	pr (yr = 1955)	fu (yr = 1996)
weekly newspaper	41.00	6.83	-0.05	0.75
doz eggs	41.00	2.70	-0.60	1.79
lb of butter	41.00	3.74	-0.62	2.79
lb of coffee	41.00	1.70	-1.00	2.00
women's winter coat	41.00	1.70	-40.00	80.00
men's suit	41.00	2.06	-65.00	150.00
car	41.00	6.05	-1,800.00	20,000.00

Assuming the increase of price is 4%, let us estimate how much each item above will cost in 5, 10, 15, and 20 years.

Walter P. Chrysler, the man who founded the Chrysler Corporation, worked as the president of Buick. While president, he earned the parent company General Motors, a profit of $48 million. He left the company at the age of 45 as a millionaire.

Table 2.2.38 Projected prices for various items with present values as prices in 1996, (I/Yr) = 4%, at periods = 5, 10, 15, and 20 years.
Type I, Class A.4 financial problem. (P/Yr) = 1, (C/Yr) = 1.

item	pr yr = 1996	fu (per = 5) yr = 2001	fu (per = 10) yr = 2006	fu (per = 15) yr = 2011	fu (per = 20) yr = 2016
weekly newspaper	-0.75	0.91	1.11	1.35	1.64
doz eggs	-1.79	2.18	2.65	3.22	3.92
lb of butter	-2.79	3.39	4.13	5.02	6.11
lb of coffee	-2.00	2.43	2.96	3.60	4.38
women's winter coat	-80.00	97.33	118.42	144.08	175.29
men's suit	-150.00	182.50	222.04	270.14	328.67
car	-20,000.00	24,333.06	29,604.89	36,018.87	43,822.46

To further appreciate the effect of inflation on price levels, consider the inflation rate in Brazil in the early to mid 1990s. This country's inflation rate reached an all-time high of 2,500% in 1993. However, with the Real Plan implemented by President Fernando Henrique Cordoso, the country's inflation rate was slashed to less than 10% in 1994. This was done by tying the new currency to the US dollar. But just consider the 2,500% inflation rate —this is equivalent to 6.85% inflation rate per day! This meant that if you bought a pound of coffee for $2.00 at the beginning of the month, with 2,500% inflation rate compounded monthly, you would have to pay $6.07 for the same pound of coffee at the beginning of the next month. (To solve this problem, set per = 30, I/Yr = 2,500, pr = 2, P/Yr = 365, C/Yr = 12).

Effect of Inflation on Investments

For short periods such as a few years, the effect of inflation on the value of money is limited. However, if money is accumulated for longer periods, such as 10 years or more, its loss of value over time can have potentially devastating results.

Assume that you want to start an investment plan in which you are putting down $100 at the end of every month into an investment account. At the end of 10 years, what will the total value of the account be? Assume that money earns 8% interest compounded monthly.

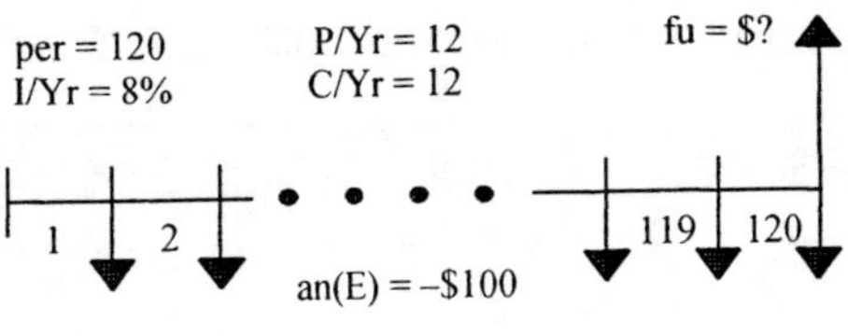

Figure 2.2.14 TVM example

The cash flow diagram is shown on the right.

Table 2.2.39 Future value of $100 annuity monthly payments.
Type II, Class C.3 financial problem, (P/Yr = C/Yr = 12), end-of-period payments.

per	(I/Yr)	fu	an(E)
120.00	8.00	18,294.60	-100.00

In today's dollars, how much is the total value of the account?

The cash flow diagram is shown on the right.

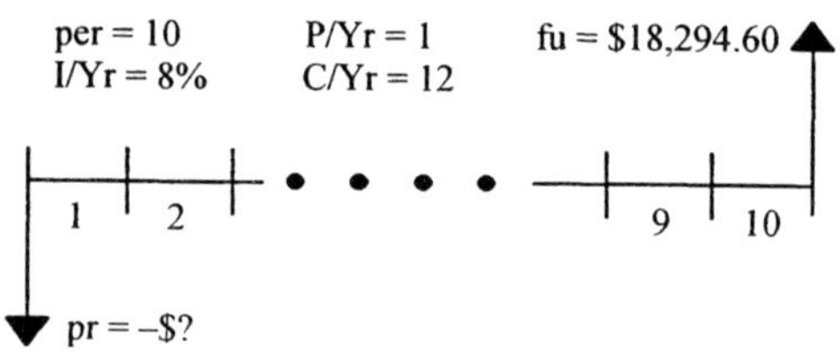

Figure 2.2.15 Calculating present value

Table 2.2.40 Present value of $18,294.60.
Type I, Class A.3 financial problem, (P/Yr = 1, C/Yr = 12).

per	(I/Yr)	pr	fu
10.00	8.00	-8,242.15	18,294.60

Therefore, the equivalent of $100 payments at the end of each month to accumulate $18,294.60 at the end of 10 years at 8% interest rate is a lump-sum payment now of $8,242.15. Note that this is considering 0% inflation.

For now, disregard the 8% interest rate. What we know is the future value, which is $18,294.60. Due to inflation alone, what is the equivalent present value at various inflation rates?

Table 2.2.41 Present value of $18,294.60 at various inflation rates.
Type I, Class A.3 financial problem, (P/Yr = 1, C/Yr = 12).

per	(I/Yr)	pr	fu
10.00	0.00	-18,294.60	18,294.60
10.00	3.00	-13,558.05	18,294.60
10.00	5.00	-11,107.77	18,294.60
10.00	7.00	-9,103.32	18,294.60
10.00	9.00	-7,463.05	18,294.60

For 0% inflation rate, the future value of $18,294.60 is also the present value.

Consider the $8,242.15 lump-sum payment. Let us look at the effect on the future value of the investment of various rates of inflation.

Table 2.2.42 Future value of $8,242.15 at various inflation rates. Type I, Class A.4 financial problem, (P/Yr = 1, C/Yr = 12).

per	(I/Yr)	pr	fu
10.00	0.00	–8,242.15	8,242.15
10.00	3.00	–8,242.15	11,121.57
10.00	5.00	–8,242.15	13,574.90
10.00	7.00	–8,242.15	16,563.93
10.00	9.00	–8,242.15	20,204.45

Although the future values are increasing as the inflation rate increases, the fact is that those monies are all worth the same, with a present value of $8,242.15. Thus, inflation results in an inflated amount of future value of money.

The technology for a "de-copying machine" has been tested and commercial units will be available in the market in early 1999. ImageX Technologies Inc. of Framingham, Mass. developed the technology, which removes toner from paper, rendering the paper reusable again. A small office unit is expected to cost $3,000 US.

2.3
Lesson 3:
FOUR METHODS TO IMPLEMENT A SAVINGS PLAN

Failing to plan is planning to fail.

Benjamin Franklin

So far, we have covered the basics of time value of money analysis by discussing the five parameters involved, including payment frequency (P/Yr) and compounding frequency (C/Yr). Types and classes of financial problems were identified and sample problems for each were shown. We've discussed interest and annuity in some detail.

One of the functions of money is to store wealth. One sacrifices the ability to spend money today to let it grow by way of earning interest. However, inflation plays a major role in whether or not the sacrifice was worth it. Thus, inflation is a very important consideration when reviewing one's personal finances.

At this point, you now have the basic foundations of personal finance. Starting from this section, we will now cover the practical applications of personal finance.

One of the most common applications of personal finance is to implement a savings plan. Most of us, I am sure have implemented a successful savings plan in the past. As a young teenager, did you save up money to buy a new bike, brand-name shoes, jackets, etc.? Maybe you had a weekly allowance from your parents. Perhaps when you were a bit older, you got a part-time job in the local grocery store or fast-food restaurant. In any case, you had to patiently set aside a few dollars and cents until you had enough money to buy what you wanted. As we grow older, finish school, and eventually hold a full-time job, we are still confronted with the savings predicament. We always say to ourselves, when I get that promotion, or when I get a higher paying job, I will be able to buy what I want. But have you found that no matter how much more income you have, you most often end up not being able to buy some of the things you really want? This is because as one's income increases, one's expenses also increase. So, to get what you really want, you need a savings plan.

Compared to the plan you had as a teenager, there are two differences. First, you are now dealing with a larger amount of money. Second, as a teenager, you deposited your money in your personal piggy bank. This time, however, you are depositing money in a bank where your money can earn interest. What are you saving for? A home theater system? A new computer? An exotic vacation with your spouse? Two of the more important reasons for implementing a savings plan are to help defray the cost of your children's education and to finance a very comfortable retirement.

There are four basic methods one can use to implement a savings plan. These are the following:

- Method 1 - lump-sum (one-time) payment
- Method 2 - annuity payment (one series of equal payments)
- Method 3 - combination of lump-sum (one-time) and annuity payments (one series of equal payments)
- Method 4 - combination of more than one lump-sum payment and several series of annuity payments

Method 1, the lump-sum payment, is usually the toughest, as it requires that you have a large sum of extra money available *today*. You do not need the money right now, but you anticipate requiring an amount of money some time in the future. Thus, a single lump-sum payment is set aside to be cashed when the money is needed. Because your money will be earning interest, the amount of money you will have to set aside is less than the future value you require. How *much* lower depends on the length of time the money will earn interest and the interest rate.

The second method, regular annuity payments, is easier, as it requires a smaller amount of money to be set aside. However, regular payments must be kept up to accumulate the required amount of money in the future. In addition to making payments every month— or every year, or whatever frequency you set for yourself— the same amount of money has to be deposited. If you cannot meet the regular payment frequency and the same payment value, the fourth method will be more appropriate for you.

The third method is a combination of the first two methods. You put down one lump-sum payment (although not as large an amount as in the pure lump-sum payment method) and then make regular, equal annuity payments. These payments, however, need not be as large as in the pure annuity payment method. Similarly as in method two, if the regular payment frequency and the regular payment value cannot be met, the fourth method will be more appropriate.

The last method for realizing a savings plan is by manually implementing the discounted cash flow (DCF) analysis. The implementation of DCF will be discussed in Section 2.7, Investment Decision Making. In this method, to accumulate the required amount of money in the future, one lays out the schedule of future payments. To assist in visualizing the payment schedule, indicate the payments along a timeline, which shows the current time on the left and the final time at the right. The payments could be several lump-sum payments, regular and irregular annuity payments, and even $0 payment value. One thing to note is that of the four methods, this is the only one that will require trial and error solution.

Let us consider a problem, which we will discuss in more detail using the four savings plan methods. After becoming familiar with the solutions, you may want to change the problem to suit your individual circumstances and find out for yourself which savings plan method suits you best.

Assume you are saving up for a major purchase five years down the road. You have estimated that you will need $10,000 at the end of five years. Use 6% per year as the rate of interest, compounded monthly.

Method 1: Lump-Sum Payment Method

As mentioned above, this method entails setting aside a large sum of money and letting it work for you by earning interest. How much do you have to put down now so that at the end of five years, you will have the $10,000 you need? (P/Yr) = 1, (C/Yr) = 12.

The cash flow diagram for this problem is shown on the right.

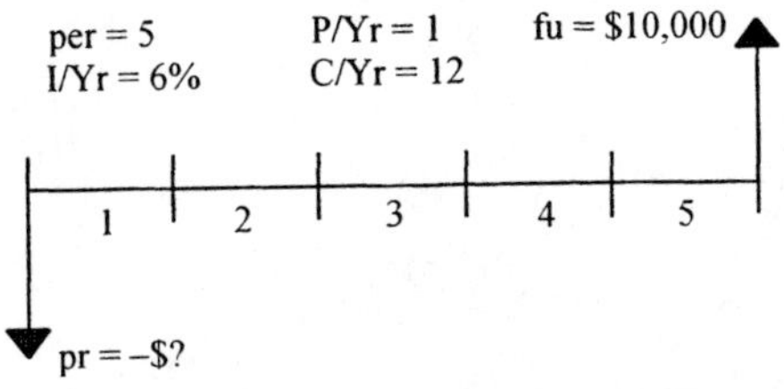

Figure 2.3.1 Lump-sum payment example

Table 2.3.1 Method 1
Type I Class A.3 financial problem, (P/Yr = 1, C/Yr = 12).

per	(I/Yr)	pr	fu
5.00	6.00	-7,413.72	10,000.00

The above table shows that if you put down a single lump-sum payment of $7,413.72 at an interest rate of 6% per year compounded monthly, the investment will accumulate to $10,000 at the end of five years.

Now, the question is, do you have the $7,413.72 to make the lump-sum payment now? If you do, great! However, most of us don't have such a sum available. Don't lose hope; there is another method you can use to accumulate the needed $10,000.

The three Star Wars films earned a total of $1.3 billion US worldwide at the box office before the re-release of the Star Wars Trilogy Special Edition. Merchandise sales, video sales and rentals added another $2.5 billion US. In 1997 dollars, this figure translates to as much as $7 billion US.

Method 2: Annuity Payment Method

This method is very convenient as it allows the accumulation of the required amount of money through regular annuity payments. Two cases will be considered:

- Case I: yearly annuity payments made at the end of each period.
- Case II: monthly annuity payments made at the end of each period.

Case I. Yearly annuity payments at the end of each year. (P/Yr) = 1, (C/Yr) = 12. As before (I/Yr) = 6%.

The cash flow diagram for the problem is shown on the right.

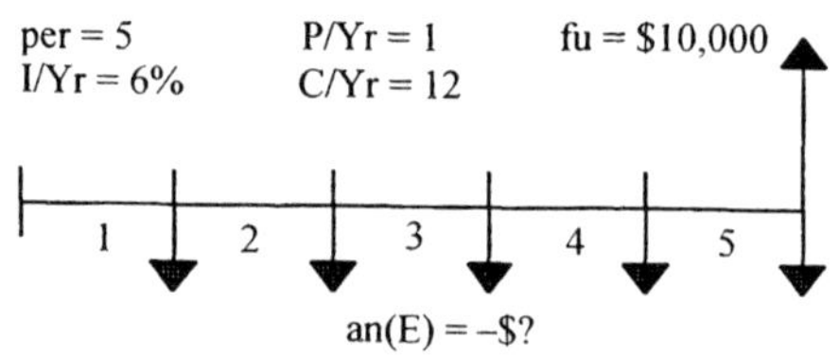

Figure 2.3.2 Method 2 – Case I example

Table 2.3.2 Method 2 – Case I, yearly annuity payments made at the end of each period.
Type II, Class C.4 financial problem, (P/Yr = 1, C/Yr = 12).

per	(I/Yr)	fu	an(E)
5.00	6.00	10,000.00	-1,768.03

The above table shows that if you were to make yearly payments of $1,768.03 at the end of each year, after five years, you would have $10,000 available.

Leonardo da Vinci painted a portrait of Mona Lisa Gherardini in 1507. It was commissioned by her merchant husband, Francesco del Giocondo, who did not like the painting and refused to pay for it. Today, it hangs in the Louvre Museum in Paris and is valued at more than $100 million US.

Case II. Annuity payments do not have to mean yearly payments. They can be monthly, weekly, etc. The only requirement is that they are made regularly. Let us take the second case and look at how much the payments will be if they are made monthly. Since the payment is monthly; (P/Yr) = 12. (C/Yr) = 12.

The cash flow diagram is shown on the right.

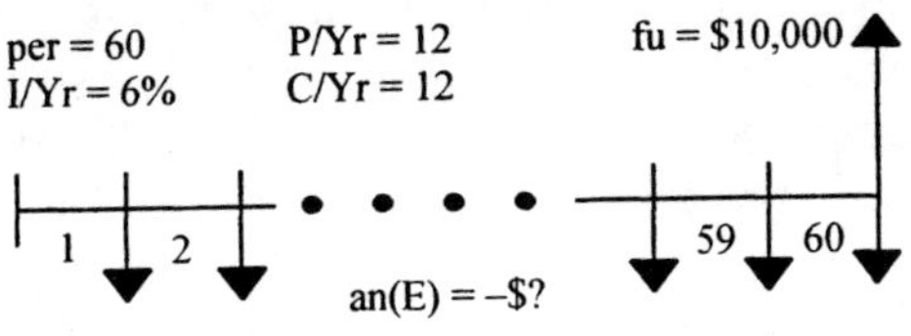

Figure 2.3.3 Method 2 – Case II example

Table 2.3.3 Method 2 — Case II, monthly annuity payments made at the end of each period.
Type II, Class C.4 financial problem, (P/Yr = C/Yr = 12).

per	(I/Yr)	fu	an(E)
60.00	6.00	10,000.00	−143.33

The monthly payment of $143.33 made at the end of each month will accumulate to $10,000 at the end of five years.

On your own, perform the calculations for cases III and IV. A summary of the results for the four cases follows.

Table 2.3.4 Summary of results for Method 2 — annuity payment.

Case	Description	P/Yr, C/Yr	per	an	total payment	total interest
I	Yearly end–of–period payment	1.00, 12.00	5.00	1,768.03	8,840.15	1,159.85
II	Monthly end–of–period payment	12.00, 12.00	60.00	143.33	8,599.80	1,400.20
III	Yearly beginning–of–period payment	1.00, 12.00	5.00	1,665.32	8,326.60	1,673.40
IV	Monthly beginning–of–period payment	12.00, 12.00	60.00	142.61	8,556.60	1,443.40

A Rolls-Royce, still the ultimate in luxury automobiles, sells at a minimum cost of $250,000 US each.

Although the total future value is $10,000 for each of the four cases above, the total interest earned is different. For end-of-period annuity payments (cases I and II), more interest is earned when the annuity payments are made more frequently (60 payments compared to 5). However, for beginning-of-period payments (cases III and IV), more interest is earned when payments are made less frequently (5 payments rather than 60).

Of the four cases, case III with less-frequent payment made at the beginning of each period, had the lowest total payment, at $8,326.60 and thus, the highest total interest, $1,673.40.

The best return on your money is achieved when a smaller payment earns more interest. The above table shows that case III provides the best return, followed by case IV, case II and finally case I. This ranking is the rule in general. Confirm for yourself the ranking by repeating the same set of calculations using your own period, future value, and interest rate.

If you are still not comfortable with the payment amount and schedule, consider the third method, which uses the combination of lump-sum (one-time) payment and annuity payments.

Method 3: Combination of Lump-Sum and Annuity Payments

The lump-sum payment always has to be made at the beginning of the first period. We will consider annuity payments made at the end and then at the beginning of each period. The two cases used in method 2 will be discussed. The scenario will be something like this.

You have $2,000 available and you would like to begin a savings plan by investing this amount at the beginning of the first period. You know that this amount will not accumulate to the $10,000, which you will need at the end of the fifth year. So, the $2,000 initial investment has to be supplemented by annuity payments.

Case I. Let us calculate the additional yearly payments you have to put into the savings account at the end of each year in order to generate the required $10,000 at the end of five years.

The cash flow diagram is shown on the right.

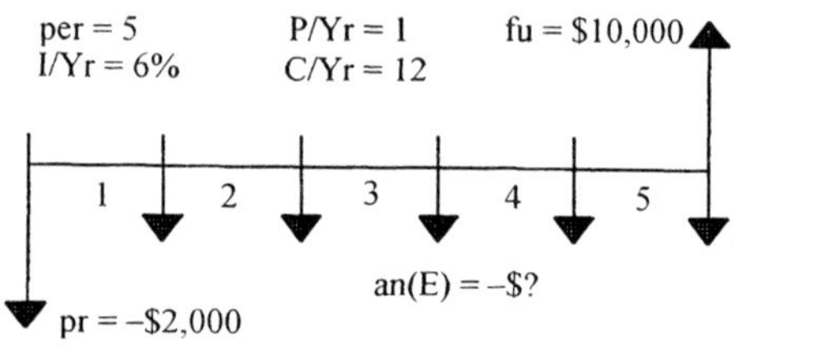

Figure 2.3.4 Method 3 – Case I example

In 1998, thirteen-year old Athina Roussel, the only child of Christina Onassis, is the sole heir to her shipping fortune, valued at about $7.5 billion US. Athina's pocket money is a mere $1.65 million US a year, or $4,520.55 US per day.

Table 2.3.5 Method 3 – Case I. Combination of lump-sum payment at the beginning of the first period and yearly payments at the end of each period. Type III, Class D.5 financial problem, (P/Yr = 1, C/Yr = 12).

per	(I/Yr)	pr	fu	an(E)
5.00	6.00	-2,000.00	10,000.00	-1,291.07

Compare this result with method 2, discussed above. The annuity payments are reduced from $1,768.03 to $1,291.07 (a reduction of $476.96) because of the $2,000 lump-sum payment.

Case II. Consider the same situation, except that payments are made monthly at the end of each period. The lump-sum payment is still $2,000, made at the beginning of the first period.

The cash flow diagram is shown on the right.

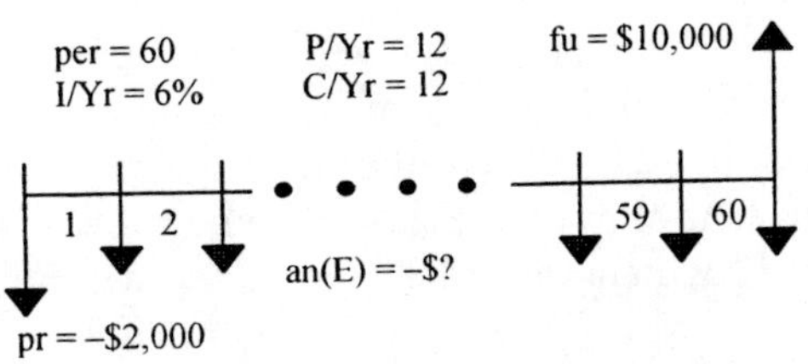

Figure 2.3.5 Method 3 – Case II example

Table 2.3.6 Method 3 – Case 2. Combination of lump-sum payment at the beginning of the first period and monthly payments at the end of each period. Type III, Class D.5 financial problem, (P/Yr = C/Yr = 12).

per	(I/Yr)	pr	fu	an(E)
60.00	6.00	-2,000.00	10,000.00	-104.66

Compare this result with method 2 case II, discussed above. Monthly payments are reduced from $143.33 to $104.66 because of the $2,000 lump-sum payment.

On your own, perform the calculations for cases III and IV. A summary of the results for the four cases follows.

South Africa is the world's largest producer of diamonds. Diamonds were first discovered there in 1866 when a farmer's children found a "sparkling pebble" which turned out to be a diamond worth $2,500 US.

Table 2.3.7 Method 3 – Combination of lump-sum payment and annuity payment, for cases I – IV.

Case	Description	P/Yr, C/Yr	per	an	total payment	total interest
I	Yearly end-of-period payment	1.00, 12.00	5.00	1,291.07	8,455.35	1,544.65
II	Monthly end-of-period payment	12.00, 12.00	60.00	104.66	8,279.60	1,720.40
III	Yearly beginning-of-period payment	1.00, 12.00	5.00	1,216.07	8,080.35	1,919.65
IV	Monthly beginning-of-period payment	12.00, 12.00	60.00	104.14	8,248.40	1,751.60

Note that the total payment column includes the $2,000 lump-sum payment.

Cases I to IV above will all accumulate $10,000 at the end of five years. But as discussed, not all will give the same return on the money, since payments and interest are different. The above table shows the best return, with this method as well. Yearly beginning-of-period payments give the largest interest earned with the smallest total payment.

Method 4: Combination of More than One Lump-Sum Payment and Irregular Annuity Payment Amounts

So far, we have looked at three methods of implementing a savings plan. These methods are suitable for those who either have a lump sum of money available or can make regular payments. If you do not have the lump sum or are doubtful whether you can make regular annuity payments, there is one last method you can use. In this section, we will manually apply the discounted cash flow (DCF) method. (In Section 2.7 Investment Decision Making, Example 7, we will apply the shortcut DCF method to the same problem.)

Method 4 is the most flexible method because you can make more than one lump-sum payment and/or series of annuity payments, each series with different payment amounts. If there is more than one payment amount for the same period, the amounts should be summed to give only one value. The only restriction of this method is that payments should not be made in the middle of a period. For example, if you choose a total period of 60 months, you should make a payment only at the beginning or at the end of each month. As $0 is considered a payment amount under method 4, every period will have a payment amount of 0 (zero) or non-zero value. It is the mathematics underlying the TVM and DCF equations that dictate that there should not be any payments between periods.

The first step in working out a savings plan using this method is to draw a cash flow diagram showing the payment schedule, that is, the amount for each period. Using your best estimate, indicate the payment amount at the appropriate period. For example:

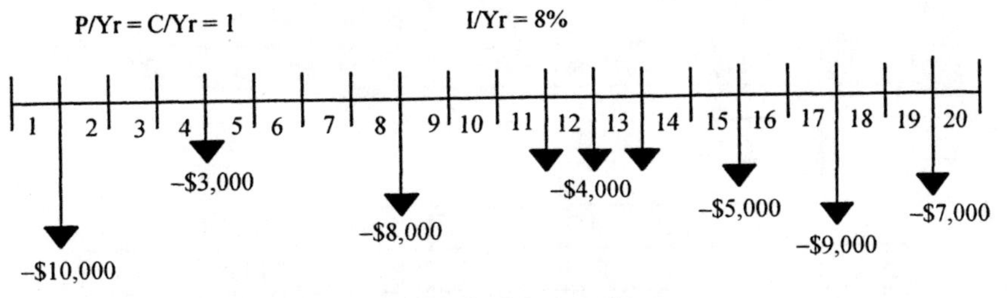

Figure 2.3.6 Method 4 example

The DCF technique involves taking each payment amount considered as future value (fu) and calculating its present value (pr) given the period (per) and interest rate (I/Yr). The present values are summed up and the total future value is calculated using TVM. If the future value calculated does not match the target amount, you will have to adjust the cash flows. Adjustments can be made either by increasing or decreasing a payment amount or series of payment amounts, or adding or deleting a cash flow. Continue adjusting, by trial and error, until the calculated future value is equal to your target value. Since we will be performing the DCF technique manually, there is no need to calculate the present value of the $0 lump-sum or annuity payments. We know that the present value of $0 will also be $0. In contrast, the shortcut method of DCF explained in Section 2.7 requires that every payment amount and frequency be considered, including payments of $0.

In this section, I will show two examples of cash flows; one with period in years and the other with period in months. The solutions to these problems are by no means the only possible ones. There are countless combinations of cash flow values that will give the same future value.

Period in Years

The savings plan problem we have been dealing with is to save $10,000 at the end of five years, with an interest rate of 6%, compounded monthly. The proposed cash flow diagram is shown on the right.

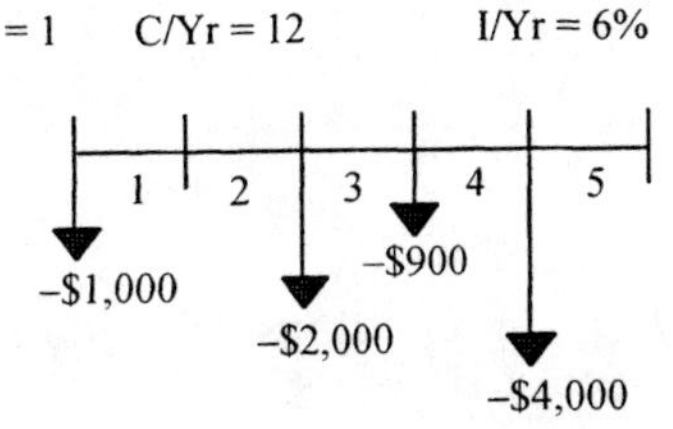

Figure 2.3.7 Method 4 example

Now, for each cash flow with an amount other than $0, calculate the present value and sum all the calculated present values. Then, use the total present value to calculate the future value.

Table 2.3.8 Present value for various cash flows with I/Yr = 6%. Type I, Class A.3 financial problem, (P/Yr = 1, C/Yr = 12).

Period (per)	Cash flow amount (fu)	Present value (pr)
0.00	−1,000.00	1,000.00
2.00	−2,000.00	1,774.37
3.00	−900.00	752.08
4.00	−4,000.00	3,148.39
		Total = 6,674.84

Table 2.3.9 Future value of the total present value. Type I, Class A.4 problem, (P/Yr = 1, C/Yr = 12).

per	(I/Yr)	pr	fu
5.00	6.00	−6,674.84	9,003.36

The calculated future value of $9,003.36 is short by $996.64 of the $10,000 target. An adjustment has to be made. Assume that you would like to limit your adjustment to only one cash flow – the smallest payment, currently set at $900. To meet the future target value, you have to increase this value to make up for the $996.64 shortfall. Repeat the calculation procedure.

Table 2.3.10 Type I, Class A.3 financial problem. I/Yr = 6%, P/Yr = 1, C/Yr = 12.

Period (per)	Cash flow amount fu)	Present value (pr)
0.00	−1,000.00	1,000.00
2.00	−2,000.00	1,774.37
3.00	−1,784.20	1,490.96
4.00	−4,000.00	3,148.39
		Total = 7,413.72

Table 2.3.11 Type I, Class A.4 financial problem. (P/Yr = 1, C/Yr = 12).

per	(I/Yr)	pr	fu
5.00	6.00	−7,413.72	10,000.00

To meet the required $10,000 at the end of 5 years, the third cash flow needs to be increased from $900 to $1,784.20. However, this is not the only solution. You could have chosen to keep the third cash flow as is and increase the first or the second cash flow. Or you could have adjusted all four cash flows. Possibilities are endless.

Period in Months

Let us solve the same problem. This time, the period is in months instead of years. As there are a total of 60 months, up to 60 present value calculations need to be performed. As this becomes a tedious task, I will not even attempt to solve this problem manually. I will however, show, the results for the Total (NPV) using the shortcut method of DCF. (The solution will be shown in Section 2.7, example 7.)

Table 2.3.12 Type I, Class A.3 financial problem. I/Yr = 6%, (P/Yr = C/Yr = 12).

Period (per)	Cash flow amount (fu)	Present value (pr)
0	395.00	.....
1 – 12	0.00	.....
13 – 25	150.00	.....
26 – 40	140.00	.....
41 – 55	210.00	.....
56 – 60	375.00	

Total (NPV) = 7,834.71

To achieve a future value of $10,000, we need the same Total (NPV) of $7,413.72 calculated earlier. The calculated total (NPV) for this series of cash flows, $7,834.71, is too high by $420.99. Adjustments to the cash flow values must be made. One of the various solutions possible is shown in the next table.

Table 2.3.13 Type I, Class A.3 financial problem. I/Yr = 6%, P/Yr = C/Yr = 12.

period (per)	cash flow amount (fu)	present value (pr)
0	300.00	.....
1 – 12	0.00	.....
13 – 25	140.00	.....
26 – 40	123.68	.....
41 – 55	210.00	.....
56 – 60	375.00	.....

Total (NPV) = 7,413.74

To achieve the Total (NPV) of $7,413.74, the lump-sum payment of $395 was changed to $300; the annuity payments of $150 were changed to $140 and the annuity payments of $140 were changed to $123.68.

Table 2.3.14 Type I, Class A.4 financial problem. (P/Yr = 1, C/Yr = 12).

per	(I/Yr)	pr	fu
5.00	6.00	-7,413.74	10,000.02

The cash flow adjustments were appropriate, as the above table shows a calculated future value of $10,000.02.

Effect of Inflation

The calculations we have covered so far for the four methods assumed 0% inflation. This means that the $10,000 we would like to make available five years from now is the same amount in today's dollars. However, if there is any inflation, what costs $1 today will cost more than a dollar in the future. Assuming 3% inflation rate compounded annually, let us calculate the expected value of $10,000 in today's money at the end of 1, 2, 3, 4 and 5 years. (Note that here, we are not considering accumulated interest, we are merely calculating the effect of inflation.)

Table 2.3.15 Future value of $10,000 today at 3% inflation rate compounded annually for various periods.
Type I Class A.4 financial problem. Assume (P/Yr) = 1, (C/Yr) = 12.

per	(I/Yr)	pr	fu
1.00	3.00	−10,000.00	10,304.16
2.00	3.00	−10,000.00	10,617.57
3.00	3.00	−10,000.00	10,940.51
4.00	3.00	−10,000.00	11,273.28
5.00	3.00	−10,000.00	11,616.17

Let us rephrase our original problem.

At the end of five years, we would like to have saved the equivalent of $10,000 in today's dollars. Assume 3% inflation rate. From Table 2.3.15, the future value of $10,000 at the end of five years due to 3% inflation is $11,616.17. Assume the same 6% interest rate compounded monthly. Let us recalculate using the first three methods for a future value of $11,616.17 instead of $10,000.

Recalculating lump-sum payment, method 1, results in the following table:

Table 2.3.16 Method 1 – Lump-sum payment. Type I Class A.3 financial problem. (P/Yr = 1, C/Yr = 12).

per	(I/Yr)	pr	fu
5.00	6.00	-8,611.91	11,616.17

Comparing these results with Table 2.3.1, you can see that you need to increase the present investment by $1,198.19 ($8,611.91 - $7,413.72) to accumulate $11,616.17 at the end of five years.

Recalculating the 4 cases for method 2 – annuity payments results in the following table:

Table 2.3.17 Method 2 – regular annuity payments. Type II, Class C.4 financial problem. Future value (fu) = $11,616.17

Case	Description	P/Yr, C/Yr	per	an	total payment	total interest
I	Yearly end–of–period payment	1.00, 12.00	5.00	2,053.78	10,268.90	1,347.27
II	Monthly end–of–period payment	12.00, 12.00	60.00	166.49	9,989.40	1,626.77
III	Yearly beginning–of–period payment	1.00, 12.00	5.00	1,934.46	9,672.30	1,943.87
IV	Monthly beginning–of–period payment	12.00, 12.00	60.00	165.66	9,939.60	1,676.57

Compare the values of 'an' with Table 2.3.4. The above table shows higher values for 'an' due to inflation. For method 3, the 4 cases will have the ultimate future value of $11,616.17. Recall that there is a lump-sum payment of $2,000 made at the beginning of the first period. The results of the calculations are shown in the table below.

Alaska was originally a part of Russia but was purchased by the US in 1867 for $7 million US. If it had been invested at 5% a year, with yearly compounding interest, this sum would be worth $3.41 billion US in 1997.

Table 2.3.18 Method 3 – combination of lump-sum and annuity payments. Future value (fu) = \$11,616.17; \$2,000 lump-sum payment at beginning of first period. I/Yr = 6% compounded monthly.

Case	Description	P/Yr, C/Yr	per	an	total payment	total interest
I	Yearly end-of-period payment	1.00, 12.00	5.00	1,576.81	9,884.05	1,732.12
II	Monthly end-of-period payment	12.00, 12.00	60.00	127.83	9,669.80	1,946.37
III	Yearly beginning-of-period payment	1.00, 12.00	5.00	1,485.21	9,426.05	2,190.12
IV	Monthly beginning-of-period payment	12.00, 12.00	60.00	127.19	9,631.40	1,984.77

Note that the total payment column includes the \$2,000 lump-sum payment. Compare the value of 'an' with Table 2.3.7.

For method 4, the analysis and solution technique will be the same as before, except that the target future value is \$11,616.17.

Summary

In this chapter, we covered four major methods to implement a savings plan. The simplest is the lump-sum payment method, method 1. It is also the most difficult to implement, especially if one does not have spare cash. However, of the three methods considered, the lump-sum payment method provides the best return on money. From our example, Table 2.3.1 shows that an investment of \$7,413.72 yields \$10,000 at the end of five years, earning a total of \$2,586.28 in interest.

The second method is the annuity payment method, method 2. It consists of annuity payments made either at the beginning or at the end of each period. A total of four cases were considered: yearly and monthly payments for beginning and end of period. Other payment frequencies; however, are possible. From Table 2.3.4, the best return on money using method 2 is the yearly payment made at the beginning of the payment period (case III).

The third method we looked at is the combined lump-sum payment and annuity payment method. The lump-sum payment is made at the beginning of the first payment period. Although four cases were considered, other cases are possible using different payment frequencies. From Table 2.3.7, the best return on money using method 3 is the yearly payment made at the beginning of the payment period (case III).

The fourth method is the most flexible, as one can lay out a schedule of cash flows consisting of several lump-sum payments or several series of annuity payments. Through manual implementation of the DCF technique, the net present value and then the future value are calculated. If the net future value does not come close to the required future value, adjustments have to be made, by trial and error, to the cash flows.

The purpose of this section is to discuss the different ways to implement a savings plan and to present the techniques used for each. After performing the calculations using Chapter 3 as a guide, you may want to refer back to this section to develop a savings plan unique to your situation. We have also recalculated the example problem taking into account the rate of inflation of 3%. You might decide instead to assume an inflation rate of 4% or 5%.

No matter which method you choose, *you* are the ultimate decision maker. You decide whether you can make a lump-sum payment, how large an annuity payment you can afford, and which of the methods will suit you best. It is very important to constantly reassess your strategy by checking on the growth of the savings plan. Remember that you started your plan based on an assumed interest rate. But we know that interest rates change daily. For this reason, I recommend performing a TVM analysis on your savings plan once a year and making appropriate adjustments to meet your goal. Perhaps you have to make an additional lump-sum payment. Or you may be able to decrease your annuity payment and still meet the required future value.

It is also possible to change from one savings method to another at any time. The amount you have accumulated at the time you decide to change your savings method will then be considered a lump-sum payment in your new cash flow diagram.

Thomas Alva Edison, the inventor of the incandescent bulb once said, "I found 5,000 ways how not to make a light bulb." He was also the inventor of the single piece, cast-concrete house, where all the parts were to be poured in a single mold. Edison's concept called for a three-storey house that would cost less than $1,200 US, complete with plumbing, heating, and lighting.

2.4
Lesson 4: LOANS AND MORTGAGES

The human species, according to the best theory I can form of it, is composed of two distinct races, the men who borrow and the men who lend.

Charles Lamb (1775-1834), British essayist

I agree 100% with Mr. Lamb's comment. I would add that *of the two races, there are more borrowers than lenders.* Even in ancient times, as we read in the section on interest, borrowing and lending was a common feature of life. The survival of both of Mr. Lamb's races seems guaranteed, as most of us will sooner or later make decisions involving loans.

For many of us, the first major purchase we face is buying a car. Cars are virtually a necessity in North America. Yet most people would find paying for a car in a lump sum very difficult. Smaller monthly payments make owning a car more affordable. Assume you replace your vehicle every seven years, that you bought your first car at about age 20 and will keep driving until about age 80. That means you will own about eight or nine vehicles in your lifetime. Do you remember the experience of applying for a loan to purchase that first car?

The next major purchase some of us will face is buying a home. This is a decision made usually during the late 20s to early 30s. The North American lifestyle is increasingly mobile. Families relocate to where the jobs are — and that means buying another home. Or you may decide to buy your second or third home to accommodate a growing family, or because you need less space when your children leave and start their own families.

Other common reasons to apply for a loan include a summer cottage or timeshare unit, a dream vacation, or education — which is an investment in yourself.

In this chapter, you will learn new concepts that will help you to make intelligent decisions about loans and mortgages. With these skills, you will become more confident the next time you purchase a car or home.

The price of gold went as high as $875 per ounce in January 21, 1980.

LOANS

Although the following discussion concerns the purchase of a new car, the concepts are equally applicable to other major purchases. I will be covering mortgages separately in this section.

The basic assumption when you apply for a loan is that you will have enough extra money to meet the regular loan repayments. This should be simple enough to check. Subtract your monthly expenses from your monthly earnings; the difference is your monthly savings, from which you will deduct your loan payments. Note, when estimating your monthly expenses, that some expenses are paid annually or semi-annually. Examples are personal insurance, property insurance, professional or union dues, etc. These have to be totaled and converted to a monthly value and summed with the regular monthly expenses to establish your average monthly expense.

To be on the conservative side, maintain an emergency fund. Remember that you calculated your *average* monthly savings. There may be times when your savings are zero, or even negative: that is, your monthly expenses exceed your monthly earnings. Then you will be glad you have an emergency fund to provide a cushion. If your average monthly savings are adequate, after allowing for an emergency fund, the idea of buying that new car is worth pursuing.

Monthly savings are more difficult to estimate when your income is variable, as it is for business owners, self-employed people, or contract workers. If your business is not undergoing great changes, an average of last year's monthly earnings can be used. The more your income varies, the more important a substantial emergency fund is.

When purchasing a car, it is usually a challenge to match the loan you can afford to the car you really want. Ideally, you would like to draw as little as possible from your savings and still be able to get that particular car model you've set your heart on. It is a balancing act. You can make the best decision if you are aware of the following:

- Your monthly payment is largely influenced by your down payment. The higher the down payment, the lower the amount of the loan you need, and therefore, the lower the monthly payment.
- At a fixed down payment, monthly payment, and loan term, as the interest rate decreases, the amount of loan you can apply for increases. You can further increase the loan amount by choosing a longer-term loan.
- At a fixed loan amount and term, as the interest rate decreases, the monthly loan payment decreases. One can further decrease the loan payment by choosing a longer-term loan.

To illustrate these concepts, let us follow Marcelo and Amanda's case.

An English court awarded a salesman $700,000 US because a car crash hurt his career. The accident made him more pleasant and less aggressive.

Know Your Limits

The difference between Marcelo and Amanda's monthly earnings and average monthly expenses is $1,500. However, they have a savings plan by which they set aside $1,000 every month. The remaining $500 therefore is used for discretionary expenses, for example, monthly payments for a new car. Marcelo has just accepted a new job requiring him to travel in the opposite direction from Amanda's place of work, so they would like to get a second car. They have money in the bank for a $5,000 down payment. Marcelo and Amanda would like to know the upper limit of the new car purchase price, considering that they have $500 available from which they can make payments.

Assuming an interest rate of 6% compounded monthly, let us look at the loan amount they can afford. First, assume a four-year term on the loan. Instead of using all the available $500, assume a monthly payment of $100. Calculate the equivalent loan amount. In TVM (time value of money) analysis, the loan amount is the present value.

Table 2.4.1 Present Value of $100 annuity payment paid at the end of each month for 48 months.
Type II, Class B.3 financial problem. (P/Yr = 12, C/Yr = 12).

per	(I/Yr)	pr	an(E)
48.00	6.00	4,258.03	-100.00

The loan equivalent therefore is $4,258.03. Let us construct a table by repeating the above calculations for 6%, 8% and 10% interest per year (I/Yr) compounded monthly; for a four-year and a five-year term loan and for monthly payments of $100, $200, $300, $400, and $500.

It is useful to generate this table, as you can quickly see the pattern of the calculated numbers. It will then be easy to find out where your current circumstances will put you and where you would want to put yourself. The table below is the result of the repeated calculations.

General Motors signed an eight-year contract with the USOC (United States Olympic Commission) to support the US team and the games in Salt Lake City. The price paid was as high as $1 billion US.

Table 2.4.2 Present Value (or equivalent loan amounts) for various monthly payments at 6%, 8%, and 10% interest rate per year for a 4– and 5–year term loan. Type II, Class B.3 financial problem. (P/Yr = C/Yr = 12). Monthly payments are made at the end of each month.

	loan amounts (pr)					
	term = 48 months (per)			term = 60 months (per)		
mo. payment (an(E))	6%	8%	10%	6%	8%	10%
-100.00	4,258.03	4,096.19	3,942.82	5,172.56	4,931.84	4,706.54
-200.00	8,516.06	8,192.38	7,885.63	10,345.11	9,863.69	9,413.07
-300.00	12,774.10	12,288.57	11,828.45	15,517.67	14,795.53	14,119.61
-400.00	17,032.13	16,384.77	15,771.26	20,690.22	19,727.37	18,826.15
-500.00	21,290.16	20,480.96	19,714.08	25,862.78	24,659.22	23,532.68

At 6% interest rate and $300 monthly payment, Marcelo and Amanda can afford a loan of $12,774.10 for a four-year term, or $15,517.67 for a five-year term. Recall that they can put down $5,000. Thus, they can afford to buy a car with a total cost of $17,774.10 paid off in four years or $20,517.67 paid off in five. If they are willing to pay the entire available $500, they can buy a car with a total cost of $26,290.16 or $30,862.78 at the four-year and five-year term respectively (still assuming 6% interest.)

The problem can also be looked at the other way around. Suppose Marcelo and Amanda would like to know the monthly payments for a given loan amount of $10,000 at 6% interest and a four-year term.

Table 2.4.3 Monthly payment for a $10,000 loan at 6% interest rate and a loan period of 4 years or 48 months.
Type II, Class B.4 financial problem. (P/Yr = C/Yr = 12). Monthly payments are made at the end of each month.

per	(I/Yr)	pr	an(E)
48.00	6.00	10,000.00	-234.85

The monthly payment therefore is $234.85. Let us construct a table by repeating the above calculations for 6%, 8%, and 10% interest per year (I/Yr) compounded monthly; for a four-year and a five-year term loan and for loan amounts of $10,000, $15,000, $20,000, and $25,000.

Salt has been used as money. In ancient Rome, Julius Caesar paid his soldiers salt instead of money. Salary in fact comes from the Latin word sal, ("salt").

Table 2.4.4 Monthly payments for various loan amounts at 6%, 8%, and 10% interest rate per year for a 4– and 5–year term loan.
Type II, Class B.4 financial problem. (P/Yr = C/Yr = 12). Monthly payments are made at the end of each month.

	monthly payments (an(E))					
	term = 48 months (per)			term = 60 months (per)		
loan amount (pr)	6%	8%	10%	6%	8%	10%
10,000.00	-234.85	-244.13	-253.63	-193.33	-202.76	-212.47
15,000.00	-352.28	-366.19	-380.44	-289.99	-304.15	-318.71
20,000.00	-469.70	-488.26	-507.25	-386.66	-405.53	-424.94
25,000.00	-587.13	-610.32	-634.06	-483.32	-506.91	-531.18

For a four-year term at 6%, $469.70 monthly payments can carry a loan of $20,000, while for a five-year term, the monthly payment amount is $386.66.

Marcelo and Amanda are not planning on using all the available $500 for monthly car loan payments. They would like to leave something extra for emergencies and have settled on $350 as the maximum monthly payment they will allow. They now want to know how much loan they can afford with the $350 monthly payment at 6%, 8%, and 10% interest rate for a four-year and a five-year term loan. The calculations will be similar to those in Table 2.4.1 but repeated for various interest rates, and periods.

Table 2.4.5 Present Value (or equivalent loan amounts) for $350 monthly payments at 6%, 8%, and 10% interest rate per year for a 4– and 5–year term loan. Type II, Class B.3 financial problem. (P/Yr = C/Yr = 12). Monthly payments are made at the end of each month.

	loan amounts (pr)					
	term = 48 months (per)			term = 60 months (per)		
monthly payment (an(E))	6%	8%	10%	6%	8%	10%
-350.00	14,903.11	14,336.67	13,799.86	18,103.95	17,261.45	16,472.88

Depending on the loan term and interest rate that Marcelo and Amanda can find, they can afford a car from a low of $18,799.86 (four-year term, 10% interest, with $5,000 down payment added to the loan amount of $13,799.86) to a high of $23,103.95 (five-year term, 6% interest with $5,000 down payment added to the loan amount of $18,103.95).

If Marcelo and Amanda visit a car dealer after working through the analyses shown above, they are sure to make better, more intelligent decisions. They know their limits exactly and will be careful not to make decisions based on emotions.

The Effects of Extending the Loan Term

But suppose Marcelo and Amanda both fall in love with a sleek beauty and decide they've just *got* to have *that* car. They agree to throw caution to the wind — after all, they have a solid emergency fund. They decide they're prepared to spend all their available $500 average monthly savings for the car loan payments. After the haggling and bargaining are over, the final price is $27,537. Let us help them decide which loan term to choose. Whichever they choose, it will be wise for them to shop around for the lowest effective interest rate for their car loan. Remember from Section 2.2, that there is a difference between nominal interest and effective interest rates.

Since they have $5,000 available for down payment, the loan they have to apply for is $22,537. To illustrate, calculate the monthly payments for a loan of $22,537 assuming a 6% interest rate and a loan term of four years.

Table 2.4.6 Monthly payment for a $22,537 loan at 6% interest rate and a loan period of 4 years or 48 months.
Type II, Class B.4 financial problem. (P/Yr = C/Yr = 12). Monthly payments are made at the end of each month.

per	(I/Yr)	pr	an(E)
48.00	6.00	22,537.00	-529.28

Let us repeat the above calculations for interest rates of 6%, 8%, and 10% at four-year and five-year term loans.

Table 2.4.7 Monthly payments for a $22,537 loan at 6%, 8%, and 10% interest rate per year for a 4– and 5–year term loan.
Type II, Class B.4 financial problem. (P/Yr = C/Yr = 12). Monthly payments are made at the end of each month.

	monthly payments (an(E))					
	term = 48 months (per)			term = 60 months (per)		
loan amount (pr)	6%	8%	10%	6%	8%	10%
22,537.00	-529.28	-550.19	-571.60	-435.70	-456.97	-478.84

The above table shows that the monthly payments are more than $500 at the four-year term loan even at 6%. These payments exceed the available average monthly savings. Marcelo and Amanda therefore have to settle for the five-year term, which produces a payment below $500. If they can find a financial institution that will provide the $22,537 loan at 6% interest, they have got themselves the best deal.

Suppose they can get that deal. By choosing a five-year rather than a four-year term, Marcelo and Amanda have lowered their monthly payments by $93.58 ($529.28 – $435.70). But the price they pay for reduced payments is higher total interest over the term of the loan.

Note from Table 2.4.4 that, for the same loan amount and the same interest rate, the five-year term loan has lower monthly payments than the four-year term loan. Let us see how much interest is paid.

Table 2.4.8 Monthly payments, total cost and total interest paid for various loans at 6% interest rate per year for a 4– and 5–year term.
(Monthly payments from Table 2.4.4)

	48 months (per)			60 months (per)		
loan amount	monthly payment (an(E))	total cost	total interest paid	monthly payment (an(E))	total cost	total interest paid
10,000.00	234.85	11,272.80	1,272.80	193.33	11,599.80	1,599.80
15,000.00	352.28	16,909.44	1,909.44	289.99	17,399.40	2,399.40
20,000.00	469.70	22,545.60	2,545.60	386.66	23,199.60	3,199.60
25,000.00	587.13	28,182.24	3,182.24	483.32	28,999.20	3,999.20

total cost = monthly payment x per
total interest paid = total cost – loan amount

Let us repeat the above calculations for interest rates of 6%, 8%, and 10% for four-year and five-year terms at the required loan of $22,537.

Table 2.4.9 Total cost and total interest paid for a loan of $22,537 at 6%, 8%, and 10% interest rate per year for a 4– and 5–year term.
Monthly payments from Table 2.4.7. (P/Yr = C/Yr = 12).

	48 months (per)			60 months (per)		
(I/Yr)	monthly payment (an(E))	total cost	total interest	monthly payment (an(E))	total cost	total interest
6.00	529.28	25,405.44	2,868.44	435.70	26,142.00	3,605.00
8.00	550.19	26,409.12	3,872.12	456.97	27,418.20	4,881.20
10.00	571.60	27,436.80	4,899.80	478.84	28,730.40	6,193.40

total cost = monthly payment x per
total interest = total cost – $22,537

The above Tables 2.4.8 and 2.4.9 show that at the same interest rate per year, more interest is paid for the five-year term than the four-year term.

Table 2.4.10 Additional interest for extending a 4–year term loan to 5 years for a loan of $22,537 at 6%, 8%, and 10% interest rates. Reference, Table 2.4.9.

(I/Yr)	additional interest				
6.00	3,605.00	–	2,868.44	=	736.56
8.00	4,881.20	–	3,872.12	=	1,009.08
10.00	6,193.40	–	4,899.80	=	1,293.60

As you can see from Table 2.4.2, extending the loan term for the same monthly payment and interest rate allows for a higher loan amount — at the expense of paying higher interest.

Let us expand on the loan amount data provided by Table 2.4.2. The result is the table below.

Table 2.4.11 Additional amount in loan due to extending a 4–year term to 5 years for different monthly payments at 6% interest rate. Down payment is $5,000. (Monthly payments and loan amounts from Table 2.4.2).

	term = 48 months (per)		term = 60 months (per)		increase in loan
monthly payments (an(E))	loan amount	total cost of car	loan amount	total cost of car	
-100.00	4,258.03	9,258.03	5,172.56	10,172.56	914.53
-200.00	8,516.06	13,516.06	10,345.11	15,345.11	1,829.05
-300.00	12,774.10	17,774.10	15,517.67	20,517.67	2,743.57
-400.00	17,032.13	22,032.13	20,690.22	25,690.22	3,658.09
-500.00	21,290.16	26,290.16	25,862.78	30,862.78	4,572.62

Note that the values under the 'total cost of car' columns were calculated by adding $5,000 (down payment) to the 'loan amount' columns. Now, how high is the penalty for the higher loan amount? Let us calculate the interest for different monthly payments for a four-year and a five-year term loan.

$1 A Year CEO Club: For the year 1994-1995, the annual salary compensation for the CEO of Ontario Hydro, the provincial utility company was $1 CDN. In 1997 the CEO of Internet software giant Netscape accepted a $1 US salary.

Table 2.4.12 Increase in interest due to extending a 4–year term loan to 5 years for different monthly payments at 6% interest rate. (Loan amounts from Table 2.4.11).

	term = 48 months (per)		term = 60 months (per)		interest increase
monthly payment (an(E))	loan amount	total interest paid	loan amount	total interest paid	
-100.00	4,258.03	541.97	5,172.56	827.44	285.47
-200.00	8,516.06	1,083.94	10,345.11	1,654.89	570.95
-300.00	12,774.10	1,625.90	15,517.67	2,482.33	856.43
-400.00	17,032.13	2,167.87	20,690.22	3,309.78	1,141.91
-500.00	21,290.16	2,709.84	25,862.78	4,137.22	1,427.38

total interest paid = (monthly payment x per) – loan amount

The examples above show the basic concepts regarding loans.

Amortization Table

Each monthly loan payment is used to pay off a portion of the original principal and a portion of the total interest. The maximum payment portion towards the total interest and the minimum payment portion towards the principal occurs on the first loan payment. Succeeding payments are apportioned so that the payment towards the interest gradually decreases and the payment towards the principal gradually increases. Thus, the maximum payment portion towards the principal and the minimum payment portion towards the interest are made on the last loan payment. The amortization table provides valuable information as to how each payment is apportioned for the principal and the interest.

To illustrate this, let us follow Marcelo and Amanda's loan arrangement. Assume that they were able to find a financial institution that will provide the $22,537 loan they want at 6% interest compounded monthly. Their monthly payment is therefore $435.70 for a five-year term (see Table 2.4.7).

How are those monthly payments apportioned to principal and interest, from the first payment (period = 1) to the last payment (period = 60)? Note that we are assuming monthly interest compounding; that is, the interest is calculated at the same frequency as the payment frequency. The nominal 6% interest rate, therefore, is also the adjusted nominal interest rate. (See Section 2.2.)

Tokyo teens spend $10 million US every year on used Nikes and other sneakers.

Table 2.4.13 Amortization table – Distribution of $435.70 monthly payment ($22,537 loan at 6% interest rate and 5–year term with payments made at the end of each period). (P/Yr = C/Yr = 12).

per	principal	principal payment	interest payment	principal balance
1.00	22,537.00	-323.01	-112.69	22,213.99
2.00	22,213.99	-324.63	-111.07	21,889.36
3.00	21,889.36	-326.25	-109.45	21,563.11
4.00	21,563.11	-327.88	-107.82	21,235.23
5.00	21,235.23	-329.52	-106.18	20,905.71
6.00	20,905.71	-331.17	-104.53	20,574.54
7.00	20,574.54	-332.83	-102.87	20,241.71
8.00	20,241.71	-334.49	-101.21	19,907.22
9.00	19,907.22	-336.16	-99.54	19,571.06
10.00	19,571.06	-337.84	-97.86	19,233.22
11.00	19,233.22	-339.53	-96.17	18,893.69
12.00	18,893.69	-341.23	-94.47	18,552.46
13.00	18,552.46	-342.94	-92.76	18,209.52
14.00	18,209.52	-344.65	-91.05	17,864.87
15.00	17,864.87	-346.38	-89.32	17,518.49
16.00	17,518.49	-348.11	-87.59	17,170.38
17.00	17,170.38	-349.85	-85.85	16,820.53
18.00	16,820.53	-351.60	-84.10	16,468.93
19.00	16,468.93	-353.36	-82.34	16,115.57
20.00	16,115.57	-355.12	-80.58	15,760.45
21.00	15,760.45	-356.90	-78.80	15,403.55
22.00	15,403.55	-358.68	-77.02	15,044.87
23.00	15,044.87	-360.48	-75.22	14,684.39
24.00	14,684.39	-362.28	-73.42	14,322.11
25.00	14,322.11	-364.09	-71.61	13,958.02
26.00	13,958.02	-365.91	-69.79	13,592.11
27.00	13,592.11	-367.74	-67.96	13,224.37
28.00	13,224.37	-369.58	-66.12	12,854.79
29.00	12,854.79	-371.43	-64.27	12,483.36
30.00	12,483.36	-373.28	-62.42	12,110.08
31.00	12,110.08	-375.15	-60.55	11,734.93
32.00	11,734.93	-377.03	-58.67	11,357.90
33.00	11,357.90	-378.91	-56.79	10,978.99

Continued, Table 2.4.13

34.00	10,978.99	-380.81	-54.89	10,598.18
35.00	10,598.18	-382.71	-52.99	10,215.47
36.00	10,215.47	-384.62	-51.08	9,830.85
37.00	9,830.85	-386.55	-49.15	9,444.30
38.00	9,444.30	-388.48	-47.22	9,055.82
39.00	9,055.82	-390.42	-45.28	8,665.40
40.00	8,665.40	-392.37	-43.33	8,273.03
41.00	8,273.03	-394.33	-41.37	7,878.70
42.00	7,878.70	-396.31	-39.39	7,482.39
43.00	7,482.39	-398.29	-37.41	7,084.10
44.00	7,084.10	-400.28	-35.42	6,683.82
45.00	6,683.82	-402.28	-33.42	6,281.54
46.00	6,281.54	-404.29	-31.41	5,877.25
47.00	5,877.25	-406.31	-29.39	5,470.94
48.00	5,470.94	-408.35	-27.35	5,062.59
49.00	5,062.59	-410.39	-25.31	4,652.20
50.00	4,652.20	-412.44	-23.26	4,239.76
51.00	4,239.76	-414.50	-21.20	3,825.26
52.00	3,825.26	-416.57	-19.13	3,408.69
53.00	3,408.69	-418.66	-17.04	2,990.03
54.00	2,990.03	-420.75	-14.95	2,569.28
55.00	2,569.28	-422.85	-12.85	2,146.43
56.00	2,146.43	-424.97	-10.73	1,721.46
57.00	1,721.46	-427.09	-8.61	1,294.37
58.00	1,294.37	-429.23	-6.47	865.14
59.00	865.14	-431.37	-4.33	433.77
60.00	433.77	-433.53	-2.17	0.24

Graceland is the late Elvis Presley's home in Memphis, Tennessee. Built in 1939 on grounds spanning 13.8 acres, Elvis bought it in 1957 for $100,000 US. Today, Graceland employs 150 tour guides for the 600,000 people who visit the Presley homestead every year.

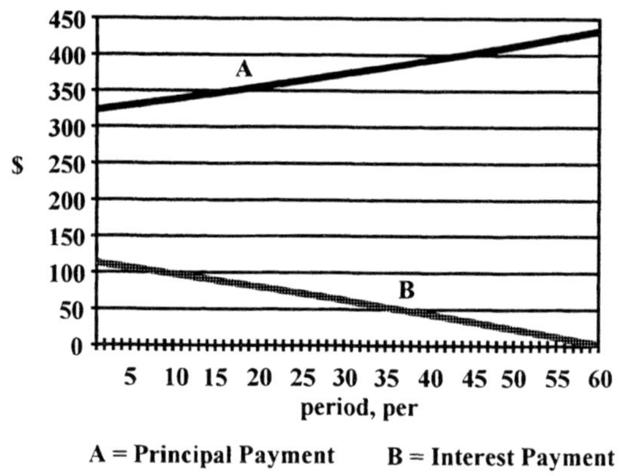

Figure 2.4.1 Plot of principal and interest payments

As the above table and figure show, the interest payments decrease throughout the life of the loan, while principal payments increase. Note that at every period, the sum of the principal and interest payments equals the monthly payment of $435.70. Later in this section, you will see that this pattern is even more marked with mortgages.

Table 2.4.13 (loan amortization) is easily calculated using the financial calculator. You can also easily calculate the total cumulative values by amortizing the payments from period 1 to 60.

Table 2.4.14 Total principal and interest payments from periods 1–60 for $22,537 loan at 6% interest rate, 5–year term and $435.70 monthly payment. (P/Yr = C/Yr = 12).

per	principal	total principal payment	total interest payment	principal balance
1–60	22,537.00	–22,536.76	–3,605.24	0.24

For the 12th Annual Garlic Festival held in 1991 in Gilroy, California, 8 tons of fresh garlic went into food preparation. This town, south of San Francisco, hosted the festival's 150,000 visitors. Chefs competed for $1,000 US in the Great Garlic Recipe Contest and Cook Off.

MORTGAGES

Not all of us will have the luck — or maybe the misfortune — to experience applying for a mortgage to purchase a home. To some people, owning a home is the dream of a lifetime. To others, it's a millstone around their necks; they'd rather avoid the whole thing. Owning a home offers several advantages:

- A forced savings plan. By making regular payments towards a durable asset, homeowners are making a form of investment — and quite a good one. A recent study in Canada confirmed that residential homes provide, on average, 12% annual compounded return over a 30-year period.
- Tax breaks. In the United States, home mortgage interest is tax-deductible (not the case in Canada).
- The pure joy of owning a home, a satisfaction you can't put any dollar value on. The home is where children are born and raised, and families spend memorable moments.

There are however, disadvantages:

- A high total interest cost, since loan amounts are much higher than, say, loans for a new car.
- A long period of indebtedness.
- Additional expenses, such as property tax and maintenance costs for such items as roof replacement and driveway repairs.

Mortgages are loans from a financial institution such as a bank, mortgage company, or mortgage broker to purchase property. A mortgage *broker* shops for mortgages from a variety of sources for you. A broker's fee is usually paid by the lender as incentive to send business the lender's way. The *amortization period* is the length of time over which the borrowed money and all interest are paid. As the mortgage typically involves large sums of money— at times more than $100,000— an amortization period of 20, 25, or even 30 years is usually selected to make monthly payments manageable. Let us look at an example.

Assume you have a $90,000 mortgage. Let's calculate the monthly payments for four-year and 25-year amortization periods at 6%, 8%, and 10% interest rate compounded monthly.

> *On average, an automobile costs $200,000 US in Singapore. This may explain why there are no traffic jams in this island country of slightly more than 3 million people.*

Table 2.4.15 Monthly payments for a $90,000 mortgage amortized over 4 years (48 months) and 25 years (300 months) for various interest rates compounded monthly.
Type II, Class B.4 financial problem. (P/Yr = C/Yr = 12). Annuity payments made at the end of each period.

per	I/Yr	pr	an(E)
48.00	6.00	90,000.00	-2,113.65
48.00	8.00	90,000.00	-2,197.16
48.00	10.00	90,000.00	-2,282.63
300.00	6.00	90,000.00	-579.87
300.00	8.00	90,000.00	-694.63
300.00	10.00	90,000.00	-817.83

The monthly payment for the 25-year amortization period has been reduced to, on average, about 30% of the payment for the four-year amortization period. Much easier to pay! Of course, as with any loan, the price of affordability is that more interest is paid. There are however, ways to reduce the total interest paid.

Your monthly mortgage payments are applied to the principal and interest. Just like loan payments, mortgage schedules are set up so that at the beginning of the amortization period, most of the payment goes to the interest. Towards the end of the amortization period, when most of the interest has already been paid, most of the mortgage payment goes towards paying off the principal. The property is also put up as collateral; that means that if the borrower defaults on the monthly payments, the *mortgagee*, or lender, can seize the property.

Although in most reference books, TVM analysis of mortgages usually assumes that the interest rate is the rate for the entire amortization period, this is not the case. This assumption is made to simplify the analysis of the mortgage problem. In reality, when you apply for a mortgage, you need to select not only an *amortization period*, but a *term* for the mortgage. It is very rare these days for financial institutions to offer a 25-year mortgage with the interest rate locked in. Instead, they offer various terms such as six months, one year, two years, three years, four years and five years. At the end of the term, you renew the mortgage for another term, which does not have to be the same as the first term, until the mortgage principal is paid. The difference between these mortgage terms is the interest rate being offered. At the shorter term, a lower interest rate is normally offered. This rate progressively increases as the term increases. For example:

The Whitbread Race has been held every four years since 1973. It covers 31,000 nautical miles and is considered the Formula One of yacht racing. It costs an average $6 to 12 million US to compete in this race. For salaries alone, $5 million US is set aside.

Table 2.4.16 Mortgage interest rates for various mortgage terms (example).

mortgage term	I/Yr
6 months	6.50
1 year	6.75
2 years	7.00
3 years	7.25
4 years	7.75
5 years	8.25

The interest rate for the term selected, together with the amortization period, will be used to calculate the monthly payments for the selected term. At the end of the term, the mortgage has to be renewed. Two things will have changed. First, the interest rate is unlikely to stay the same, since rates change every day. Second, the amortization period will be reduced. Depending on the interest rate for the selected term and the remaining amortization period, the monthly payment for the renewed mortgage may be higher or lower than for the last mortgage term. This process of term expiration and renewal continues until the mortgage principal and total interest are paid.

Let us take an example.

Assume you have a mortgage of $95,000 and you selected a 25-year amortization period and a five-year term. At the five-year term, the interest rate is 8.5%, compounded monthly. Calculate the monthly payment at the end of each period.

Table 2.4.17 Calculation of monthly mortgage payment made at the end of each period for 25–year term (300 months) at 8.5% compounded monthly. Type II, Class B.4 financial problem. (P/Yr = C/Yr = 12).

per	I/Yr	pr	an(E)
300.00	8.5	95,000.00	-764.97

The monthly payment is $764.97. At the end of five years, using the amortization function of the financial calculator, the status of the mortgage is as follows:

In 1921, $1 US was worth 81 German marks. By July 1923, $1 US was worth 1 million German marks.

Table 2.4.18 Status of mortgage after the first 5-year term (60 months). Refer to Table 2.4.14 for the financial calculator keystrokes.

per	principal balance	principal paid	interest paid	remaining amortization period (months)
1-60	88,147.32	-6,852.68	-39,045.52	240.00

Assuming you renewed your mortgage for another five years but this time the interest rate was 8%, calculate the new monthly mortgage payment.

Table 2.4.19 Calculation of monthly mortgage payment made at the end of each period for 2nd 5-year term at 8%.
Type II, Class B.4 financial problem. (P/Yr = C/Yr = 12).

per	I/Yr	pr	an(E)
240.00	8.00	88,147.32	-737.30

The monthly payment is $737.30. At the end of the 2nd five-year term, using the amortization function of the financial calculator shows that the status of the mortgage is as follows:

Table 2.4.20 Status of mortgage after 2nd 5-year term (60 months). Refer to Table 2.4.14 for the financial calculator keystrokes.

per	principal balance	principal paid	interest paid	remaining amortization period (months)
1-60	77,151.48	-10,995.84	-33,242.16	180.00

Repeating the above calculations, there would be three more five-year mortgage terms to completely pay off the principal of $95,000 amortized at 25 years. This assumes that the calculated monthly payments per five-year term are not increased or decreased. Below is a table that summarizes the status of the mortgage over the 25-year period.

In the late 1980s, tuition at the law school of the University of Toronto in Canada was $1,300. Eight years later, it was at $4,500. Using time value of money analysis, this represents an inflation rate of 16.79% per year.

Table 2.4.21 Summary of 5 consecutive 5-year term mortgages of $95,000 amortized over 25 years with different interest rates at renewal. (P/Yr = C/Yr = 12).

per	I/Yr	monthly payment	principal balance	principal paid	interest paid	remaining amortization period
300.00	8.50	-764.97	88,147.32	-6,852.68	-39,045.52	240.00
240.00	8.00	-737.30	77,151.48	-10,995.84	-33,242.16	180.00
180.00	9.00	-782.52	61,773.70	-15,377.78	-31,573.42	120.00
120.00	8.50	-765.91	37,330.77	-24,442.93	-21,511.67	60.00
60.00	8.00	-756.93	0.20	-37,330.57	-8,085.23	
			TOTALS	-94,999.80	-133,458.00	

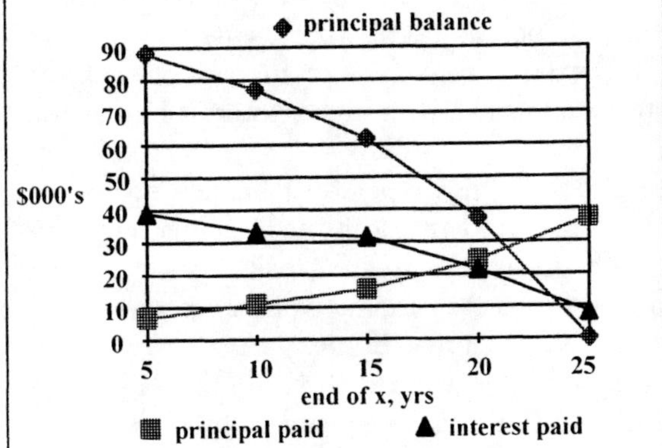

Figure 2.4.2 Principal balance, principal and interest paid for sample mortgage

The total principal paid is $94,999.80 plus the balance of $0.20 will give a total of $95,000, the original principal. In return to borrowing this money, the total interest paid is $133,458.00. Notice as you go down the above table, the total principal paid increased from $6,852.68 at the end of the first five-year term to $37,330.57 at the end of the fifth five-year term. For total interest paid, the amount decreased from $39,045.52 at the end of the first five-year term to $8,085.23 at the end of the fifth five-year term.

As I said, in most reference books, mortgages are calculated as if the purchaser could get a single 25-year term mortgage. How much difference does it make that the mortgage is actually renewed over several terms? Let us look at the same example, but this time work it through as a single 25-year term mortgage. Assume the same $95,000 mortgage amortized over 25 years with a 25-year term at 8.4% interest rate (the average of the interest rates over the five terms in the previous example) compounded monthly.

Table 2.4.22 Status of $95,000 mortgage at the end of 25–year term amortized for 25 years at 8.4% interest compounded monthly.
(P/Yr = C/Yr = 12).

per	I/Yr	monthly payment	principal balance	principal paid	interest paid
300.00	8.4	-758.57	4.99	-94,995.01	-132,575.99

The total principal paid will still add up to $95,000 ($94995.01 + $4.99). The total interest paid is $132,575.99, which is $882.01 less than the amount of $133,458.00 from the previous example. The difference is a mere 0.66% of the total interest: close enough for decision making. This is why most reference books use the simpler single-term mortgage calculation.

Which is better, a short-term or a long-term mortgage? People who select a longer term, such as five years, gain stability and predictability. They know that the monthly mortgage payments will remain the same for the next five years and therefore they can make other financial commitments such as home improvements, vacation, or purchasing a new vehicle. Others choose a shorter term, such as six months or one year, for the lower interest rates. They are willing to take the risk of a higher interest rate at renewal time in exchange for the money saved.

A home purchase is a very major personal finance decision as it entails long-term financial commitment. Feeling confident about the basic math involved in mortgages should help you make the right decisions. This section will provide you with the knowledge and math skills to talk confidently with the mortgage officer at your bank or financial institution about what you need to purchase that new home.

Typically, purchasing a home requires three things. First, unless you just won the lottery, you will need a financial institution to lend you the mortgage. Second, although not absolutely necessary, the services of a real estate agent can be very useful. As a home purchaser, you do not pay the agent anything. The agent is paid by the seller a commission from proceeds of the sale. Agents will be happy to work with you in locating your new home. They can set up appointments for you to view suitable homes and can give valuable advice. Lastly, you will need a lawyer to make sure that there are no outstanding bills, liens, or litigation against the property you intend to purchase and to take care of the legal aspects of the sale.

Before you can qualify for a mortgage, you have to satisfy the financial institution that you pass two test ratios. The first is the gross debt-to-service ratio: your monthly mortgage payment, property tax, and heating must not be more than 30-32% of your monthly income, excluding irregular income such as overtime. Second, the cost of carrying the home plus all other loans should not be more than 33-36% of your income.

In 1995, about $180 million US was spent to market the message that a diamond is connected with love and romance.

Pierre and Michelle's Home-Buying Saga

Let us follow Pierre and Michelle in their first experience in purchasing a home.

Pierre and Michelle have been married for five years and have been saving up so they can purchase their first home. They have saved $50,000. From this amount, they will deduct the required fees for the lawyer, moving expenses, and new appliances for the new home. A major portion of the money will be used as a down payment. They feel now is the right time to make the move and so they have contacted a real estate agent. They've been shown several homes and liked several of them. But when they considered purchasing one of those houses, and how it could affect them financially, they decided to take a step back and set some realistic targets.

The first thing that Pierre and Michelle did was to get an idea of their combined monthly earnings and average monthly expenses (not counting their current rent). The difference between these amounts is their average monthly savings. After setting aside an emergency fund, the savings from which they can make their monthly mortgage payments is $1,100. From the accumulated $50,000 in their savings account, they plan to use $40,000 as down payment. Next, Pierre and Michelle would like to know the upper limit of the home purchase price.

Let us calculate the mortgage loan amount they can afford from the available $1,100 per month at 20- and 25-year term mortgage. (As we have seen, although they will not get this term, the results will be close enough.) Below is a table that shows loan amounts at various monthly payments and at different interest rates for a 20-year and 25-year term mortgage. The table is a result of repeated calculations, as was done for Table 2.4.1 in the loan sub-section.

London Bridge was a stone structure built in the 12th century that spanned the Thames River in the City of London. In 1968, it was sold for $2,460,000 US. Its masonry facing was dismantled and shipped across the Atlantic. Over 10,000 tons of carefully numbered stones were reassembled on a core of reinforced concrete at Lake Havasu City, Arizona as a tourist attraction. The assembly cost was $6,900,000 US. The new London Bridge was rededicated and opened on October 10, 1971.

Table 2.4.23 Loan amounts for various monthly payments at different interest rates and at 20- and 25-year amortization.
Type II, Class B.3 financial problem. (P/Yr = C/Yr = 12). Monthly payments made at the end of each month.

	loan amounts (pr)					
	term = 240 months (per)			term = 300 months (per)		
mo. payment (an(E))	6%	8%	10%	6%	8%	10%
-100.00	13,958.08	11,955.43	10,362.46	15,520.69	12,956.45	11,004.72
-200.00	27,916.15	23,910.86	20,724.92	31,041.37	25,912.90	22,009.45
-300.00	41,874.23	35,866.29	31,087.39	46,562.06	38,869.36	33,014.17
-400.00	55,832.31	47,821.72	41,449.85	62,082.75	51,825.81	44,018.89
-500.00	69,790.39	59,777.15	51,812.31	77,603.43	64,782.26	55,023.62
-600.00	83,748.46	71,732.58	62,174.77	93,124.12	77,738.71	66,028.34
-700.00	97,706.54	83,688.00	72,537.23	108,644.80	90,695.17	77,033.06
-800.00	111,664.62	95,643.43	82,899.69	124,165.49	103,651.62	88,037.78
-900.00	125,622.69	107,598.86	93,262.16	139,686.18	116,608.07	99,042.51
-1,000.00	139,580.77	119,554.29	103,624.62	155,206.86	129,564.52	110,047.23

Thus, at 8% interest rate and $700 monthly payment, for example, Pierre and Michelle can afford a loan of $83,688.00 or $90,695.17 for a 20-year and 25-year term respectively. Recall that they can put down $40,000. Thus, they can afford to buy a home with a total cost of $123,688.00 or $130,695.17. If they are willing to pay $1,000 monthly, still assuming 8% interest, they can purchase a home with a total cost of $159,554.29 or $169,564.52 at a 20-year and 25-year term respectively.

Now, look at the problem from the other angle; Pierre and Michelle would like to know the monthly payments for a given loan amount at 8% interest and at a 20-year and 25-year amortization.

Titanic, the luxury ocean liner that struck an iceberg and sank in the North Atlantic, taking with it 1,493 passengers and crew, was built at a cost of over $8 million US. The 1997 movie Titanic, *produced by James Cameron and Jon Landau, cost around $200 million US.*

Table 2.4.24 Monthly payments for various loans at 6%, 8%, and 10% for a 20-year and 25-year term loan.
Type II, Class B.4 financial problem. (P/Yr = C/Yr = 12). Monthly payments made at the end of each month.

	monthly payments (an(E))					
	term = 240 months (per)			term = 300 months (per)		
loan amount (pr)	6%	8%	10%	6%	8%	10%
50,000.00	-358.22	-418.22	-482.51	-322.15	-385.91	-454.35
60,000.00	-429.86	-501.86	-579.01	-386.58	-463.09	-545.22
70,000.00	-501.50	-585.51	-675.52	-451.01	-540.27	-636.09
80,000.00	-573.14	-669.15	-772.02	-515.44	-617.45	-726.96
90,000.00	-644.79	-752.80	-868.52	-579.87	-694.63	-817.83
100,000.00	-716.43	-836.44	-965.02	-644.30	-771.82	-908.70

The table above is generated by repeated calculations, as was done for Table 2.4.3. If Pierre and Michelle pursue their home purchase efforts equipped with the information shown in Tables 2.4.23 - 2.4.24, they are surely going to make better decisions. With such a heavy financial commitment, it pays to do the extra work.

Let us follow through with Pierre and Michelle's case. As with any loan, a longer amortization period will produce a lower monthly payment but at the price of increased total interest on the loan.

Table 2.4.25 Total cost and total interest paid for various loan amounts at 8% interest rate.
Monthly payments an(E) are from Table 2.4.24.

	term = 240 months (per)			term = 300 months (per)			
loan amount	payment (an(E))	total cost	total interest	payment (an(E))	total cost	total interest	interest increase
50,000.00	418.22	100,372.80	50,372.80	385.91	115,773.00	65,773.00	15,400.20
60,000.00	501.86	120,446.40	60,446.40	463.09	138,927.00	78,927.00	18,480.60
70,000.00	585.51	140,522.40	70,522.40	540.27	162,081.00	92,081.00	21,558.60
80,000.00	669.15	160,596.00	80,596.00	617.45	185,235.00	105,235.00	24,639.00
90,000.00	752.80	180,672.00	90,672.00	694.63	208,389.00	118,389.00	27,717.00
100,000.00	836.44	200,745.60	100,745.60	771.82	231,546.00	131,546.00	30,800.40
110,000.00	920.08	220,819.20	110,819.20	849.00	254,700.00	144,700.00	33,880.80
120,000.00	1,003.73	240,895.20	120,895.20	926.18	277,854.00	157,854.00	36,958.80
130,000.00	1,087.37	260,968.80	130,968.80	1,003.36	301,008.00	171,008.00	40,039.20

total cost = payment x per
total interest = total cost – loan amount

As you can see from the above table, the total interest paid on a $100,000 loan is $100,745.60 for a 20-year amortization and a 20-year term. Keeping the amount and interest rate constant but lengthening the term and mortgage to 25 years gives total interest of $131,546.00 — an increase of $30,800.40.

As we have seen in previous examples, at the same monthly payments and interest rate, you can increase your loan amount by extending the amortization period. Let us see by how much the loan amount is increased.

Table 2.4.26 Increase in loan from 20-year to 25-year amortization at various monthly payments and at 8% interest rate. Loan amounts from Table 2.4.23.

	20 year term		25 year term		
monthly payments (an(E))	loan amount	total value of home	loan amount	total value of home	increase in loan
-500.00	59,777.15	99,777.15	64,782.26	104,782.26	5,005.11
-600.00	71,732.58	111,732.58	77,738.71	117,738.71	6,006.13
-700.00	83,688.00	123,688.00	90,695.17	130,695.17	7,007.17
-800.00	95,643.43	135,643.43	103,651.62	143,651.62	8,008.19
-900.00	107,598.86	147,598.86	116,608.07	156,608.07	9,009.21
-1,000.00	119,554.29	159,554.29	129,564.52	169,564.52	10,010.23

increase in loan = loan amount (25-yr term) - loan amount (20-yr term)

The "total value of home" column was calculated by adding $40,000 (the available down payment) to the "loan amount" column. Assuming Pierre and Michelle are willing to pay out a maximum of $800 monthly mortgage payments, at 8%, they can afford to buy a house with a total price of $95,643.43 + $40,000.00 = $135,643.43 with a 20-year amortization or $103,651.62 + $40,000.00 = $143,651.62 with a 25-year amortization.

Table 2.4.27 Total interest paid at 8% interest rate, monthly mortgage payment of $800, with 20- and 25-year term. Loan amount from Table 2.4.26.

	term = 240 months term (per)			term = 300 months term (per)		
monthly payment (an(E))	loan amount	total cost	total interest paid	loan amount	total cost	total interest paid
-800.00	95,643.43	192,000.00	-96,356.57	103,651.62	240,000.00	-136,348.38

total cost = monthly payment x per

total interest paid = total cost - loan amount

Choosing an amortization period of 25 rather than 20 years adds $39,991.81 to the total interest paid ($136,348.38 - $96,356.57). This is quite a sum of money. Although they can afford a more expensive house with a 25-year mortgage — $143,651.62, which is just $8,008.19 more than the $135,643.43 they can afford with a 20-year mortgage — it is a very easy decision to choose the 20-year mortgage because of the interest savings.

All the calculations shown above were performed with the help of a financial calculator. It is always useful to generate a table of values, as you can see the pattern and where your unique situation will place you.

Assuming Pierre and Michelle are successful in purchasing a home with a mortgage of $95,643.43 at 8% interest amortized at 20 years, their monthly payment will be $800.

Pierre and Michelle's Mortgage Amortization Table

The usefulness of the financial calculator does not end here. With it, we can generate Pierre and Michelle's amortization table. Let us see how much of their monthly payment goes towards paying off the principal and how much to interest.

Table 2.4.28 Distribution of $800 monthly payment; $95,643.43 loan at 8% interest rate and 20-year amortization in increments of 10 months. (P/Yr = C/Yr = 12).

per	principal payment	interest payment	principal balance
1.00	-162.38	-637.62	95,481.05
10.00	-172.38	-627.62	93,970.07
20.00	-184.23	-615.77	92,181.75
30.00	-196.88	-603.12	90,270.57
40.00	-210.41	-589.59	88,228.07
50.00	-224.87	-575.13	86,045.24
60.00	-240.31	-559.69	83,712.48
70.00	-256.82	-543.18	81,219.44
80.00	-274.47	-525.53	78,555.11
90.00	-293.33	-506.67	75,707.74
100.00	-313.48	-486.52	72,664.75
110.00	-335.02	-464.98	69,412.69
120.00	-358.03	-441.97	65,937.20
130.00	-382.63	-417.37	62,222.93
140.00	-408.92	-391.08	58,253.48
150.00	-437.01	-362.99	54,011.33
160.00	-467.03	-332.97	49,477.74
170.00	-499.12	-300.88	44,632.68

Continued, Table 2.4.28

180.00	-533.41	-266.59	39,454.76
190.00	-570.06	-229.94	33,921.09
200.00	-609.22	-190.78	28,007.24
210.00	-651.08	-148.92	21,687.10
220.00	-695.81	-104.19	14,932.74
230.00	-743.61	-56.39	7,714.34
240.00	-794.70	-5.30	0.02

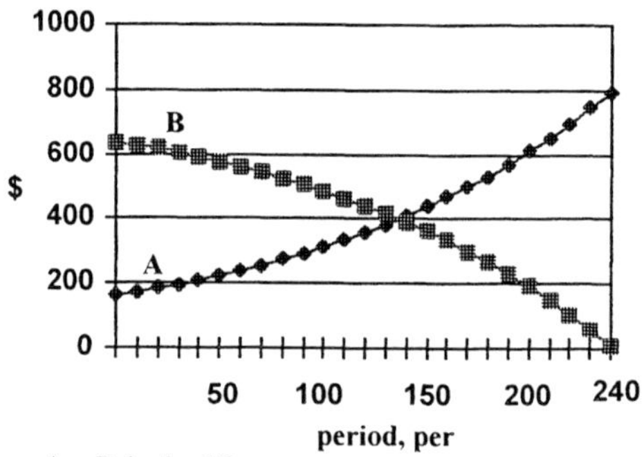

Figure 2.4.3 Principal payment and interest payment for above example

As the above table and figure show, the interest payments are decreasing from a maximum value of $637.62 and the principal payments are increasing from a minimum of $162.38. Note that in every period, the sum of the principal and interest payments equals the monthly payment of $800.00. For the first payment, the amount used to pay a portion of the total interest is about four times more than the amount used to reduce the principal. Compare with Table 2.4.13 in the loans sub-section above.

The Canadian Mortgage

The calculations we've just shown are valid for mortgages where interest is compounded monthly (C/Yr = 12), at the same frequency as the mortgage payment (P/Yr = 12).

However, for Canadian mortgages, the interest is compounded semi-annually, that is, (C/Yr = 2). The mortgage payment frequency is as before, monthly, (P/Yr = 12). If you need a review of how to handle interest rates when the interest compounding frequency is not the same as the payment frequency, refer to Section 2.2.

A financial calculator's built-in functions make mortgage calculations very easy. Let us repeat the calculations as shown in Table 2.4.27 but this time for a Canadian mortgage, using C/Yr = 2 or semi-annual interest compounding. The table below compares the result with those from Table 2.4.27 (C/Yr = 12).

Table 2.4.29 Total interest paid at 8% nominal interest rate compounded semi-annually (C/Yr = 2) and monthly (C/Yr = 12) for the same mortgage payments of $800 for C/Yr = 12 and $792.27 for C/Yr = 2.

		240 months term			300 months term		
C/Yr	mthly paymt	loan amount	total cost	totl int paid	loan amount	total cost	totl int paid
2.00	-792.27	95,643.43	190,144.80	-94,501.37	103,807.07	237,681.00	-133,873.93
12.00	-800.00	95,643.43	192,000.00	-96,356.57	103,651.62	240,000.00	-136,348.38

With a 20-year amortization, monthly compounding of interest (C/Yr = 12) results in $1,855.20 more total interest than semi-annual compounding (C/Yr = 2) ($96,356.57 – $94,501.37). With a 25-year amortization, the increase in interest is $2,474.45 ($136,348.38 – $133,873.93).

What is the effect of the frequency of compounding interest on the monthly payment? For the same mortgage loan of $95,643.43, let us calculate the monthly payment for monthly (C/Yr = 12), semi-annual (C/Yr = 2) and annual (C/Yr = 1) interest compounding with a 20-year amortization and a nominal interest rate of 8%.

Table 2.4.30 Monthly payment and interest saved for various interest compounding at 8% nominal interest rate, loan of $95,643.43 and 20-year amortization.

Type II, Class B.4 financial problem. (P/Yr = 12).

C/Yr	per	pr	an	total cost	total interest	interest saved
12.00	240.00	95,643.43	-800.00	192,000.00	96,356.57	0.00
2.00	240.00	95,643.43	-792.27	190,144.80	94,501.37	1,855.20
1.00	240.00	95,643.43	-783.46	188,030.40	92,386.97	3,969.60

As interest compounding becomes less frequent, the monthly payment decreases, and the interest saved for the loan increases.

Michael Jordan, the star player of the Chicago Bulls, signed a one-year contract for $30 million US.

SUMMARY

1. For the same interest rate and the same loan or mortgage, the monthly payment is lower when the term or amortization period is longer.
2. For the same interest rate and a given monthly loan payment, as the term or amortization period is increased, the affordable loan or mortgage increases.
3. The longer the loan term or amortization period, the more interest is paid.
4. Lower monthly payments and increased loans come with a price: higher total interest.
5. The monthly loan or mortgage payment is used to pay off the principal and the interest. From the first payment, the total interest paid starts from a maximum value and decreases towards the end of the term. The repayment on the principal, on the other hand, starts from a minimum value at the first payment and increases towards the end of the term.
6. Interest on short-term loans (usually three to five years) is much lower than the principal amount. However, interest on mortgages (typically ranging from 15 to 30 years) usually exceeds the principal amount.
7. You do not need a personal computer with amortization software or amortization booklets to determine your mortgage amortization table. The built-in functions of a financial calculator make this task extremely easy.
8. Typical US mortgages have interest compounded monthly, the same frequency as the payment frequency. Canadian mortgages, however, have the interest compounded semi-annually.
9. Less frequent interest compounding means less interest and is therefore a better deal for the borrower for loan and mortgage applications. However, for savings applications, *more* frequent interest compounding is a better deal.

The first edition of the Encyclopaedia Britannica was published in 1768–1771. Mozart was a young boy; Napoleon was a baby and Washington, Jefferson, and Adams were about to declare a new nation. Buyers paid £12 for the complete set. Approximately 3,000 sets were printed and a few have survived.

2.5
Lesson 5:
PLANNING FOR THE CHILDREN'S EDUCATION

Education costs money, but so does ignorance.

Sir Claus Moses, German-born English academic

I believe education is the greatest gift parents can bestow on their children. History has shown time and time again that, despite humble and poor beginnings, great men and women have emerged and influenced our society because they strove and completed their education.

I myself am a parent with two children. While they were still young, my wife and I started a forced savings plan to help finance their university education. A "forced" savings plan is any arrangement by which you commit yourself to automatically making regular periodic payments. You don't have to decide every month whether to put money away or spend that money on some immediate temptation. Human nature being what it is, most of us find some forced plan necessary to meet our long-term goals. We chose a registered education savings plan (RESP). There are other ways to cover the costs of post-secondary education, including university loans and scholarships, public and private sector scholarships, and student bank loans.

If you are planning to save for your children's education, this chapter will prove very useful. We will cover how to estimate the future value of the education fund required for a university or college education, how to implement a savings plan now, the effects of delaying the start of this savings plan, and the effect of inflation.

In 1998, the highest amount paid for a Web address on the Internet is $3.35 million US. Compaq Computer Corp., which owns the search engine Alta Vista, paid Jack Marshall the said amount for the web site name. Mr. Marshall started up his company, Alta Vista Technology Inc., and bought cyber-rights in 1994.

Before you start your calculations, you need to know the values for the following items. If you don't know actual amounts, estimate.

1. the number of years until the child will start university
2. the number of years the child will attend university
3. current yearly education cost, which includes tuition, room and board, and transportation costs
4. the rate of inflation
5. the interest rate that money will earn
6. interest compounding per year, C/Yr

Item 1 is a function of the age of the child. Depending on the educational system, a child might start university between the ages of 16 and 19. For item 2, four years is the standard length of course studies to obtain a university degree. For item 3, reference books are available giving yearly costs for various universities. In Canada, an excellent guide is the yearly publication of Maclean's Canadian University Guide. Items 4 and 5 are the current values for inflation and interest rate respectively. Item 6 is the interest compounding, whether yearly (C/Yr = 1), monthly (C/Yr = 12) or any other frequency.

In the TVM calculations, you will assume that the values for items 4 and 5 remain constant for the entire period being considered. However, we know for a fact that this is not the case. This is why I recommend that you repeat the calculations every year using current inflation and interest rates, and adjust the lump-sum or annuity payments into the savings plan. This is the only way to ensure that you're on track for your target future value.

The key to planning for the children's education is to calculate the future value of the education fund required at the time the child starts university or college education. The solution technique is as follows:

1. Calculate the present value of the total cost of university or college education.
2. Calculate the equivalent future value, using as period the number of years before the child goes to university; consider the effect of inflation.
3. Use one of the four savings methods discussed in Section 2.3 to save for the future education fund.

Table 2.5.1 shows the tabular format for the above three steps. In the third step, the table suggests using method 3, a combination of lump-sum and annuity payments.

Deep Space 4/Champollion is a NASA project that requires building an unmanned spacecraft that will land on a comet, collect samples, launch from the comet surface, link up with an orbiter, and then return the samples to earth. To be launched in the spring of 2003, it has a total budget of $180 million US.

Table 2.5.1 Steps to implement a savings plan for a child's education.

Steps	per	I/Yr	pr	fu	an
Step 1	years in university or college	nominal rate	? (calculate)	(0.00)	yearly education cost
Step 2	period until start of post-secondary education	inflation rate	present value of education fund	? (calculate)	(0.00)
Step 3	period until start of post-secondary education	nominal rate	present value of education fund	future value of education fund	? (calculate)

▒ = parameter not required

To illustrate the above-mentioned solution technique, let us use an example.

Vincenzo and Sophia have been married for five years. They live comfortably and own two vehicles and a home. They have a three-year-old son Giuseppe. Since they know the value of a university education, Vincenzo and Sophia would like to start an education fund that their son can use for four years of university. He is not expected to start university for another 15 years.

In the above example, the current year is 1996. In North America, school usually starts in September. The funds should be made available a few months before. Assume that the yearly education expenses will be withdrawn from the education fund every June starting in June 2011 and for the next three years.

In Canada, based on 1996 figures, it costs, on average, $12,000 per year to cover the cost of tuition, books, room and board, transportation, and other miscellaneous expenses. Assume that the savings fund to be set up for Giuseppe will earn 8% interest per year, compounded monthly, and the rate of inflation is 3%, also compounded monthly.

Step 1

The first step is to use June 1996 as the reference point for the present time. Calculate the present value of the four-year fund needed, at a $12,000 yearly education cost, taking into account that money earns 8%. See the figure below for the cash flow diagram. For our calculation, period (per) = 4, I/Yr = 8%, annuity payment (an(B)) = –$12,000, P/Yr = 1, and C/Yr = 12. Note that the annuity is made at the beginning of each period.

> *Women's athletics are on a roll. For example, in 1987, University of Notre Dame spent $880,000 US per year on women's athletics. Ten years later, in 1997, the annual budget reached almost $3.8 million US.*

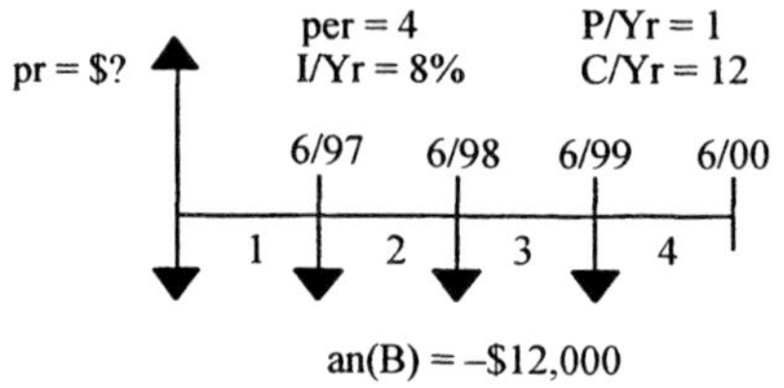

Figure 2.5.1 Present value of education fund

Table 2.5.2 Present value of $12,000 yearly education cost, taking into account 3% inflation compounded monthly and money earns 8% interest compounded monthly. Payments are made at the beginning of each period. I/Yr to be used is the nominal interest rate of 8% compounded monthly.

Type II, Class B.3 financial problem. (P/Yr = 1, C/Yr = 12).

per	I/Yr	pr	an(B)
4.00	8.00	42,758.55	-12,000.00

Step 2

The calculated present value is the total education fund that would be required if Giuseppe is to start university in September 1996. However, since he will be starting university 15 years from June 1996, we have to calculate the fund's future value, taking into account the inflation rate of 3%.

Table 2.5.3 Future value of $42,758.55 due to 3% inflation compounded monthly.

Type I, Class A.4 financial problem. (P/Yr = 1, C/Yr = 12).

per	I/Yr	pr	fu
15.00	3.00	-42,758.55	67,021.11

The calculated future value represents the total amount for a four-year university education 15 years from June 1996 due to the 3% inflation. This will be the target education fund amount required to guarantee that Giuseppe will have funds for his four-year university education.

The electric shaver, invented by Jacob Schick, was first sold in 1931 in the US for $25 US.

Step 3

There are four methods to implement a savings plan, as discussed in Section 2.3. Although Table 2.5.1 suggests using method 3 in this step, Table 2.5.4 shows the monthly payments using method 2 savings plan implementation. Note that the I/Yr to be used is 8%, the nominal interest rate that money earns.

Table 2.5.4 Monthly payments (an) made at beginning of each period for the next 15 years to accumulate $67,021.11 at 8% interest compounded monthly.
Type II, Class C.4 financial problem. (P/Yr = C/Yr = 12).

per	I/Yr	fu	an(B)
180.00	8.00	67,021.11	–192.40

Vincenzo and Sophia have to put into Giuseppe's education fund $192.40 at the beginning of each month for 15 years in order to accumulate $67,021.11.

To check our calculations, let us track the depletion of the education fund as Giuseppe goes through 4 years of university. Before we can do this, we need to estimate how the $12,000 yearly cost of education increases due to 3% inflation compounded monthly.

Table 2.5.5 Increase of $12,000 yearly cost of education due to 3% inflation compounded monthly.
Type I, Class A.4 financial problem. (P/Yr = 1, C/Yr = 12).

per	I/Yr	pr	fu
15.00	3.00	–12,000.00	18,809.18

Thus, the $12,000 cost of each year's education (in terms of present value) has a future value of $18,809.18. Using this value, let us follow through the depletion of Giuseppe's education fund.

Table 2.5.6 Depletion of Giuseppe's education fund of $67,021.11 starting June 2011 until June 2014. The fund earns 8% interest compounded monthly.
Type I, Class A.4 financial problem. (P/Yr = 1, C/Yr = 12).

beginning of year		money at beginning of year	yearly education cost	remainder to be invested	money at end of year (principal + int)
June 2011	1st year	67,021.11	18,809.18	48,211.93	52,213.50
June 2012	2nd year	52,213.50	18,809.18	33,404.32	36,176.86
June 2013	3rd year	36,176.86	18,809.18	17,367.68	18,809.19
June 2014	4th year	18,809.19	18,809.18	0.01	

The Canadian Bankers Association has recently published a booklet, *Saving for Your Children's Education.* In this booklet, example data was shown for the following scenario: inflation rate is 5%, money earns 8%, yearly education cost is $10,000 for a student living away from home. The first three columns of the table below are data from the booklet while the next two columns are calculated values using the solution method just explained in this section. The last two columns show the difference and percent difference between the two monthly savings payments. Financial calculations use factors of the form: $(1 + in)^{per}$. Small deviations from rounding-off procedures can result in widely differing values. Example, $(1 + 0.0601)^{100} = 342.52$, whereas $(1 + 0.0600)^{100} = 339.30$. Obviously there were two different rounding-off procedures for the two sets of data below. This difference makes it all the more important to update these calculations yearly.

Table 2.5.7 Comparison of calculated values for estimated education fund and monthly savings payment.

yrs to attend university	estimated education fund	monthly savings payment	estimated education fund	monthly savings payment	monthly pymnt diff.	% diff.
2	42,000	1,600	39,437	1,515	-85	5.31
4	46,000	820	43,480	771	-49	5.96
6	51,000	560	47,937	522	-38	6.79
8	56,000	425	52,850	397	-28	6.59
10	62,000	345	58,267	321	-24	6.96
12	68,000	290	64,240	271	-19	6.55
14	75,000	250	70,824	234	-16	6.40
16	83,000	220	78,084	206	-14	6.36
18	92,000	200	86,087	184	-16	8.00

Summary: Effects of Inflation

Our example regarding Giuseppe's education fund assumes an inflation rate of 3%. If all the parameters remained the same, repeating similar calculations for other rates of inflation result in Table 2.5.8. Refer to Tables 2.5.2 - 2.5.4 on how to calculate pr, fu and an(B).

Table 2.5.8 Present, future values, and monthly payments (beginning-of-period payments) at 8% interest, with inflation of 0%, 3%, 4%, and 5%. Assume years before starting university is 15 years (three-year-old child).

inflation	pr	fu	an(B)
0%	42,758.55	42,758.55	-125.84
3%	42,758.55	67,021.11	-192.40
4%	42,758.55	77,833.46	-223.44
5%	42,758.55	90,378.91	-259.45

Effect of Savings Fund Interest Rate

The above example used 8% interest rate. If the rate is 10%, the result is the summary Table 2.5.9 shown below. Refer to Tables 2.5.2 - 2.5.4 on how to calculate pr, fu and an(B).

Table 2.5.9 Present, future values, and monthly payments (beginning-of-period payments) at 10% interest rate at 0%, 3%, 4%, and 5% inflation rates; assume years before starting university is 15 years (three-year-old child).

inflation	pr	fu	an(B)
0%	41,596.34	41,596.34	-99.53
3%	41,596.34	67,964.61	-156.01
4%	41,596.34	80,051.10	-181.18
5%	41,596.34	94,288.02	-210.38

The monthly payments under the annuity (an(B)) column are lower than those for 8% interest rate simply because money was earning a higher interest at 10%.

Effect of Period

Our example so far has involved a three-year-old child who will start attending university in 15 years. Let us now see the effect of period on the present, future, and annuity values. Table 2.5.10 shows the calculated values when starting an education fund for a newborn child with 18 years before starting university. Table 2.5.11, on the other hand, applies to a 13-year old child, with five years before starting university. Refer to Tables 2.5.2 - 2.5.4 on how to calculate pr, fu, and an(B).

Table 2.5.10 Present value, future value, and monthly payments (beginning-of-period payments) at 8% interest rate at 0%, 3%, 4%, and 5% inflation rates. Years before starting university is 18 years (newborn child).

inflation	pr	fu	an(B)
0%	42,758.55	42,758.55	-88.47
3%	42,758.55	73,324.54	-151.72
4%	42,758.55	87,739.47	-181.55
5%	42,758.55	104,972.60	-217.21

Notice that the calculated monthly payments (an(B)) are lower compared to Table 2.5.8 (for three-year-old child), because there is an additional three years during which money can work for you by earning additional interest. Let us now consider the case for a 13-year old child.

Table 2.5.11 Present, future values, and monthly payments (beginning-of-period payments) at 8% interest rate at 0%, 3%, 4%, and 5% inflation rates. Years before starting university is 5 years (for 13-year-old child).

inflation	pr	fu	an(B)
0%	42,758.55	42,758.55	-578.08
3%	42,758.55	49,669.05	-671.51
4%	42,758.55	52,208.04	-705.83
5%	42,758.55	54,874.56	-741.88

Because of a very short period of time for money to earn interest, the monthly payments are much higher compared to the previous cases of a three-year old child (Table 2.5.8) and a newborn child (Table 2.5.10). This is, of course, due to the effect of compounding interest. If you can afford to start your savings plan when the child is still young, it will prove easier in the long run.

Savings Plan Implementation

Section 2.3 discussed the four methods of implementing a savings plan. In Table 2.5.4, we used method 2 to calculate the required payments to accumulate the desired education fund of $67,021.11. We will now revisit the first three saving methods, and apply them to our example. If you're interested in the fourth method, you can work out a schedule on your own.

Recall our assumptions about Vincenzo and Sophia's situation.

1. Giuseppe has 15 years before he starts university.
2. Giuseppe will be attending a four-year university course.
3. In 1996, the yearly cost of education for a student living away from home is $12,000.
4. Money is earning interest at 8% per year.
5. Inflation is assumed to be 3% per year.
6. Monthly interest compounding, C/Yr = 12.

The present value of the cost of four years' education is $42,758.55 (see Table 2.5.2). Applying 3% inflation to the present value for 15 years resulted in the future value of $67,021.11 (see Table 2.5.3). This is the estimated value of Giuseppe's education fund available in June 2011. He will attend university starting September 2011.

The James Bond movie film series has grossed more than $1 billion US worldwide from ticket sales since 1961.

Single Lump-Sum Payment (Method 1)

We can calculate the equivalent lump-sum payment required to accumulate $67,021.11.

Table 2.5.12 Present value of $67,021.11 at 8% interest compounded monthly, period of 15 years.
Type I, Class A.3 financial problem. (P/Yr = 1, C/Yr = 12).

per	I/Yr	pr	fu
15.00	8.00	-20,266.92	67,021.11

What is the effect if starting up Giuseppe's education fund is delayed? We can repeat the above calculation for various periods (per).

Table 2.5.13 Increasing lump-sum payments when saving for Giuseppe's education fund is delayed.
Type I, Class A.3 financial problem.

yr fund started	per	I/Yr	pr	fu
1996	15.00	8.00	-20,266.92	67,021.11
1997	14.00	8.00	-21,949.06	67,021.11
1998	13.00	8.00	-23,770.82	67,021.11
1999	12.00	8.00	-25,743.79	67,021.11
2000	11.00	8.00	-27,880.51	67,021.11
2001	10.00	8.00	-30,194.58	67,021.11
2002	9.00	8.00	-32,700.72	67,021.11
2003	8.00	8.00	-35,414.86	67,021.11
2004	7.00	8.00	-38,354.28	67,021.11
2005	6.00	8.00	-41,537.66	67,021.11
2006	5.00	8.00	-44,985.27	67,021.11
2007	4.00	8.00	-48,719.02	67,021.11
2008	3.00	8.00	-52,762.68	67,021.11
2009	2.00	8.00	-57,141.96	67,021.11
2010	1.00	8.00	-61,884.71	67,021.11
2011	0.00	8.00	-67,021.11	67,021.11

The company with the most millionaires employed is Microsoft Corp. By mid-1998, the company has more than 2,000 millionaires.

You can see how every year Vincenzo and Sophia put off starting Giuseppe's education fund increases the lump-sum payment needed to accumulate the required future fund value of $67,021.11. The lump-sum amount starts from a low of $20,266.92 and rises to $67,021.11 — the value needed when no savings plan is implemented.

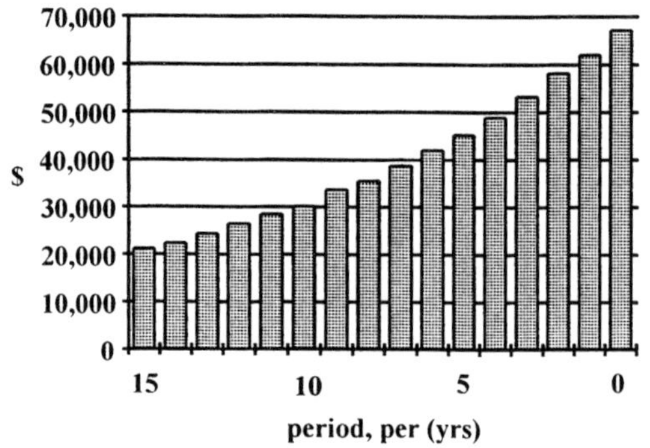

Figure 2.5.2 Lump-sum payments when education fund is delayed

The Queen Elizabeth II, operated by Cunard, is a transatlantic cruise liner that travels between New York City and Southampton, England. It is the world's fastest passenger ship at 32.5 knots cruising speed, capable of carrying 2,850 passengers and crew. In 1993, a first-class round-trip luxury cabin cost $57,500 US during July and August. At low season during April-May and November-December, it cost $44,000 US.

Periodic Annuity Payments (Method 2)

Yearly Payments

Table 2.5.14 Yearly payments at the beginning of each period when saving for Giuseppe's education fund is delayed. 8% interest rate compounded monthly. Type II, Class C.4 financial problem. (P/Yr = 1, C/Yr = 12).

yr fund started	per	I/Yr	fu	an(B)
1996	15.00	8.00	67,021.11	-2,226.52
1997	14.00	8.00	67,021.11	-2,501.31
1998	13.00	8.00	67,021.11	-2,823.02
1999	12.00	8.00	67,021.11	-3,203.46
2000	11.00	8.00	67,021.11	-3,658.75
2001	10.00	8.00	67,021.11	-4,211.41
2002	9.00	8.00	67,021.11	-4,894.00
2003	8.00	8.00	67,021.11	-5,755.35
2004	7.00	8.00	67,021.11	-6,872.16
2005	6.00	8.00	67,021.11	-8,372.26
2006	5.00	8.00	67,021.11	-10,485.75
2007	4.00	8.00	67,021.11	-13,672.78
2008	3.00	8.00	67,021.11	-19,007.02
2009	2.00	8.00	67,021.11	-29,709.42
2010	1.00	8.00	67,021.11	-61,884.71

The yearly payment at the beginning of each period starts from a low of $2,226.52 to a high of $61,884.71.

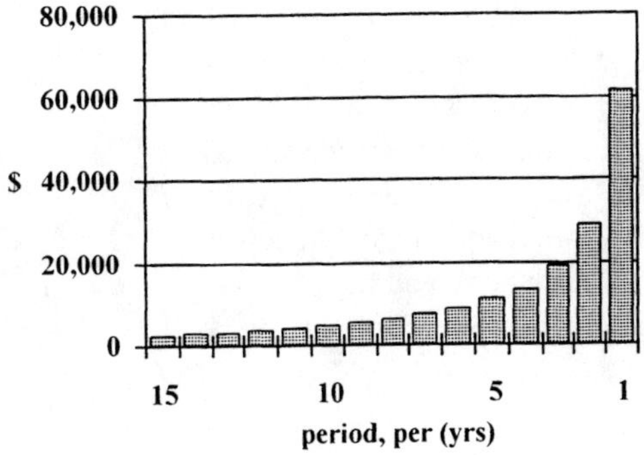

Figure 2.5.3 Yearly payments for education fund started at various points

Monthly Payments

Table 2.5.15 Monthly payments at the beginning of each period when saving for Giuseppe's education fund is delayed. 8% interest rate compounded monthly. Type II, Class C.4 financial problem. (P/Yr = C/Yr = 12).

yr fund started	per	I/Yr	fu	an(B)
1996	15 x 12	8.00	67,021.11	-192.40
1997	14 x 12	8.00	67,021.11	-216.14
1998	13 x 12	8.00	67,021.11	-243.94
1999	12 x 12	8.00	67,021.11	-276.82
2000	11 x 12	8.00	67,021.11	-316.16
2001	10 x 12	8.00	67,021.11	-363.92
2002	9 x 12	8.00	67,021.11	-422.90
2003	8 x 12	8.00	67,021.11	-497.33
2004	7 x 12	8.00	67,021.11	-593.84
2005	6 x 12	8.00	67,021.11	-723.47
2006	5 x 12	8.00	67,021.11	-906.10
2007	4 x 12	8.00	67,021.11	-1,181.50
2008	3 x 12	8.00	67,021.11	-1,642.44
2009	2 x 12	8.00	67,021.11	-2,567.26
2010	1 x 12	8.00	67,021.11	-5,347.60

If Vincenzo and Sophia start Giuseppe's education fund in June 1996, the current year for the problem, they will have to put aside $192.40 at the beginning of each month for 15 years to accumulate $67,021.11. The longer they wait to start, the higher the payment. If they wait until one year before Giuseppe starts university, they will have to pay $5,347.60 at the beginning of every month.

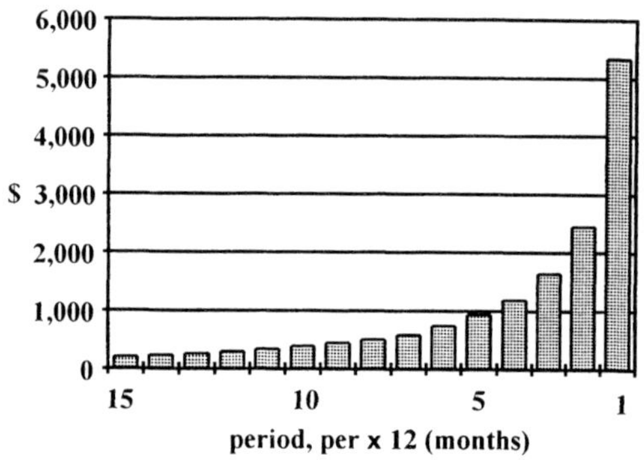

Figure 2.5.4 Monthly payments for various periods of starting up the education fund

Combination of Lump–Sum and Annuity Payments (Method 3)

Combination of Lump-Sum and Yearly Payments

Table 2.5.16 Yearly payments at the beginning of each period when saving for Giuseppe's education fund is delayed. 8% interest rate compounded monthly with lump–sum payments of $0, $1,000, $5,000, and $10,000. Future value = $67,021.11.
Type III, Class D.5 financial problem. (P/Yr = 1, C/Yr = 12).

yr fund started	per	an(B) pr = 0.00	an(B) pr = -1,000.00	an(B) pr = -5,000.00	an(B) pr = -10,000.00
1996	15.00	−2,226.52	−2,116.66	−1,677.22	−1,127.92
1997	14.00	−2,501.31	−2,387.35	−1,931.51	−1,361.71
1998	13.00	−2,823.02	−2,704.26	−2,229.22	−1,635.42
1999	12.00	−3,203.46	−3,079.03	−2,581.28	−1,959.10
2000	11.00	−3,658.75	−3,527.52	−3,002.60	−2,346.45
2001	10.00	−4,211.41	−4,071.93	−3,514.03	−2,816.65
2002	9.00	−4,894.00	−4,744.34	−4,145.70	−3,397.40
2003	8.00	−5,755.35	−5,592.83	−4,942.79	−4,130.22
2004	7.00	−6,872.16	−6,692.98	−5,976.28	−5,080.40
2005	6.00	−8,372.26	−8,170.70	−7,364.47	−6,356.68
2006	5.00	−10,485.75	−10,252.66	−9,320.29	−8,154.82
2007	4.00	−13,672.78	−13,392.14	−12,269.55	−10,866.32
2008	3.00	−19,007.02	−18,646.78	−17,205.84	−15,404.66
2009	2.00	−29,709.42	−29,189.50	−27,109.81	−24,510.19
2010	1.00	−61,884.71	−60,884.71	−56,884.71	−51,884.71

The youngest of the billionaires in the US is Bill Gates, the co-founder of Microsoft of Seattle, Washington. He was 20 when the company was established. He became a billionaire at the age of 31.

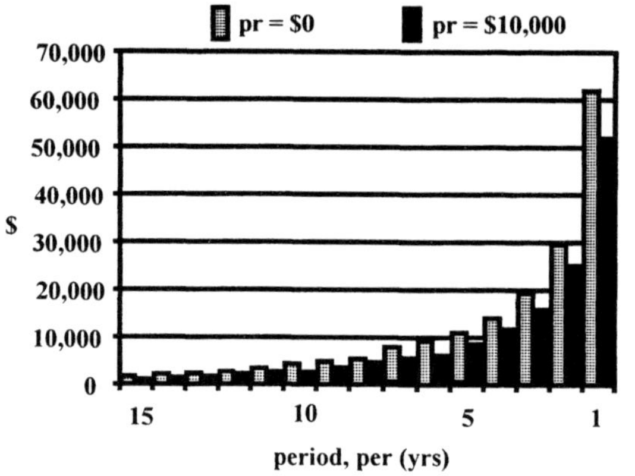

Figure 2.5.5 Yearly payments for various periods of starting up the education fund with different present values

Manhattan Island in New York was purchased from Native North American indians in 1626 by Peter Minuit, who represented the Dutch West India Company. He traded the land for beads, trinkets, and cloth worth about 60 Dutch guilders, or $24 US. If this money had been invested, today it would be worth more than $50 billion US.

Combination of Lump-Sum and Monthly Payments

Table 2.5.17 Monthly payments at the beginning of each period when saving for Giuseppe's education fund is delayed. 8% interest rate compounded monthly with lump-sum payments of $0, $1,000, $5,000, and $10,000. Future value = $67,021.11.
Type III, Class D.5 financial problem. (P/Yr = C/Yr = 12).

yr fund started	per	an(B) pr = 0.00	an(B) pr = -1,000.00	an(B) pr = -5,000.00	an(B) pr = -10,000.00
1996	15 x 12	–192.40	–182.91	–144.93	-97.47
1997	14 x 12	–216.14	–206.30	–166.91	–117.67
1998	13 x 12	–243.94	–233.68	–192.63	–141.32
1999	12 x 12	–276.82	–266.07	–223.05	–169.29
2000	11 x 12	–316.16	–304.82	–259.46	–202.76
2001	10 x 12	–363.92	–351.87	–303.66	–243.39
2002	9 x 12	–422.90	–409.97	–358.24	–293.58
2003	8 x 12	–497.33	–483.29	–427.12	–356.90
2004	7 x 12	–593.84	–578.36	–516.42	–439.01
2005	6 x 12	–723.47	–706.05	–636.38	–549.30
2006	5 x 12	–906.10	–885.96	–805.39	–704.68
2007	4 x 12	–1,181.50	–1,157.25	–1,060.24	–938.98
2008	3 x 12	–1,642.44	–1,611.31	–1,486.80	–1,331.15
2009	2 x 12	–2,567.26	–2,522.33	–2,342.62	–2,117.98
2010	1 x 12	–5,347.60	–5,261.19	–4,915.54	–4,483.48

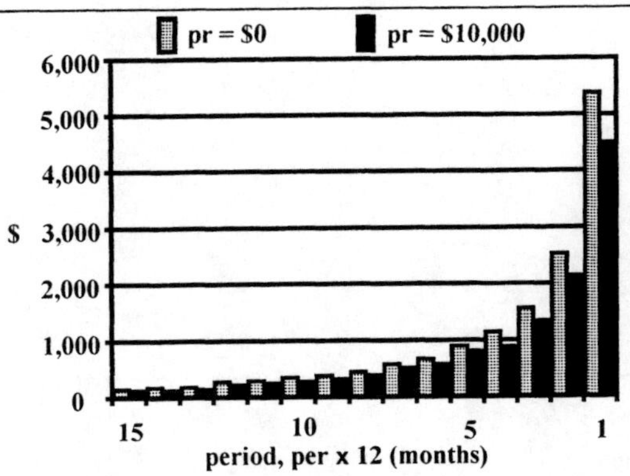

Figure 2.5.6 Monthly payments for various periods of starting up the education fund for different present values

Variations to the Calculations

There are several possible variations of the analyses we've just performed. First, we assumed that the child would take a four-year university course. You could, instead, assume the child would take a two-year college course, or a seven- to eight-year medical course. Maybe you plan to cover 50% or 75% of your child's education expenses, leaving the rest for the child to cover through summer jobs, scholarships, or loans. We chose a period of 15 years before the child attends university, and then did the same calculations for periods three and 18 years. Of course, other periods are possible. The inflation rates we used were 0%, 3%, 4%, and 5%; you could try it with 1% inflation. Likewise, we worked out monthly and yearly payments. You could try bi-monthly, quarterly, or semi-annual payments. The combinations are endless and will be specific to your particular situation. My intent is to teach you the techniques. From there, you should be able to perform similar calculations using your unique situation. As you will see if you follow the calculations in Chapter 3, they are done easily with a financial calculator.

Westinghouse Electric Corp., a household name in consumer appliance as well as a recognized name in the power generation business, changed its name to CBS Inc., effective December 1, 1997. It has agreed to sell its power generation business to Siemens AG of Germany for $1.53 billion US cash. It plans to become a media company after purchasing CBS television network.

2.6
Lesson 6: PLANNING FOR RETIREMENT

You can be young without money but you can't be old without it.

Tennessee Williams (1911-1983) US dramatist

It is sad to think that the most certain thing about our lives is that they will end. I am reminded of somebody who said, "we begin to die on the day that we are born." Since this is our inevitable destiny, we are all striving to make the best of life; to live it, to enjoy it, and to cherish its memorable moments.

Some people intentionally make no plans for the future. They do not believe in saving, but choose to live for the present. There are others, however, who make plans because they want to ensure a comfortable and rewarding retirement when the time comes. I belong to the second group. If you do too, you will find the basic techniques to plan for the future discussed in this section very useful.

Retirement means different things to people of different ages. If you are in your early 20s and just starting your first job, retirement is generally something you do not worry too much about. You're usually more concerned about buying your first car, a new stereo, a new computer, new clothes, etc. Setting aside money for retirement is usually at the very bottom of the list. However, as we mature and commit ourselves to buying a house or starting a family and raising children, our perspective in life changes. What used to be at the bottom of the list slowly creeps up to the top. Starting from the late 30s and early 40s, we begin to take retirement seriously. We start asking, am I saving enough for a comfortable retirement? Finally, when we hit retirement age, around late 50s to mid-60s, if we have done our homework well when we had the opportunity, we can start to enjoy life in style and comfort.

The billionaire oil magnate John D. Rockefeller once owned Standard Oil. In 1906, the US State Department charged Standard Oil with an oil monopoly. The result was its break-up in 1911 into smaller companies: Esso, Mobil, Chevron, and Amoco.

YOUR EARNING POTENTIAL

Have you ever wondered how much you are capable of earning in all of your working years? Assume you start employment at age 23 with a starting salary of $20,000 a year, get a yearly salary increase of 2% compounded annually, and work until age 65, what is the cumulative value of your total earnings at age 65?

To simplify calculations, we will assume an annual end-of-period payment, although bi-weekly or monthly payments are more common.

Table 2.6.1 Future value of $20,000 a year increasing 2% per year for 43 years. Use end-of-period payments.
Type II, Class C.3 financial problem. (P/Yr = C/Yr = 1). Period (per) = 65 − 23 + 1 = 43.

per	I/Yr	fu	an(E)
43.00	2.00	1,343,189.36	-20,000.00

Even with a modest 2% annual increase, the total accumulated value is over one million dollars, at $1,343,189.36! This is the pool of money from which you will meet your living expenses and also fund any savings plans. Will your lifestyle be to live for the present or will it be to plan for a comfortable retirement?

Let us repeat the same calculations for various periods, per = 43, 35, 25, and 15; for yearly increases of 2%, 3%, and 4% compounded annually; and for starting salaries of $20,000, $30,000, $40,000, $50,000, $60,000, $80,000, and $100,000. Table 2.6.2 shows the accumulated future values (rounded off to the nearest dollar).

The tables and figures below show that most of the accumulated future values are over a million dollars. Even starting at age 31 with a salary of $20,000, and a 2% annual salary increase, the accumulated future value is close to one million, $999,890.

The Mexican War of 1846–1848 led to the Treaty of Guadalupe Hidalgo, which provided that the US would purchase from Mexico, for $15 million US, a block of land comprising 3 million square km, which now forms part of New Mexico and California.

Table 2.6.2 Total earnings at the end of age 65 for various starting salaries, ages and yearly increases.
Type II, Class C.3 financial problem. (P/Yr = C/Yr = 1). Use end-of-period payments.

	Age			
	23	31	41	51
	per = 43	per = 35	per = 25	per = 15
Starting Salary	2% yearly increase			
20,000	1,343,189	999,890	640,606	345,868
30,000	2,014,784	1,499,834	960,909	518,803
40,000	2,686,379	1,999,779	1,281,212	691,737
50,000	3,357,973	2,499,724	1,601,515	864,671
60,000	4,029,568	2,999,669	1,921,818	1,037,605
80,000	5,372,757	3,999,558	2,562,424	1,383,473
100,000	6,715,947	4,999,448	3,203,030	1,729,342

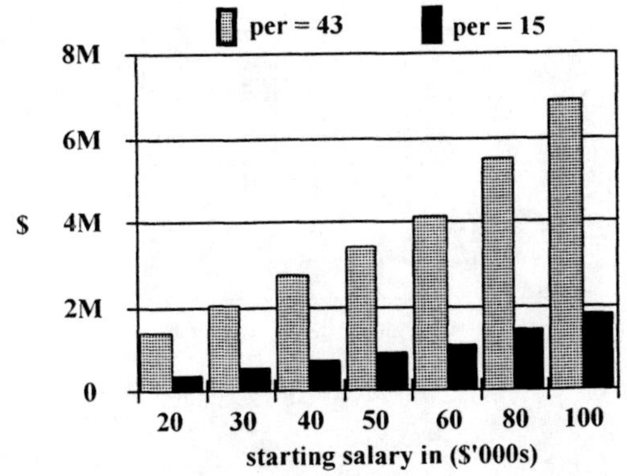

Figure 2.6.1 Total earnings at end of age 65 at 2% yearly increase

In the 1800s during the Industrial Revolution, shoes that were mass-produced could be worn on either foot. Only the rich could afford custom-made shoes that had a right and a left.

Continued, Table 2.6.2

Starting Salary	Age 23 per = 43	Age 31 per = 35	Age 41 per = 25	Age 51 per = 15
	3% yearly increase			
20,000	1,709,678	1,209,242	729,185	371,978
30,000	2,564,517	1,813,862	1,093,778	557,967
40,000	3,419,356	2,418,483	1,458,371	743,957
50,000	4,274,195	3,023,104	1,822,963	929,946
60,000	5,129,034	3,627,725	2,187,556	1,115,935
80,000	6,838,711	4,836,967	2,916,741	1,487,913
100,000	8,548,389	6,046,208	3,645,926	1,859,891

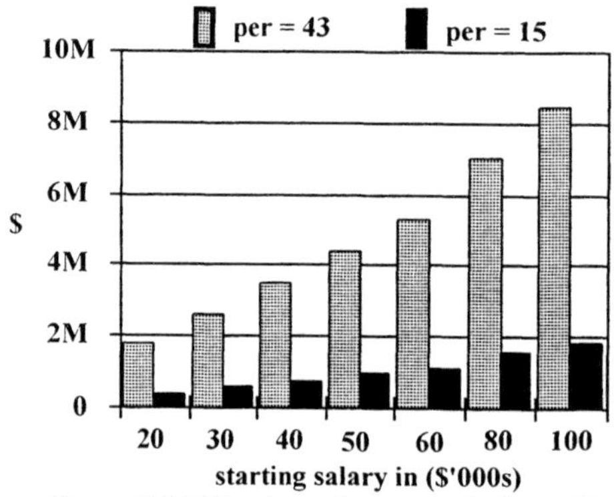

Figure 2.6.2 Total earnings at end of age 65 at 3% yearly increase

It takes about seven years for a pearl-producing oyster to make an average-sized pearl. The largest pearl weighed more than 14 lbs. and was found at Palawan, Philippines in 1934. In 1971 it was valued at $4.08 million US.

Continued, Table 2.6.2

	Age			
	23	31	41	51
	per = 43	per = 35	per = 25	per = 15
Starting Salary	**4% yearly increase**			
20,000	2,200,248	1,473,045	832,918	400,472
30,000	3,300,371	2,209,567	1,249,377	600,708
40,000	4,400,495	2,946,089	1,665,836	800,944
50,000	5,500,619	3,682,611	2,082,295	1,001,179
60,000	6,600,743	4,419,133	2,498,755	1,201,415
80,000	8,800,991	5,892,178	3,331,673	1,601,887
100,000	11,001,238	7,365,222	4,164,591	2,002,359

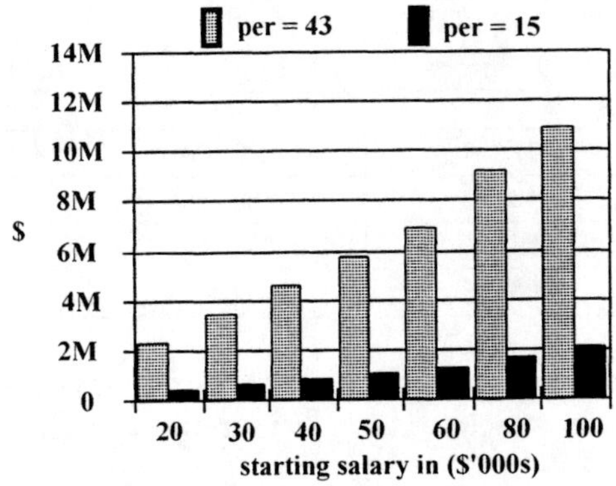

Figure 2.6.3 Total earnings at end of age 65 at 4% yearly increase

In 1997, Canadians contributed a record $80 billion CDN in new money, boosting the total mutual fund assets value to $280 billion CDN. In 1996, $41 billion in new money was attracted, with total mutual fund assets at $211.8 billion.

Let us look in more detail at that 23-year old who stands to earn a total income of $1,343,189 by the end of age 65.

If this person saves $100 per month in those 43 working years, what is the accumulated value of the savings, assuming money earns 8% interest compounded monthly?

Table 2.6.3 Future value of $100 a month, for 43 years at 8% per year compounded monthly. Use beginning-of-period payments.
Type II, Class C.3 financial problem. (P/Yr = C/Yr = 12).

per	I/Yr	fu	an(B)
43 x 12	8.00	450,478	-100.00

For various interest rates:

Table 2.6.4 Future values at the end of age 65 for various monthly savings amount. Interest is compounded monthly. Monthly payments are made at the beginning of each period. Period = 43 x 12.
Type II, Class C.3 financial problem. (P/Yr = C/Yr = 12).

savings amount	total savings	future value at 6% interest	future value at 8% interest	future value at 10% interest
50.00	25,800	212,731	225,239	431,959
100.00	51,600	243,463	450,478	863,919
150.00	77,400	365,194	675,716	1,295,878
200.00	103,200	486,925	900,955	1,727,838

This young person not only has the potential to earn more than a million dollars for a life's work, but also, by investing wisely, to actually retire with a million dollars saved.

Hong Kong's newest airport, called Chek Lap Kok, was built at a cost of $20 billion US. The land on which it sits is a man-made platform 6 km long and 3.5 km wide. Some 10 tonnes of soil, mud, and sand were moved every second for three years. Opened in July 1998, it is designed to serve 35 million passengers and nine million tonnes of cargo each year.

STARTING EARLY

When considering saving up for retirement, your number one ally — if it is still available to you — is *time*. Let us follow the different paths taken by two friends Ingrid and Natasha.

Ingrid started saving for retirement early. On her 18th birthday, she set aside $2,000. She set aside the same amount on her 19th, 20th and 21st birthday. In total, she put down $8,000 towards her retirement. Let us calculate the future value of her retirement savings at the end of age 65, assuming 8% interest compounded monthly.

The cash flow diagram is as follows:

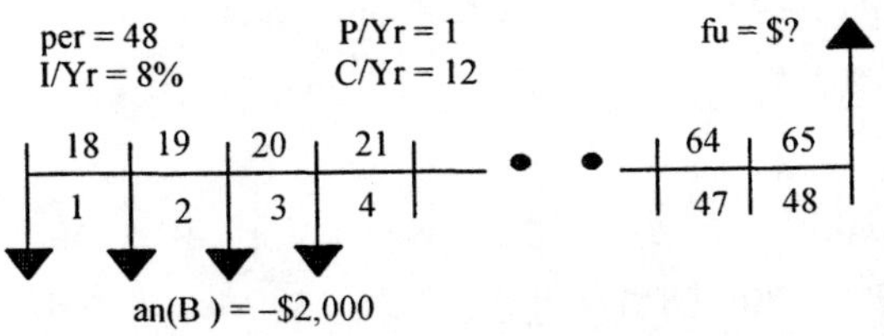

Figure 2.6.4 Ingrid's $8,000 investment

There are two parts to the problem. First, let us calculate the present value of the four annual payments of $2,000.

Table 2.6.5 Present value of $2,000 a year for four years, per = 4 at 8% interest compounded monthly. Use beginning–of–period payments.
Type II, Class B.3 financial problem. (P/Yr = 1, C/Yr = 12).

per	I/Yr	pr	an(B)
4.00	8.00	7,126	-2,000.00

The next step is to calculate the future value of $7,126.

Table 2.6.6 Future value of $7,126.
Type I, Class A.4 financial problem. (P/Yr = 1, C/Yr = 12).

per	I/Yr	pr	fu
48.00	8.00	-7,126	327,342

Natasha, on the other hand, decided to wait 10 years before starting her retirement savings. On her 28th birthday, she set aside $1,000 and did the same every year thereafter until age 65. Natasha's total savings are $38,000. Let us calculate the future value of the retirement savings at the end of age 65, assuming 8% interest compounded monthly. The cash flow diagram is as follows:

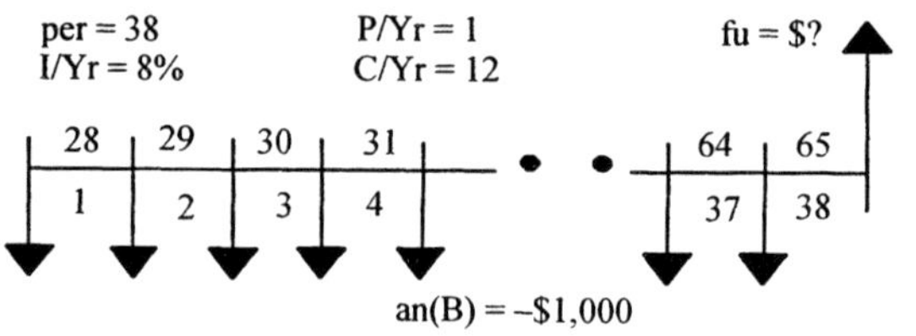

Figure 2.6.5 Natasha's $38,000 investment

Table 2.6.7 Future value of $1,000 a year for 38 years at 8% interest compounded monthly. Use beginning-of-period payments.
Type II, Class C.3 financial problem. (P/Yr = 1, C/Yr = 12).

per	I/Yr	fu	an(B)
38.00	8.00	256,991	-1,000.00

Comparing the results therefore:

Table 2.6.8 Summary results for Ingrid's and Natasha's savings accounts for yearly payments made at the beginning of each period.

	Ingrid	Natasha
Total amount saved	$8,000	$38,000
Total future value at end of age 65	$327,342	$256,991
Total interest earned	$319,342	$218,991

Ingrid's retirement savings earned $100,351 ($319,342 – $218,991) more than Natasha's. Ingrid was able to take advantage of the positive effect of time on her savings.

As you can see, Ingrid made the best decision by putting down $8,000 towards retirement early in her life. Natasha could not even match Ingrid's total accumulated money even though she set aside nearly five times as much.

Let us redo the calculations, this time using yearly end-of-period payments.

The price of each space shuttle was about $600 million US. The shuttle space program cost about $9 billion US.

Table 2.6.9 Present value of $2,000 a year for 4 years at 8% interest compounded monthly (for Ingrid's retirement savings). Payments made at the end of each period.
Type II, Class B.3 financial problem. (P/Yr = 1, C/Yr = 12).

per	I/Yr	pr	an(E)
4.00	8.00	6,580	-2,000.00

The next step is to calculate the future value of $6,580.

Table 2.6.10 Future value of $6,580.
Type I, Class A.4 financial problem. (P/Yr = 1, C/Yr = 12).

per	I/Yr	pr	fu
48.00	8.00	-6,580	302,261

Table 2.6.11 Future value of $1,000 a year for 38 years at 8% interest compounded monthly (for Natasha's retirement savings). Payments made at the end of each period.

per	I/Yr	fu	an(E)
38.00	8.00	237,295	-1,000.00

Comparing the new results:

Table 2.6.12 Summary results for Ingrid's and Natasha's savings accounts for yearly payments made at the end of each period.

	Ingrid	Natasha
Total amount saved	$8,000	$38,000
Total future value at end of age 65	$302,261	$237,295
Total interest earned	$294,261	$199,295

Ingrid's retirement savings earned $94,966 more than Natasha's ($294,261 - $199,295). However, Ingrid's earnings were $25,082 lower than in the previous case where the yearly payments were made at the beginning of the period.

According to a 1998 National Science Board report, US expenditures on R&D exceeded $200 billion for the first time in 1997.

Tips: Start early to save up for retirement; use beginning-of-period payments for series of equal payments to generate greater interest earnings.

We have seen how yearly payments made at the beginning of the period provided greater interest earnings. How does it compare with monthly payments? Let us redo the calculations but this time using monthly payments made at the beginning of each period. For Ingrid, the monthly payment is $2,000/12 = $167 for 48 months (4 years x 12). Natasha's monthly payment is $1,000/12 = $83 for 456 months (38 years x 12).

Table 2.6.13 Present value of $167 a month for 48 months at 8% interest compounded monthly (for Ingrid's retirement savings). Payments made at the beginning of each period.
Type II, Class B.3 financial problem. (P/Yr = C/Yr = 12).

per	I/Yr	pr	an(B)
48.00	8.00	6,886	-167.00

The next step is to calculate the future value of $6,886.

Table 2.6.14 Future value of $6,886 (for Ingrid's retirement savings). Payments made at the beginning of each period.
Type I, Class A.4 financial problem. (P/Yr = C/Yr = 12).

per	I/Yr	pr	fu
48 x 12	8.00	-6,886	316,318

Table 2.6.15 Future value of $83 a month for 38 years at 8% interest compounded monthly (for Natasha's retirement savings). Payments made at the beginning of the period.
Type II, Class C.3 financial problem. (P/Yr = C/Yr = 12).

per	I/Yr	fu	an(B)
38 x 12	8.00	246,842	-83.00

Financial services companies led all other firms in Internet advertising at $2 million CDN in 1997. For every four sites that sell advertising space, three are likely to be rented by a financial services company.

Comparing again the results:

Table 2.6.16 Summary results for Ingrid's and Natasha's savings accounts for monthly payments made at the beginning of each period.

	Ingrid	**Natasha**
Total amount saved	$8,016	$37,848
Total future value at end of age 65	$316,318	$246,842
Total interest earned	$308,302	$208,994

This time, Ingrid's earnings were $99,308 more than Natasha's.
The overall summary is as follows:

Table 2.6.17 Summary results for Ingrid's and Natasha's savings accounts for yearly payments made at the beginning and end of each period and monthly payments made at the beginning of each period.

	Yearly payment at beginning of each period		**Yearly payment at end of each period**		**Monthly payment at beginning of each period**	
	Ingrid	Natasha	Ingrid	Natasha	Ingrid	Natasha
Total amount saved	$8,000	$38,000	$8,000	$38,000	$8,016	$37,848
Total future value at end of age 65	$327,342	$256,991	$302,261	$237,295	$316,318	$246,842
Total interest earned	$319,342	$218,991	$294,261	$199,295	$308,302	$208,994
Difference	$100,351		$94,966		$99,308	

It makes sense that payments at the beginning of the year earn more interest than monthly payments, simply because the money is earning interest longer. At each yearly payment, the entire amount is available to start earning interest, whereas with monthly payments, only at the end of the 12th month is the entire yearly amount available to earn interest.

Similarly, it is not surprising that payments made at the beginning of each month earned more interest than payments made at the end of each year. This is because with the monthly payment, some of the money is already earning interest in the early part of the year.

Tips: For series of payments, the greatest interest is earned for yearly payments made at the beginning of each year; next best are monthly payments made at the beginning of each month.

ESTABLISHING YOUR RETIREMENT FUND

In Canada, the government encourages citizens to save for retirement. They are encouraged to set aside money for retirement in a registered retirement savings plan (RRSP). The interest earned is not taxed until the funds are withdrawn. The other advantage to the plan is that, depending on your taxable income and the amount of contribution for the year, the government gives back a portion of the money during income tax filing time in the form of allowable deductions to income.

In the US, the 401(k) retirement plan (so named as it was authorized in Section 401 (k) of the US Internal Revenue Code) permits employees to have part of their income regularly withheld and invested, with taxes deferred until money is withdrawn.

I used to ignore the annual rush of people trying to beat the end of February deadline for RRSP contributions in Canada. However, over the past few years, I have begun to seriously consider the promotion newsletters put out by the various financial institutions wanting to get a piece of my RRSP business. These newsletters discuss, among other topics, how to maximize the tax benefits from RRSP contributions. They are full of charts, tables, and graphs to emphasize the impact of interest compounding, and the advantages of "cost-averaging" when buying stocks, bonds, and mutual funds. Some of the tables show how much one has to save now based on number of years to retirement, desired retirement income, number of retirement years, and the interest rate. Some newsletters take into account inflation while others do not.

To take a more proactive role in your own retirement plans, the first thing you need to do is to perform time value of money calculations. You need to consider any accumulated RRSP savings you already have. It is also important to take into account the effect of inflation. TVM analysis can help in answering the following question: "for the retirement income that I want, am I saving enough, too little, or too much?"

If you're already saving enough, there is nothing more to do. Simply keep setting aside the same amount of money every year for your retirement. However, if you are not saving enough, you will need to know how much more to set aside every year in order to reach your desired retirement income. On the other hand, if you are saving too much, you would like to know how much less to set aside every year and still achieve your desired retirement income. The extra cash freed up could become discretionary income to be used for present needs or it can be saved for major purchases in the future.

These are the steps to be taken in order to plan for one's retirement:

1. Decide how much, in today's dollars you want as monthly income when you retire and for how long you want to fund your retirement. Then, calculate the present value of the retirement fund.
2. Calculate the equivalent future value, using as period the number of years before retirement starts; consider the effect of inflation.
3. Use one of the four savings methods (as discussed in Section 2.3) to begin building your retirement fund.

Table 2.6.18 charts these three steps. In the third step, the table suggests using method 3, combined lump-sum and annuity payments.

Table 2.6.18 Steps to calculate the monthly savings payments at the beginning of each period for total months prior to retirement in order to receive the required monthly retirement income.

Steps	per	I/Yr	pr	fu	an
Step 1	retirement period	nominal rate	? (calculate)	(0.00)	req'd periodic retirement income
Step 2	period to retirement	inflation rate	present value of retirement fund	? (calculate)	(0.00)
Step 3	period to retirement	nominal rate	lump-sum payment	future value of retirement fund	? (calculate)

▒ = parameter not required

Let's take an example.

John and Mary have been planning for their retirement. They currently have a retirement fund of $100,000. If they would like to receive $4,000 retirement income at the beginning of each month for 20 years, how much should they save at the beginning of each month if they have 15 more years before they start retiring? Assume that money earns 8% interest and that the rate of inflation is 3%. Both interest rates are compounded monthly.

Step 1

Since payments are monthly, P/Yr = 12. The period to be used is 20 years, or 240 months. Note that during the 20 years of retirement, money will earn interest at the rate of 8%. The technique is to calculate the present value of the monthly retirement income available at the beginning of each month. Given period (per) = 240, I/Yr = 8%, P/Yr = 12, C/Yr = 12 and annuity payment (an(B)) = $4,000, let us calculate the present value (pr) with a time reference of today. Note that the annuity payment is made at the beginning of the payment period.

In 1997, the operating budget of the University of Notre Dame, in Indiana was $388 million US. This is more than $1 million a day!

Table 2.6.19 Present value of $4,000 monthly retirement income, taking into account 3% inflation compounded monthly and money earning 8% interest compounded monthly. Monthly payments are made at the beginning of each period. Type II, Class B.3 financial problem. (P/Yr = C/Yr = 12).

per	I/Yr	pr	an(B)
240.00	8.00	-481,405	4,000.00

Step 2

The calculated present value is the retirement fund that would be required if John and Mary were to retire today. However, since they will be starting retirement 15 years from now, we have to calculate the fund's future value, taking into account the inflation rate. The period to be used is 15 years, or 180 months.

Table 2.6.20 Future value of $481,405 due to 3% inflation compounded monthly.
Type I, Class A.4 financial problem. (P/Yr = C/Yr = 12).

per	I/Yr	pr	fu
180.00	3.00	-481,405	754,570

The calculated future value represents the value of the retirement fund 15 years from now due to 3% inflation. This will be the target amount that will need to be accumulated to guarantee that John and Mary will have funds for their retirement.

Step 3

There are four methods to implement a savings plan, as discussed in Section 2.3. Table 2.6.21 shows the monthly payments using method 3. Note that the I/Yr to be used is 8%, the nominal interest rate that money earns. The current value of the retirement fund is $100,000. Period is 15 years, or 180 months.

Table 2.6.21 Monthly payments required for the next 15 years to accumulate $754,570 at 8% interest compounded monthly. Payments made at the beginning of each period.
Type III, Class D.5 financial problem. (P/Yr = C/Yr = 12).

per	I/Yr	pr	fu	an(B)
180.00	8.00	-100,000.00	754,570	-1,217

The solution technique just discussed is the same one used for calculating your children's education fund covered in Section 2.5. In that section, we compared data from the booklet published by the Canadian Bankers Association and calculated values from the solution technique. The comparison Table 2.5.7 showed that the solution technique is in close agreement with the data from the booklet. The difference is due to different rounding-off procedures between the two techniques.

Similarly, in this section, let us compare the solution technique to published data from a financial institution. For example, Bank of Montreal published an RRSP (Registered Retirement Savings Plan) Personal Check-up Planner. In it, an example retirement calculation was shown with the following scenario: a person has an existing $20,000 retirement fund and plans to retire in 25 years; money earns 10% compounded annually; inflation is at 5% per year, also compounded annually. The problem is to calculate the yearly savings payment towards retirement if the person wants to receive $1,500 per month to supplement other sources of retirement income for 20 years. Assume beginning-of-period payments. The answer to the problem was $2,970. In addition to showing how $2,970 was calculated, the personal planner showed the financial factors for various years to retirement. By following the example, I calculated the yearly savings payment for various years to retirement. The second column in Table 2.6.22 below shows the results. The third column shows the calculation results using the solution technique discussed in this section. The last two columns show the difference and percent difference between the calculated values. Similar to Section 2.5, the difference can be explained by the differing rounding-off procedures of the two techniques.

Table 2.6.22 Comparison of calculated values for estimated yearly savings payment.

years to retirement	yearly savings payment	yearly savings payment	yearly payment difference	% difference
5	26,084	25,882	-202	0.77
10	12,068	12,040	-28	0.23
15	7,192	7,212	20	0.28
20	4,610	4,663	53	1.15
25	2,970	3,050	80	2.69
30	1,826	1,927	101	5.53
35	982	1,101	119	12.12

The Ice Hotel in northern Sweden is built from scratch in the village of Jukkasjarvi, 200 km north of the Arctic Circle in Lapland. Unheated cabins at the Ice Hotel, which can be as cold as −37° C, cost $75 to $100 US. The heated cabins cost $25 US.

The above calculations (Tables 2.6.19 - 2.6.21) can be repeated for various years to retirement, monthly payments, and interest rates. Tables 2.6.23 - 2.6.26 show the monthly payments to finance a monthly retirement income of $3,000 or $4,000 in today's dollars for 20 years, taking into account an existing retirement fund of $10,000, $50,000, $100,000, and $150,000. The calculations assume interest rates of 4%, 6%, and 8% compounded monthly for various years to retirement. Beginning-of-period payments are also assumed.

When using the financial calculator to calculate the monthly payments, be careful to enter the existing retirement fund as a cash outflow (negative value) and the future value of the retirement fund as a cash inflow (positive value).

The calculated value in brackets, for example, (+$5) in Table 2.6.24 indicates that the lump-sum payment of $50,000 at 8% nominal interest rate with 3% inflation is more than enough to provide, in today's dollars, $3,000 of monthly retirement income for 20 years. Thus, instead of setting money aside at the beginning of every month, the fortunate plan holder can actually *withdraw* $5 monthly for 40 years from the savings fund and still have the required $3,000 monthly retirement payment for 20 years. Similar interpretations apply to others that show bracketed positive values.

Table 2.6.23 Monthly payments to finance $3,000 and $4,000 monthly retirement income for 20 years if $10,000 retirement fund has already been started. Money earns 4%, 6%, and 8% interest, compounded monthly; 3% inflation, compounded monthly; various years to retirement. Use beginning-of-period payments. (P/Yr = C/Yr = 12).

Years to retirement	$3,000 monthly retirement income			$4,000 monthly retirement income		
	4%	6%	8%	4%	6%	8%
40.00	-1,347	-642	-272	-1,810	-875	-385
30.00	-1,705	-965	-518	-2,289	-1,306	-715
20.00	-2,397	-1,579	-1,026	-3,216	-2,129	-1,395
15.00	-3,079	-2,173	-1,530	-4,131	-2,925	-2,071
10.00	-4,436	-3,337	-2,525	-5,948	-4,487	-3,407
5.00	-8,490	-6,779	-5,469	-11,382	-9,103	-7,359

According to the Motion Picture Association of America, in 1998 it costs an average of $53 million US to produce a film, about double what it cost in 1992. Another $22 million per film is added for TV and newspaper marketing ads.

Table 2.6.24 Monthly payments to finance $3,000 and $4,000 monthly retirement income for 20 years if $50,000 retirement fund has already been started. Money earns 4%, 6%, and 8% interest, compounded monthly; 3% inflation, compounded monthly; various years to retirement. Use beginning-of-period payments. (P/Yr = C/Yr = 12).

Years to retirement	$3,000 monthly retirement income			$4,000 monthly retirement income		
	4%	6%	8%	4%	6%	8%
40.00	-1,180	-423	(+5)	-1,643	-656	-109
30.00	-1,515	-726	-227	-2,099	-1,067	-424
20.00	-2,156	-1,294	-693	-2,975	-1,844	-1,063
15.00	-2,785	-1,837	-1,150	-3,836	-2,589	-1,691
10.00	-4,032	-2,896	-2,043	-5,544	-4,045	-2,925
5.00	-7,756	-6,001	-4,663	-10,648	-8,334	-6,553

Table 2.6.25 Monthly payments to finance $3,000 and $4,000 monthly retirement income for 20 years if $100,000 retirement fund has already been started. Money earns 4%, 6%, and 8% interest, compounded monthly; 3% inflation, compounded monthly; various years to retirement. Use beginning-of-period payments. (P/Yr = C/Yr = 12).

Years to retirement	$3,000 monthly retirement income			$4,000 monthly retirement income		
	4%	6%	8%	4%	6%	8%
40.00	-972	-150	(+350)	-1,435	-382	(+237)
30.00	-1,277	-428	(+138)	-1,861	-769	-59
20.00	-1,854	-937	-278	-2,673	-1,487	-647
15.00	-2,416	-1,417	-675	-3,467	-2,170	-1,217
10.00	-3,528	-2,343	-1,440	-5,040	-3,492	-2,322
5.00	-6,838	-5,048	-3,656	-9,730	-7,372	-5,546

Disney's third full-length animated feature film was Sleeping Beauty. It took Disney six years and $6 million US to complete the project. It was released in January 29, 1959. At 2% inflation rate compounded yearly, the cost in 1998 is about $13 million US. At 3% inflation, it is about $19 million US.

Table 2.6.26 Monthly payments to finance $3,000 and $4,000 monthly retirement income for 20 years if $150,000 retirement fund has already been started. Money earns 4%, 6%, and 8% interest, compounded monthly; 3% inflation, compounded monthly; various years to retirement. Use beginning-of-period payments. (P/Yr = C/Yr = 12).

Years to retirement	$3,000 monthly retirement income			$4,000 monthly retirement income		
	4%	6%	8%	4%	6%	8%
40.00	-764	(+124)	(+695)	-1,227	-108	(+582)
30.00	-1,039	-129	(+502)	-1,623	-471	(+305)
20.00	-1,552	-581	(+138)	-2,371	-1,131	-232
15.00	-2,047	-997	-200	-3,098	-1,750	-742
10.00	-3,023	-1,791	-838	-4,535	-2,940	-1,719
5.00	-5,921	-4,086	-2,649	-8,812	-6,410	-4,539

RETIREMENT FUND HAS NOT BEEN STARTED

If the retirement fund has not been started, Tables 2.6.27 - 2.6.29 provide the payment values for methods 1 and 2 of the savings implementation

Table 2.6.27 Lump-sum payment values (Method 1) to provide $2,000, $3,000, $4,000 monthly retirement income for 20 years at 4%, 6%, and 8% interest rates compounded monthly for various years to retirement. Payments are made at the beginning of each period; inflation is 3%. (P/Yr = C/Yr = 12).

Years to retirement	$2,000 monthly payment			$3,000 monthly payment		
	4%	6%	8%	4%	6%	8%
40.00	-222,231	-84,882	-32,874	-333,346	-127,323	-49,311
30.00	-245,532	-114,450	-54,077	-368,297	-171,675	-81,115
20.00	-271,275	-154,319	-88,954	-406,913	-231,478	-133,432
10.00	-299,719	-208,075	-146,327	-449,578	-312,113	-219,490

From the University of Miami comes a job satisfaction guarantee. In the fall of 1997 if a student graduates with a B average and does not find a suitable job six months after graduating, the student is eligible to receive up to 18 credit hours towards a graduate engineering degree in the university. The tuition value for these credits is approximately $17,000 US.

Continued, Table 2.6.27

Years to retirement	$4,000 monthly payment		
	4%	6%	8%
40.00	-444,461	-169,764	-65,748
30.00	-491,063	-228,900	-108,153
20.00	-542,551	-308,637	-177,909
10.00	-599,437	-416,150	-292,654

Table 2.6.28 Yearly payment values (Method 2) to provide $2,000, $3,000, $4,000 monthly retirement income for 20 years at 4%, 6%, and 8% interest rates compounded monthly for various years to retirement. Payments are made at the beginning of each period; inflation is 3%. (Steps 1 and 2, P/Yr = 1, C/Yr = 12). (Step 3, P/Yr = C/Yr = 12).

Years to retirement	$2,000 monthly payment			$3,000 monthly payment		
	4%	6%	8%	4%	6%	8%
40.00	-10,908	-5,426	-2,628	-16,362	-8,140	-3,942
30.00	-13,766	-7,973	-4,561	-20,650	-11,959	-6,842
20.00	-19,306	-12,846	-8,553	-28,959	-19,269	-12,830
10.00	-35,637	-26,840	-20,409	-53,456	-40,261	-30,614

Years to retirement	$4,000 monthly payment		
	4%	6%	8%
40.00	-21,815	-10,853	-5,255
30.00	-27,532	-15,946	-9,123
20.00	-38,611	-25,691	-17,107
10.00	-71,274	-53,681	-40,818

The world's first industrial computer was installed in 1959 at Texaco's No. 1 Polymerization Unit at its refinery in Port Arthur, Texas. The Ramo-Wooldridge RW-300 computer used was about the size of an office desk and cost $98,000 US.

Table 2.6.29 Monthly payment values (Method 2) to provide $2,000, $3,000, $4,000 monthly retirement income for 20 years at 4%, 6%, and 8% interest rates compounded monthly for various years to retirement. Payments are made at the beginning of each period and inflation is 3%. (P/Yr = C/Yr = 12).

Years	$2,000 monthly payment			$3,000 monthly payment		
to retirement	4%	6%	8%	4%	6%	8%
40.00	-926	-465	-227	-1,389	-697	-341
30.00	-1,168	-683	-394	-1,752	-1,024	-591
20.00	-1,638	-1,100	-739	-2,458	-1,650	-1,109
10.00	-3,024	-2,299	-1,764	-4,537	-3,448	-2,645

Years	$4,000 monthly payment		
to retirement	4%	6%	8%
40.00	-1,851	-929	-454
30.00	-2,337	-1,366	-788
20.00	-3,277	-2,200	-1,478
10.00	-6,049	-4,597	-3,527

The Presidential Suite at the Four Seasons Hotel in New York City provides a view of Manhattan in all directions. The suite occupies the entire 52nd floor of the hotel. It has two bedrooms, a living room and a dining room. In 1997, it cost $7,100 US a night.

WHAT CAN YOU AFFORD TO SAVE?

Calculations can be looked at from the opposite point of view as well.

You have already started a retirement fund of $50,000. You want to find out what monthly retirement income (in today's dollars) you can expect during your 20 years of retirement if you set aside $1,000 or $2,000 at the beginning of each month from now until start of retirement.

Let us calculate the answer assuming various periods to retirement, nominal interest rates of 4%, 6%, and 8%, and 3% inflation rate.

Table 2.6.30 Monthly retirement payments in today's dollars for 20 years with existing $50,000 retirement fund. Money earns 4%, 6%, and 8% interest compounded monthly; 3% inflation, compounded monthly; various years to retirement. Use beginning-of-period payments. (P/Yr = C/Yr = 12).

Years to retirement	-$1,000 monthly savings payment			-$2,000 monthly savings payment		
	4%	6%	8%	4%	6%	8%
40.00	2,611	5,482	11,850	4,771	9,786	20,658
30.00	2,119	3,803	6,923	3,831	6,732	11,997
20.00	1,589	2,466	3,830	2,810	4,284	6,536
15.00	1,302	1,887	2,723	2,254	3,217	4,570
10.00	995	1,351	1,817	1,656	2,221	2,952
5.00	663	844	1,062	1,009	1,275	1,591

Table 2.6.31 Steps to calculate the expected monthly retirement income for the monthly savings payments made at the beginning of each period for total months prior to retirement.

Steps	per	I/Yr	pr	fu	an
Step 1	period to retirement	nominal rate	lump–sum payment	? (calculate)	periodic savings payment
Step 2	period to retirement	inflation rate	? (calculate)	future value of retirement fund	(0.00)
Step 3	retirement period	nominal rate	present value of retirement fund	(0.00)	? (calculate)

▒ = parameter not required

The values in Table 2.6.30 are the calculated values from step 3 of Table 2.6.31. For reference see the financial calculator keystrokes to solve the second row (period = 30) on Table 2.6.30.

There are endless scenarios that we could analyze — with different periods, rates of inflation, desired incomes, etc. — but there would not be enough pages in this book to cover all of them. Once you understand the fundamentals, and know how to use a financial calculator, you should have the confidence and know-how to solve your unique personal finance problems.

Let me stress again the importance of repeating your calculations at least once a year to update the assumed nominal interest rate, inflation rate, and other parameters used in the TVM analysis.

The third-largest retail industry in the US is the travel industry. The Travel Industry Association of America projects the annual travel spending in the US alone in 1998 will be $473 billion US and will be growing steadily.

2.7
Lesson 7: *INVESTMENT DECISION MAKING*

An investment in knowledge pays the best interest.

Benjamin Franklin

In the last four sections, we dealt with the practical applications of time value of money (TVM) analysis. This section will focus on investment decision making using discounted cash flow (DCF) analysis. As in the previous four sections, all examples were solved using the financial calculator.

Both TVM and DCF analyses are techniques used to analyze personal finance problems. TVM, as you've seen, can be used to analyze lump-sum payments, series of annuity payments, or a combination. In the problems we've looked at so far, there was never more than one lump-sum payment. If there was a series of payments, the amounts were the same and made at regular intervals, either at the end or at the beginning of each period. We also used the cash flow diagram to visualize the outflow (negative $ value) or inflow (positive $ value) of the payments. An example of a cash flow diagram that combines lump-sum and annuity payments is shown below.

Figure 2.7.1 on the right shows a single lump-sum payment of $1,000 and annuity payments of $200 made at the end of each of the 15 payment periods. P/Yr shows a value of 1, which means that the annuity payments are made annually. Thus, the total period consists of 15 years. The I/Yr is 8% and compounded annually as indicated by the value of 1 for C/Yr. The future value of these payments is $8,602.59.

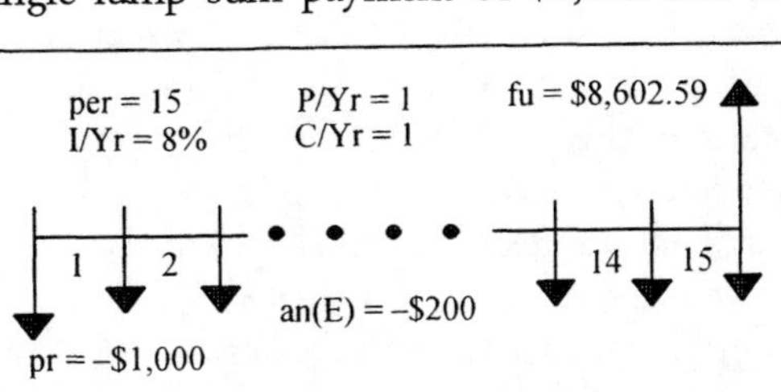

Fig. 2.7.1 Example cash flow diagram for TVM analysis

The Bowmore distillery in Scotland produces the most expensive malt whiskey that can be bought off the shelf. It cost $9,750 US a bottle in 1998.

DISCOUNTED CASH FLOW (DCF) ANALYSIS

There are several important differences between DCF analysis and TVM analysis:

1. In TVM, there can be no more than one lump-sum payment (the present value for Type I, II and III problems) while in DCF, there can be two or more lump-sum payments, which may be of different amounts.
2. In TVM, there may be only one series of annuity payment (Type II and III problems) while in DCF, there can be several series of annuity payments, and each series may have a different amount.
3. In TVM, the lump-sum or annuity payment is always greater than $0. In DCF, $0 is a valid payment amount. Therefore, in the DCF cash flow diagram, each period has a payment value.
4. In TVM an annuity payment is made at either the beginning or at the end of each period. In DCF, there may be periods where the payment amount is different or has the value of $0.

However, the two techniques do share several similarities:

1. Both TVM and DCF use the parameters I/Yr, P/Yr, and C/Yr.
2. Both TVM and DCF use the cash flow diagram for visual representation of the problem.
3. Both TVM and DCF require that payments, whether lump-sum or annuity, are made exactly at the beginning or at the end of a payment period, never in the middle.

In DCF analysis, the payments are referred to as cash flows. There is an initial cash flow occurring at the beginning of the first period (CF0). This can be a value equal to $0 or greater than $0 and can be an inflow or an outflow. For each of the next and succeeding cash flows (CFi), a frequency attribute is also assigned (Ni). Thus, if the next cash flow value is a series of equal payments, they can be grouped by assigning a cash flow value and its frequency. A cash flow value of $0 is valid. Therefore, except for the cash flow at the beginning of the first period, each period needs to have a cash flow entry and its frequency. A positive cash flow indicates money received while a negative cash flow indicates money paid out.

A typical cash flow diagram for a DCF analysis problem is shown on the right.

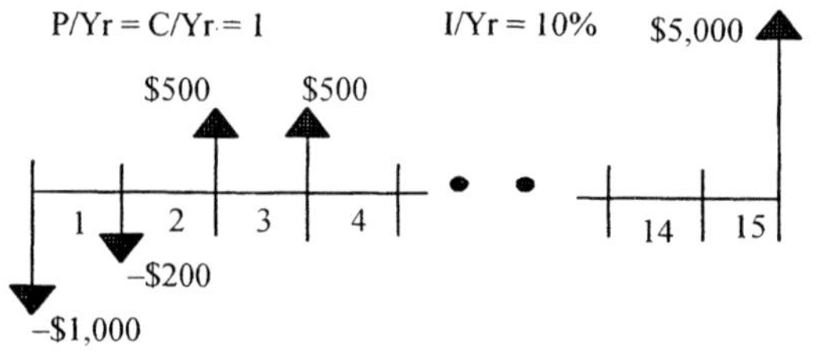

Figure 2.7.2 Cash flow diagram for DCF analysis

The tiny Cayman Islands, famous as a tax haven, have 540 banks represented there.

The cash flow diagram shows an initial cash flow paid out in the amount of CF0 = -$1,000. This was followed by another outgoing cash flow of CF1 = -$200 and frequency of N1 = 1, made at the end of the first period. At the end of the second and third period, equal cash flows of $500 are received. They can be grouped into a cash flow of CF2 = $500 and frequency of N2 = 2. From the end of the fourth to the fourteenth period, the cash flow can be represented as a group with cash flow value of CF3 = $0 and frequency is N3 = 11. Finally, at the end of the 15th period, a cash flow of CF4 = $5,000 is received with frequency of N4 = 1. Interest, I/Yr is 10% and P/Yr = C/Yr = 1.

Table 2.7.1 Financial calculator data entry of values for DCF analysis.

cash flow	frequency
CF0 = -1,000.00	
CF1 = -200.00	N1 = 1.00
CF2 = 500.00	N2 = 2.00
CF3 = 0.00	N3 = 11.00
CF4 = 5,000.00	N4 = 1.00

Given the cash flow schedule, which consists of cash flow values CF0, CF1, etc., frequency of cash flow value Ni, the interest rate I/Yr, payment frequency P/Yr, and interest compounding frequency C/Yr, only two parameters are calculated by the DCF method: NPV (net present value) and IRR (internal rate of return). Both parameters are useful in evaluating an investment to see if it meets profit objectives.

The calculation of the net present value requires determining the equivalent present values for all the cash flows and summing the calculated present values. An investment is worth pursuing if the NPV calculates to a positive value. This indicates that you are exceeding your profit objectives —which is good! The higher the NPV, the more attractive the investment. A value of 0 (zero) for NPV indicates the investment revenue target has been exactly met. A negative NPV indicates that the investment revenue target has not been met.

IRR is the rate of return required that gives NPV = 0. In other words, it is the rate of return at which the investor's objective is exactly met. IRR is an important number as it can be used as a yardstick to determine the lower limit of the rate of return that would meet the investment objective.

DCF analysis is a short-cut solution to the method of TVM analysis for Type I Class A.3 financial problems (see Section 2.1, Table 2.1.12). Take this statement as a given right now; I'll prove it later in this section.

Let us look at several examples to illustrate the NPV and IRR calculations. Remember that these calculations only give you information you can use in making your decision. The best decision for you will depend on many factors — your own needs, opportunities and goals.

A pair of Levis jeans in Singapore cost $130 US in 1998.

Example 1: Short Term Investment

An investor has been purchasing stocks over a period of three months. The purchase values were: $10,000, $500, and $3,000. It has been 18 months since the initial investment and his stock portfolio is now worth $20,000. If his target is a rate of return of 20%, will he have met his target if he sells now?

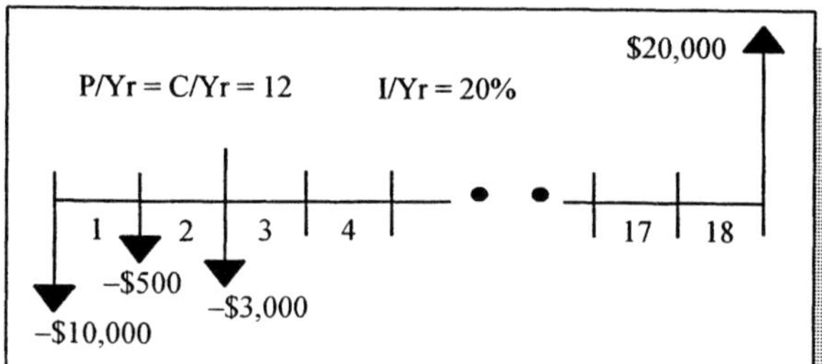

Figure 2.7.3 Example 1

The cash flow diagram is shown on the right.

Table 2.7.2 Financial calculator data entry of values for Example 1. I/Yr = 20%, P/Yr = C/Yr = 12.

cash flow	frequency
CF0 = –10,000.00	
CF1 = –500.00	N1 = 1.00
CF2 = –3,000.00	N2 = 1.00
CF3 = 0.00	N3 = 15.00
CF4 = 20,000.00	N4 = 1.00

NPV = $1,458.80, IRR = 27.22% (2.27% periodic interest; monthly rate). A positive NPV value indicates an achievable return. In fact, up to 27.22% IRR, the return on his investment is satisfied.

Example 2: Leasing Income

A building owner offers a private commercial bank a 10-year lease. The lease payments start at $35,000 per month and increase by 15% every two years. The payments are made at the beginning of each month. What is the expected net present value of the lease payments if the rate of interest is 10%?

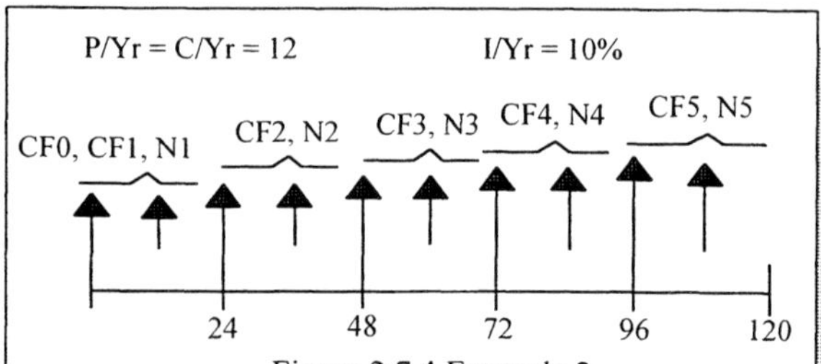

Figure 2.7.4 Example 2

The cash flow diagram is shown on the right.

Table 2.7.3 Financial calculator data entry of values for Example 2.
I/Yr = 10%, P/Yr = C/Yr = 12.

cash flow	frequency
CF0 = 35,000	
CF1 = 35,000	N1 = 23
CF2 = 35,000 x 1.15 = 40,250	N2 = 24
CF3 = 40,250 x 1.15 = 46,288	N3 = 24
CF4 = 46,288 x 1.15 = 53,231	N4 = 24
CF5 = 53,231 x 1.15 = 61,216	N5 = 24

NPV = $3,407,611.54. Note that there is no IRR solution as there is no sign change in the cash flows.

Example 3: Discounted Contract

A lender has offered to sell you a contract, which has the following cash flows:

Table 2.7.4 Cash flow values for the discounted contract.
I/Yr = 20%, P/Yr = C/Yr = 12.

End of Month	Value
3.00	2,000
10.00	5,000
11.00	5,000
20.00	1,000
24.00	4,000
30.00	10,000

As an investor, you are always on the lookout for a better return on your investments. You currently have some cash in an investment account earning 15%. You would like to see what purchase price you could offer for the contract and expect a rate of return of 20%.

The cash flow diagram is shown below.

Charles Babbage of England first proposed the concept of the first computer. The British government contributed £17,000 and Babbage himself £6,000. Dubbed the Analytical Machine, Babbage worked on it from 1822 to 1871. It required several thousand moving parts and was never completed, as the technology to produce these parts was not available.

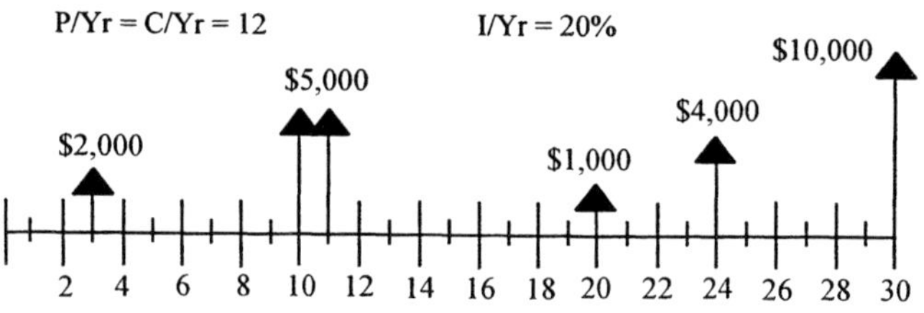

Figure 2.7.5 Example 3

Table 2.7.5 Financial calculator data entry of values for Example 3. I/Yr = 20%, P/Yr = C/Yr = 12.

cash flow	frequency
CF0 = 0.00	
CF1 = 0.00	N1 = 2.00
CF2 = 2,000.00	N2 = 1.00
CF3 = 0.00	N3 = 6.00
CF4 = 5,000.00	N4 = 2.00
CF5 = 0.00	N5 = 8.00
CF6 = 1,000.00	N6 = 1.00
CF7 = 0.00	N7 = 3.00
CF8 = 4,000.00	N8 = 1.00
CF9 = 0.00	N9 = 5.00
CF10 = 10,000.00	N10 = 1.00

NPV = $19,809.21.

As an investor, you must purchase the contract for $19,809.21 in order to achieve the 20% return.

If the seller is asking $21,000, what would your yield be?

In this case CF0 = -$21,000. Calculating for NPV gives a value of -$1,190.79. The IRR is 16.07% per year. The investment therefore is not attractive since NPV calculates to a negative value. This is supported by the fact that the calculated IRR is 16.07% (rate at which NPV = 0), several percentage points lower than your required 20% rate of return.

In 1997, NASA, the US space agency, which operates the space shuttle, spent about $10,000 US per pound to get it into space orbit.

Example 4: Real Estate Investment

A real estate investor purchased a home and has been renting it out for almost three years. She bought the house at a cost of $150,000. She also spent $20,000 refurbishing the house to make it suitable for renting. She has been receiving a monthly income of $1,500 since four months after the purchase. She is thinking of selling the property at a price of $180,000. If she does so, will she have achieved her original goal of a 12% return on her investment?

The cash flow diagram for the problem is shown on the right.

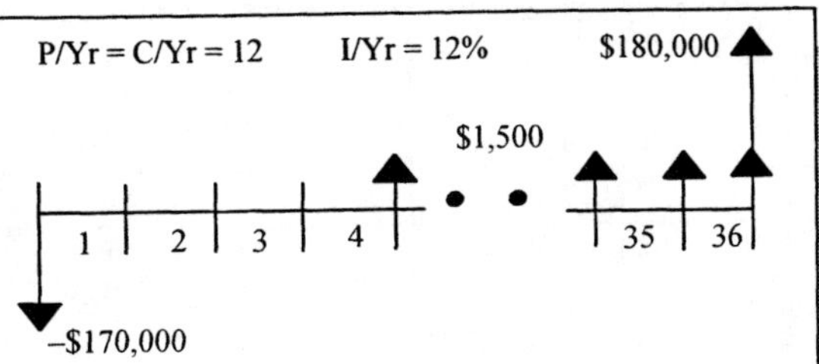

Figure 2.7.6 Example 4

Table 2.7.6 Financial calculator data entry of values for Example 4. I/Yr = 12%. P/Yr = C/Yr = 12.

cash flow		frequency	
CF0 =	–170,000.00		
CF1 =	0.00	N1 =	3.00
CF2 =	1,500.00	N2 =	32.00
CF3 =	181,500.00	N3 =	1.00

NPV = –$3,443.73, IRR = 11.22% (0.94% periodic interest; monthly rate). If the investor sells the property, she will not have met her target of 12% return.

Example 5: Selling a Small Business

You started your own small business five years ago. Your initial investment was $75,000 and had the cash flows shown below. Next year, you expect the revenue to be $45,000. How much additional money would you need from selling the business in order to generate a rate of return of 25%?

The cash flow diagram is shown on the right.

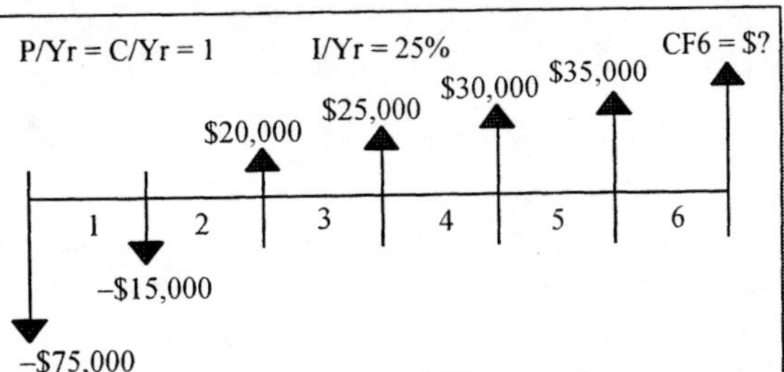

Figure 2.7.7 Example 5

Table 2.7.7 Financial calculator data entry of values for Example 5. I/Yr = 25%. P/Yr = C/Yr = 1.

cash flow		frequency	
CF0 =	-75,000.00		
CF1 =	-15,000.00	N1 =	1.00
CF2 =	20,000.00	N2 =	1.00
CF3 =	25,000.00	N3 =	1.00
CF4 =	30,000.00	N4 =	1.00
CF5 =	35,000.00	N5 =	1.00
CF6 =	?	N6 =	1.00

This problem is solved by trial and error. The procedure is to assume a value for CF6 and calculate NPV. The correct value for CF6 is one where the NPV is closest to 0.

Table 2.7.8 NPV and IRR for various values of CF6.

CF6	NPV	IRR
90,000.00	-14,050.24	19.85
100,000.00	-11,428.80	20.91
110,000.00	-8,807.36	21.92
120,000.00	-6,185.92	22.89
130,000.00	-3,564.48	23.81
140,000.00	-943.04	24.69
142,500.00	-287.68	24.91
143,500.00	-25.54	24.99
145,000.00	367.68	25.12

Since you are expecting an income from the business of $45,000 in the year you are planning to sell the business, you could have met the target of 25% with a selling price of $98,500 ($143,500 - $45,000).

The USS Enterprise was the first nuclear-powered aircraft carrier. Launched on September 24, 1960 at Newport News, Virginia, at a cost of $445 million US, it had eight pressurized water-cooled nuclear reactors. With 440 officers and 4,160 enlisted men, it was designed to carry 100 aircraft.

COMBINATION OF DCF AND TVM ANALYSES

There are personal finance applications that require using both the time value of money (TVM) and discounted cash flow (DCF) analyses. Two such applications are calculating the net future value and wrap-around mortgages. Let us look at representative example for each.

Example 6: Net Future Value

You have been making deposits for several months into an interest-bearing account. Future deposits are planned and you would like to know what the value of the account will be 20 months after the first deposit. The investment account is earning 9.5% compounded monthly.

The cash flow diagram showing the past deposits and the future planned deposits is shown on the right.

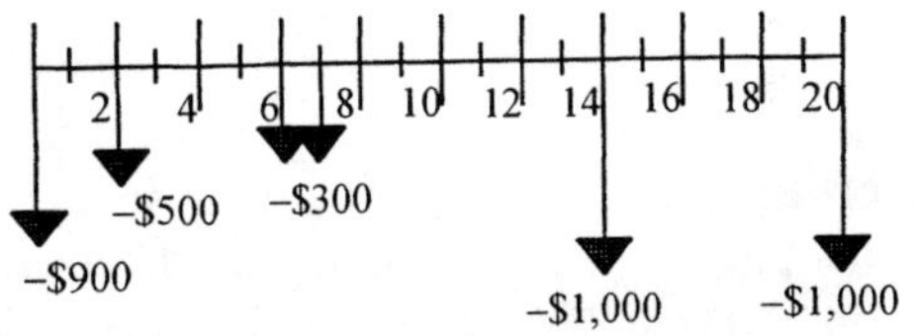

Figure 2.7.8 Example 6

Table 2.7.9 Financial calculator data entry of values for Example 6.
I/Yr = 9.5%. P/Yr = C/Yr = 12.

cash flow	frequency
CF0 = -900.00	
CF1 = 0.00	N1 = 1.00
CF2 = -500.00	N2 = 1.00
CF3 = 0.00	N3 = 3.00
CF4 = -300.00	N4 = 2.00
CF5 = 0.00	N5 = 6.00
CF6 = −1,000.00	N6 = 1.00
CF7 = 0.00	N7 = 5.00
CF8 = −1,000.00	N8 = 1.00

NPV = –$3,711.78.

Henry Luce bought the name Life *in 1936 from John Mitchell, an illustrator of a weekly humor magazine, for $92,000 US. Luce's* Life *magazine first appeared on October 1936. Each issue sold a million copies, making it one of the most successful magazines ever.*

Using time value of money analysis to calculate the future value:

Table 2.7.10 Type I, Class A.4 financial problem.
I/Yr = 9.5%. P/Yr = C/Yr = 12.

per	I/Yr	pr	fu
20.00	9.5	-3,711.78	4,345.85

The future value of the NPV is $4,345.85.

Example 7: Savings Method 4 (Section 2.3)

In Section 2.3, in the second example of method 4, I said I would give the solution to the total net present value later. Here it is. The target was to save $10,000 over five years, with five unequal payments greater than $0, and using a period of months. From the cash flow information of Table 2.3.12, the data for the DCF method is the following:

Table 2.7.11 DCF analysis data entry values for the calculator.
I/Yr = 6%. P/Yr = C/Yr = 12.

period (per)	cash flow	frequency
0	CF0 = 395.00	
1 – 12	CF1 = 0.00	N1 = 12.00
13 – 25	CF2 = 150.00	N2 = 13.00
26 – 40	CF3 = 140.00	N3 = 15.00
41 – 55	CF4 = 210.00	N4 = 15.00
56 – 60	CF5 = 375.00	N5 = 5.00

NPV = $7,834.71

The future value of $10,000 at I/Yr = 6% is a present value of $7,413.72 (see Table 2.3.11). Table 2.3.13 shows the adjusted cash flow that will give an NPV of $7,413.74.

The next table shows the data for the DCF solution.

In 1997, the perfume industry was a $15 billion industry. Since the launching of Chanel No.5 over 75 years ago, it has earned more than $1 billion US in sales.

Table 2.7.12 DCF analysis data entry values for the calculator.
I/Yr = 6%. P/Yr = C/Yr = 12.

period (per)	cash flow	frequency
0	CF0 = 300.00	
1 – 12	CF1 = 0.00	N1 = 12.00
13 – 25	CF2 = 140.00	N2 = 13.00
26 – 40	CF3 = 123.68	N3 = 15.00
41 – 55	CF4 = 210.00	N4 = 15.00
56 – 60	CF5 = 375.00	N5 = 5.00

NPV = $7,413.74.

Example 8: Wrap-Around Mortgages

Besides banks, financial institutions, relatives, and friends, another source of borrowed money is your principal residence. It is possible to borrow against the real estate equity of your home. Most often, this money is used to finance a small business.

A wrap-around mortgage combines mortgage refinancing and borrowing against real estate equity. Solving this type of problem requires using both the TVM and DCF analyses.

Assume your original mortgage was for $100,000. At 8% interest rate compounded monthly, amortized over 20 years (240 months), your monthly payment at the end of each period is $836.44. You have already made 200 payments and therefore have 40 more payments left.

From your amortization schedule, at the end of 200 payments (calculated easily with a financial calculator, as shown in Section 2.4):

Balance remaining	= $29,282.90
Principal paid out	= -$70,717.10
Interest paid out	= -$96,570.90

You are planning on starting a small business and would like to borrow money from the equity of your home. You need $50,000 to finance your new venture. You've found a lender who is willing to "wrap" a new mortgage of $79,282.90 ($29,282.90 + $50,000) for 10 years at 11%. What is your new monthly payment and what is the rate of return the lender is getting on the wrap-around mortgage?

First we need to use TVM analysis to calculate your new monthly payments.

Jeans were first made in 1850 by Levi Strauss. Rivets were added in 1874. These riveted jeans sold for $13.50 US a dozen.

Table 2.7.13 Type II, Class B.4 financial problem.
I/Yr = 11%, P/Yr = C/Yr = 12.

per	I/Yr	pr	an(E)
120.00	11.00	79,282.90	-1,092.12

The new monthly payment therefore is $1,092.12. Next, we use DCF analysis to calculate the IRR. The cash flow diagram from the lender's point of view is:

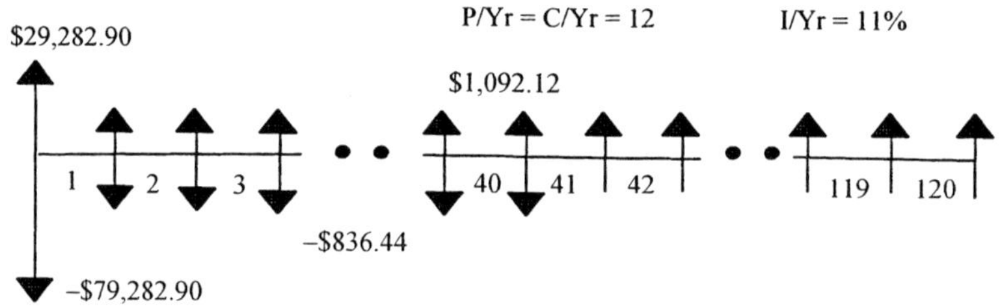

Figure 2.7.9 First cash flow diagram for example 8

Table 2.7.14 DCF analysis data entry values for the calculator.
I/Yr = 11%. P/Yr = C/Yr = 12.

cash flow	frequency
CF0 = 29,282.90 – 79,282.90 = –50,000.00	
CF1 = 1,092.12 – 836.44 = 255.68	N1 = 40.00
CF2 = 1,092.12	N2 = 120 – 40 = 80.00

The final cash flow diagram is as follows:

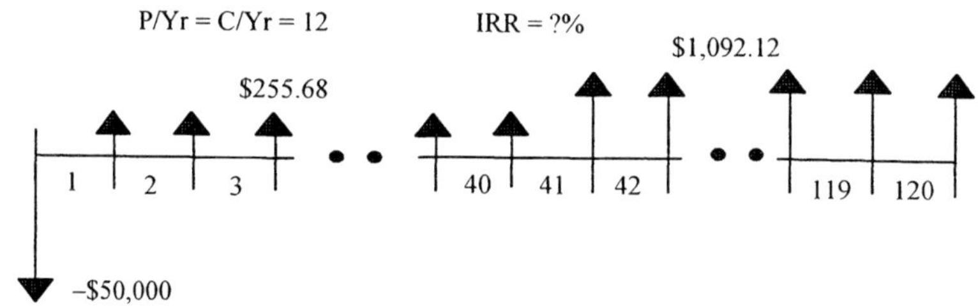

Figure 2.7.10 Second cash flow diagram for example 8

NPV = $1,379.04, IRR = 11.50%

Problems with IRR Calculation

The procedure used to calculate IRR is a repetitive one. There are various types of cash flow diagrams depending on the sign changes of the cash flow. The number of cash flow sign changes affects the confidence one should put in the calculated IRR. Although this is a problem for calculating IRR, it is not a problem for calculating NPV. There is one and only one answer for NPV for every cash flow problem.

Cash Flow Diagram with No Sign Changes

Although one can calculate NPV for cash flows with no sign change, there is no solution for IRR calculation. A valid series of cash flow for IRR calculation requires at least one positive and one negative cash flow, therefore, a minimum of one sign change.

The figure on the right shows a cash flow diagram with no sign change.

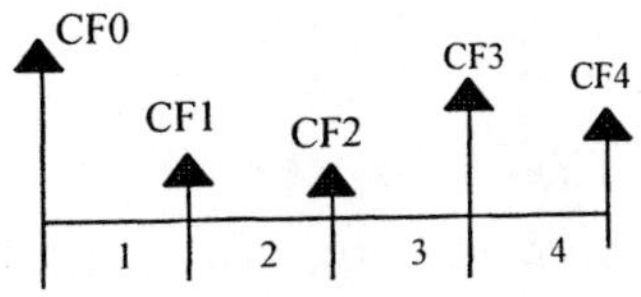

Figure 2.7.11 Cash flow diagram with no sign change for the cash flows

Cash Flow Diagram with Only One Sign Change

For a series of cash flows that have only one sign change, there is only one solution for IRR.

The figure on the right shows a cash flow diagram with one sign change, from CF0 to CF1. This is a valid cash flow series for IRR calculation.

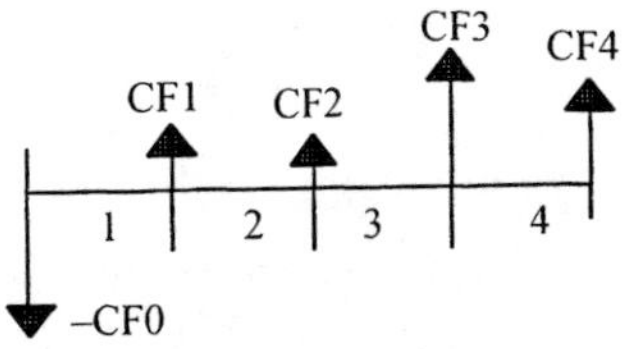

Figure 2.7.12 Cash flow diagram with one sign change for the cash flows

In 1978, Hughes Space and Communications Company won the $172 million US contract from NASA Ames to design and build the Galileo probe to capture priceless data as it plunges into the hellish atmosphere of Jupiter. The probe first blasted into space on Oct 18, 1989 and had the encounter with Jupiter on Dec 7, 1995.

Cash Flow Diagram with More than One Sign Change

For a series of cash flows with two or more sign changes, there may be as many solutions as there are sign changes. One should be careful in making investment decisions on the calculated IRR if the cash flow series has more than one sign change.

The example cash flow diagram on the right shows three sign changes, from CF0 to CF1, CF2 to CF3 and CF3 to CF4. This cash flow series may have one, two or three solutions for IRR.

Example 9 below shows how to handle cash flow problems with more than one sign change.

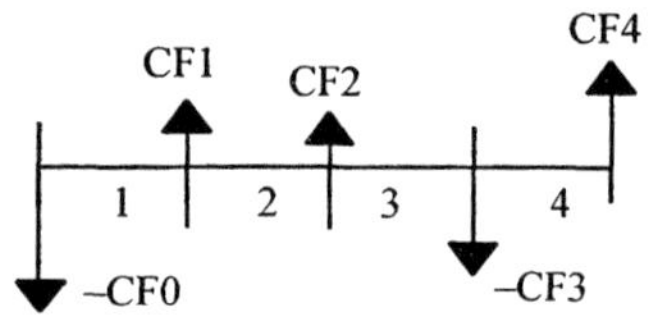

Figure 2.7.13 Cash flow diagram with three sign changes for the cash flows

Example 9: Net Present Value (5 Sign Changes)

A small business was established 10 years ago. The owner started the company with $75,000. Over the years the revenue from the business was used to finance and expand the business. A new computer system was installed, the business moved to a bigger office space, more employees were hired, etc..

Below is the cash flow diagram showing the inflows and outflows of cash. The owner could sell the business now for $685,000. If he is expecting 25% return on his investment, will he meet this investment objective if he sells now?

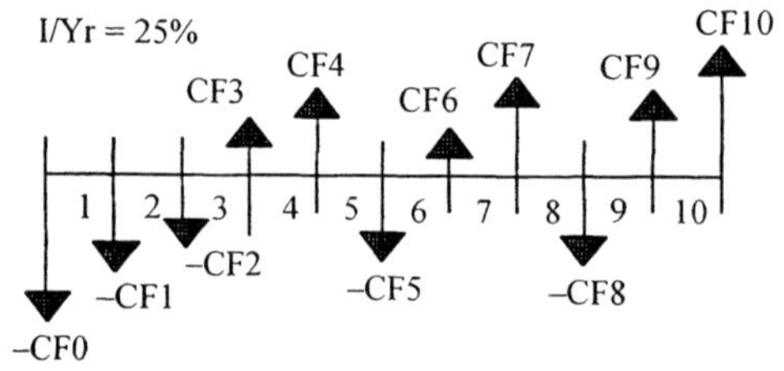

Figure 2.7.14 Cash flow diagram for example 9

The most successful professional athlete turned ad man is Michael Jordan. In 1997, he was paid $47 million US for endorsing products. His 1997 earnings from basketball were $31 million US.

Table 2.7.15 DCF analysis data entry values for the financial calculator. I/Yr = 25%. P/Yr = C/Yr = 1.

cash flow	frequency
CF0 = -75,000.00	
CF1 = -50,000.00	N1 = 1.00
CF2 = -40,000.00	N2 = 1.00
CF3 = 40,000.00	N3 = 1.00
CF4 = 60,000.00	N4 = 1.00
CF5 = -30,000.00	N5 = 1.00
CF6 = 10,000.00	N6 = 1.00
CF7 = 60,000.00	N7 = 1.00
CF8 = -30,000.00	N8 = 1.00
CF9 = 80,000.00	N9 = 1.00
CF10 = 685,000.00	N10 = 1.00

NPV = -$10,914.48

Since there is more than one sign change, the correct procedure to determine IRR is by trial and error. Assume an interest rate and calculate NPV. The interest rate for which NPV is closest to zero (0) is the correct value for IRR.

Table 2.7.16 Trial and Error Method to calculate IRR for cash flow problems with more than one sign change.

Interest Rate (I/Yr)	NPV
1.00	635,169.45
10.00	219,357.33
15.00	106,101.50
20.00	34,835.26
23.00	5,051.74
23.60	-28.67
25.00	-10,914.48
35.00	-60,638.97

On June 1, 1997, Donovan Bailey (Canada) and Michael Johnson (US) ran the 150 meters for the title of the world's fastest man. The entire race was over in about 15 seconds, with Donovan Bailey winning the $1.5 million US purse. This is equivalent to getting paid about $100,000 per second.

Thus, the IRR for the cash flow problem is 23.60%. If the investor sells his business now, he will have achieved a return on investment of 23.6%, slightly lower than his expectation of 25%.

LONGHAND SOLUTION VIA TVM ANALYSIS

As mentioned at the beginning of this section, DCF analysis is a short-cut method of TVM analysis for Type I Class A.3 problems. Let us demonstrate this by using TVM to solve example 9. Note that after performing TVM calculation, the sign for the calculated present value should be reversed to have the same sign as the given future value.

Table 2.7.17 Equivalent TVM analysis solution to sample problem 9.
Type I Class A.3 financial problem, I/Yr = 25%, P/Yr = C/Yr = 1.

per	I/Yr	pr	fu
0.00	25.00	-75,000.00	-75,000.00
1.00	25.00	-40,000.00	-50,000.00
2.00	25.00	-25,600.00	-40,000.00
3.00	25.00	20,480.00	40,000.00
4.00	25.00	24,576.00	60,000.00
5.00	25.00	-9,830.40	-30,000.00
6.00	25.00	2,621.44	10,000.00
7.00	25.00	12,582.91	60,000.00
8.00	25.00	-5,033.16	-30,000.00
9.00	25.00	10,737.42	80,000.00
10.00	25.00	73,551.31	685,000.00
		total = -10,914.48	

The total amount, therefore, is identical to NPV = -$10,914.48 using the method of DCF analysis.

In the DCF method to solve for IRR, we used trial and error because there is more than one sign change. In this method, we assumed a rate of return and calculated NPV. IRR is the rate of return at which NPV is closest to 0. We tried rates of return from 1% to 35%, as shown in Table 2.7.16. For the TVM method, the procedure becomes more tedious since we have to repeat the procedure at different rates of return. Let's try a rate of return of 23%. The result is shown in the table below.

Star Wars was responsible for the mega-marketing of major movies for products such as novels, toys, souvenir shirts, and many others. Before the release of Star Wars in 1977, consumers globally spent $5 billion US for licensed merchandise. In 1990, this figure approached $66 billion US.

Table 2.7.18 Equivalent TVM analysis solution to above problem.
Type I Class A.3 financial problem. I/Yr = 23%, P/Yr = C/Yr = 1.

per	I/Yr	pr	fu
0.00	23.00	-75,000.00	-75,000.00
1.00	23.00	-40,650.41	-50,000.00
2.00	23.00	-26,439.29	-40,000.00
3.00	23.00	21,495.36	40,000.00
4.00	23.00	26,213.85	60,000.00
5.00	23.00	-10,656.04	-30,000.00
6.00	23.00	2,887.81	10,000.00
7.00	23.00	14,086.90	60,000.00
8.00	23.00	-5,726.38	-30,000.00
9.00	23.00	12,414.92	80,000.00
10.00	23.00	86,425.01	685,000.00
		total - 5,051.73	

The total of $5,051.73 is the same as in Table 2.7.16 with NPV = $5,051.74 at a rate of return of 23%.

Using TVM analysis, you would need to repeat these calculations for the other rates of return. You will quickly realize the benefits of the DCF method.

Complex Problems

Even if a solution exists, the calculator may not be able to calculate IRR if the cash flow problem is very complex. An Error Message appears on the calculator display. So I recommend using the IRR only for problems with only one sign change. On cash flow problems with more than one sign change, use NPV to make the investment appraisal.

The century's biggest party was Expo 98 held in Lisbon, Portugal from May 22 to September 30, 1998. Its theme was "The Oceans, a Heritage for the Future." It was also a celebration of the 500th anniversary of Portuguese navigator Vasco de Gama's voyage around the Cape of Good Hope to reach India, which opened a trade route between Europe and the spice-rich Far East. It was a $3.4 billion US extravaganza, which drew 8.5 million visitors.

PART 2
EXERCISES

3

HANDS-ON EXERCISES USING THE FINANCIAL CALCULATOR

The rich advantage of good exercise.

William Shakespeare

3.1
INTRODUCTION TO HANDS-ON EXERCISES

Chapter 3 will focus on hands-on exercises using the financial calculator. There are several brands of financial calculators available in the market. They should not be confused with scientific calculators, which have arithmetic, algebraic, logarithmic, trigonometric, and memory functions. Depending on the model of the scientific calculator, some even have binary, octal, hexadecimal, and boolean functions, plus programming and graphing capabilities. These calculators are excellent for scientific and engineering applications. They *can* also be used for financial calculations, if you know the financial formulas. You will also need to break the calculation problem into small, manageable units especially if you are not using the programmable type. In other words, scientific calculators are very cumbersome to use for financial calculations. To illustrate, take the simple equation for calculating the future value of an ordinary annuity (end-of-period payments, an(E)). The basic financial equation is:

$$pr = \frac{pr}{an(E)} \times an(E) = \frac{(1 + in)^{per} - 1}{(in \times (1 + in)^{per})} \times an(E) \qquad \textit{equation (3.1)}$$

where pr = present value, an(E) = annuity or equal payments, in = periodic interest rate and per = number of periods of annuity payments

For example, let's take the case of René. He recently won in a lottery and will be receiving $20,000 at the end of each year for the next 20 years. Assuming money is earning 8% per year compounded yearly, what is the present value of René's winnings?

A quarter of the world's known oil reserve lies under the territorial boundaries of Saudi Arabia. At about 160 million billion barrels of oil, it was worth $8 trillion US in 1997.

Using a scientific calculator with one memory, to calculate the present value of the winnings, René will need to calculate the periodic interest (in). From equation 2.1.2, in = (8/(100 x 1)) = 0.08. Then, he has to calculate $(1+.08)^{20}$ and store the resulting value, 4.66096 to memory. To calculate the numerator of equation 3.1, subtract 1 from 4.66096 and then divide by 0.08 and divide the result by the stored value, 4.66096. The calculated value is multiplied by the equal payments of $20,000. The final result is $196,362.95.

Performing this same calculation using a financial calculator is very simple. Assume the calculator is Texas Instruments, BA II Plus. The first advantage is you don't need to know the formulas. They are "burned-in" to the calculator. Secondly, the number of keystrokes required is minimal. Simply reset the TVM memories of the calculator. Then, enter 20 for a key labeled N, 8 for the key labeled I/Y, -20,000 for the key labeled PMT and 1 for P/Y and C/Y. Then to calculate present value, simply press the keys 'CPT' followed by the key 'PV'. The display of the calculator shows $196,362.95, which is the answer to the problem.

If the problem involves calculating the periodic interest rate (in), the formula in equation 3.1 becomes:

$$0 = (1 + in)^{per} - \frac{1}{1 - \frac{pr}{an(E)} \times in} \qquad \text{equation (3.2)}$$

Solving equation 3.2 for (in) requires repeated calculations involving trial and error to search for the right value of (in) so that the right side of equation 3.2 equates to zero (0). If you do this on a scientific calculator, your fingertips will be sore from all the keystrokes due to the trial and error procedure. Using the financial calculator, however, just enter the values to the appropriate memory keys and press the memory key for the unknown variable, I/Y. The calculator performs the repeated calculations automatically.

Let us follow our example with René.

When René learned about his winnings, he began to seriously consider his longtime dream of opening up a retail business. He went to his bank and borrowed $40,000 to finance the business. His payments are $850 at the end of each month for 60 months. Calculate the rate of interest, I/Y on René's loan.

In equation 3.2, (per) is 60, (pr) is 40,000 and (an(E)) is -850. Using a scientific calculator, you have to find a value for (in) by trial and error so that the right side of the equation equals to zero (0). But suppose you have a Texas Instruments BA II Plus. Simply reset the memories then store 60 for N memory, -850 for PMT memory and 40,000 for PV memory. Then press the 'CPT' key followed by the I/Y key. The result is 10.01% (for P/Y = C/Y = 12).

Another advantage to using financial calculators is elimination of rounding off problems. To illustrate, let us consider a Type I problem.

Assume you have \$5,000 and you would like to put it in a savings account for 100 months earning 8% interest compounded monthly. What is the value of your money at the end of 100 months?

The equation to calculate the future value given the present value, interest rate, and period is;

$$fu = (fu/pr) \times pr = (1 + in)^{per} \times pr \qquad \textit{equation (3.3)}$$

where pr = present value, fu = future value, in = periodic interest rate and per = number of periods

From equation 2.1.1,

$$per = (P/Yr) \times Yr = (12) \times (100/12) = 100$$

From equation 2.1.2,

$$in = \frac{(I/Yr)}{100 \times (P/Yr)} = \frac{8}{100 \times 12}$$

Thus, equation 3.3 yields,

$$fu = (fu/pr) \times pr = \left(1 + \frac{8}{100 \times 12}\right)^{100} \times 5{,}000 = \$9{,}717.15$$

Note that in the above calculation, I used 8/(100 x 12) rather than rounding off the calculated value to 0.0067. If the rounded–off value is used, it will yield:

$$fu = (fu/pr) \times pr = (1 + 0.0067)^{100} \times 5{,}000 = \$9{,}749.38$$

Rounding off gives a final result \$32.23 over the correct value. This problem is avoided with a financial calculator. Table 3.1.1 below (from Section 2.1, Table 2.1.13) shows data entry for the financial calculator and the solution to the problem.

The Memphis-based Fed-Ex, or Federal Express Corp. was founded by Fred Smith in 1973. In the 1998 fiscal year, its revenue is worth \$13.3 billion US. The story goes that Mr. Smith developed the idea for an overnight delivery service while at Yale University; however the term paper that presented the proposal was not well received by his professor.

Table 3.1.1 (Refer to Table 2.1.13)
Type I, Class A.4 financial problem. P/Yr = C/Yr = 12.

per	I/Yr	pr	fu
100.00	8.00	-5,000.00	9,717.15

Have I convinced you that a financial calculator will save you a great deal of time and trouble?

All financial calculators have the basic financial equations built-in. Most of them also have statistics, arithmetic, and some algebraic functions. Some even have logarithmic functions. Each brand of financial calculators uses different names for the calculator keys representing present value, future value, period, annuity payments, and interest rate. As you will see in our hands-on examples, the financial calculators are all in close agreement on the final solution to a given problem.

Six brands of financial calculator are covered in this chapter. They include:

- two models from Texas Instruments: BA-35 Solar and BA II Plus
- one model from Hewlett-Packard: HP 10B
- two models from Sharp: EL-733A and EL-735
- one model from Casio: FC-100

The above listed financial calculators are by no means the only ones available. Hewlett-Packard also has three special models, all priced above $100 (1996 CDN retail price):

- HP19B II Business Consultant for MBA students and executives
- HP17B II Financial Calculator for accounting, banking and finance professionals
- HP12C Financial Calculator for professionals in real estate, banking and finance

For the kind of problems covered in this book, you don't need any of the expensive financial calculators. This chapter will only cover the first six financial calculator models, which are all priced under $50 (1996 CDN $). First we will summarize the calculator's features and capabilities, as stated in the product manual for each. We will then cover sample calculations from Sections 2.1 to 2.7. Problems that were flagged with a key symbol [ ] are worked out in calculator keystrokes for all six financial calculators. Once you have learned the functions of your own calculator, you can easily adapt the method shown.

The Edison Co. in the US produced the first 10-inch and 12-inch long-playing records in 1926. They had 450 grooves to the inch, were made of phenolic, and played at 80 rpm. The 12-minute disc cost $1.75 and the 20-minute disc $2.50 US.

Tables comparing the capabilities of the six financial calculators follow in Section 3.2.

As you read Chapter 2, you had to take the numbers shown in the examples on faith. To reinforce understanding the discussions in Chapter 2, pre-selected examples were chosen. In Sections 3.3 to 3.6, I will show you, step by step, the calculator keystrokes required to work out the answers yourself. The purpose of these exercises is to help you build the confidence to start using the financial calculator for your own unique circumstances to make better personal finance decisions.

The Liberty Bell is the most famous bell in America. It weighs 2,080 pounds and was rung on July 8, 1776 to announce the signing of the Declaration of Independence. The citizens of Pennsylvania bought it from England in 1752 for $300 US.

3.2 COMPARATIVE TABLES ON FINANCIAL CALCULATORS

The five tables in this section show the differences between the six financial calculators considered in this book. The information contained in these tables is intended to assist the reader in deciding which model to purchase. For example, in North America especially, the separator used for numbers greater than one thousand is a comma (,) that is; 1,000.99. However, in Europe, period (.) is used, that is; 1.000,99. As personal finance is a universal subject, a reader in Europe would most likely prefer TI BA II Plus or the HP 10B. See Table 3.2.3 under Special Functions.

Table 3.2.1 shows the various functions used to differentiate the six financial calculators. They include mathematical, financial and other functions. Table 3.2.2 expands on the various mathematical and financial functions while Table 3.2.3 expands on the other functions.

Table 3.2.4 shows the interest rate entries used for TVM problems. The key for interest rate may be either of in% or I/Yr. Finally, Table 3.2.5 is for DCF applications. It shows the maximum ranges for the cash flow groups (CFi), the frequencies (Ni) and DCF interest data entry.

Mr. Alois Ruf, proprietor of Ruf Automobile GmBh near Munich, Germany, has been remanufacturing and modifying stock Porsches. His latest creation, the CTR-2, with a Porsche 911 body, can reach a top speed of 340 kph. It is powered by a 520-horsepower engine and costs about $120,000 US.

Table 3.2.1 Comparison of different financial calculators' functions.

FUNCTIONS	TI BA-35 Solar (a)	TI BA II Plus (b)	HP 10B (c)
math	✓	✓	✓
constant		✓	✓
trigonometric		✓	
logarithmic	✓	✓	✓
statistical	1 var, 2 var	1 var, 2 var, +	1 var, 2 var
memory	1	10	16
date		yes	
FINANCIAL FUNCTIONS			
TVM analysis	✓	✓	✓
interest conversion	✓	✓	✓
mortgage & amortization schedule	✓	✓	✓
DCF analysis		✓	✓
percentage calculation	✓	✓	✓
depreciation		✓	
profit margin	✓	✓	✓
breakeven		✓	
bond calculation		✓	
financial database			
OTHERS			
Special Functions	✓	✓	✓
calculator case	hard	hard	soft
auto power OFF	yes	yes	yes
battery power	solar	battery	battery
self-test			yes
dim display			yes
Retail Price (1996 CDN $)	under $30.00	under $50.00	under 50.00

✓, yes = function available ▒ = function not available

McDonald's popular Big Mac, as of 1998, is now available in more than 100 countries. On average, it costs $2.42 in the United States. In Switzerland however, it costs $4.02 US and in China, it costs $1.16 US.

Continued, Table 3.2.1

FUNCTIONS	Sharp EL-733A (d)	Sharp EL-735 (e)	Casio FC-100 (f)
math	✓	✓	✓
constant		✓	✓
trigonometric			
logarithmic	✓	✓	✓
statistical	1 var, 2 var	1 var, 2 var	1 var, 2 var, +
memory	1	1	7
date		yes	yes
FINANCIAL FUNCTIONS			
TVM analysis	✓	✓	✓
interest conversion	✓	✓	✓
mortgage & amortization schedule	✓	✓	✓
DCF analysis	✓	✓	✓
percentage calculation	✓	✓	✓
depreciation			
profit margin	✓	✓	✓
breakeven			
bond calculation		✓	
financial database		✓	
OTHERS			
Special Functions	✓	✓	✓
calculator case	soft	soft	soft
auto power OFF	yes	yes	yes
battery power	battery	battery	battery
self–test			
dim display			
Retail Price (1996 CDN $)	under $50.00	under $50.00	under $50.00

✓, yes = function available ▢ = function not available

The list of products purchased via the Internet is topped by PC hardware and software. Dell Computers is one company that has cashed in on the trend. In the third quarter of 1997, Dell's on-line sales averaged $3 million US per day.

Table 3.2.2 Details of the various functions.

math	divide, multiply, subtract, add, square, square root, inverse, power, percentage, change sign
constant	store a number and an operation for repetitive calculations
trigonometric	sin, cos, tan, arcsin, arccos, arctan, hyperbolic, and hyperbolic arc functions
logarithmic	natural logarithm, natural antilogarithm (exponential)
statistical	All models have 1–variable and 2–variable statistical functions; '+' indicates TI BA II Plus and Casio FC–100 have four regression models for 2 variable statistics: linear, logarithmic, exponential, and power.
memory	All financial calculations require memory and registers for per, I/Yr, pr, fu, an and others; in addition the number shown indicates the additional memory or register available.
date	calculate number of days between 2 dates; date and day of the week until a specified number of days (from a starting date)
TVM analysis	calculate per, I/Yr, pr, fu, an
interest conversion	nominal & effective interest rates conversion given compounding periods; for TVM calculations, only TI BA II Plus use both P/Yr and C/Yr. All others use APR and EFF/Yr
mortgage & amortization schedule	calculate principal paid, interest paid and outstanding balance
DCF analysis	calculate NPV and IRR
percentage calculation	calculate percentages, percent change, add–ons, discounts
depreciation	Only TI BA II Plus provides this function. User has choice from 6 depreciation methods; straight–line, sum–of–the–years'–digit, declining–balance, DB method with crossover to SL, French SL and French DB.
profit margin	calculate cost, selling price, and profit margin
breakeven analysis	Only TI BA II Plus has this function; calculate breakeven point and sales level required for a specified profit.
bond calculation	Only TI BA II Plus and Sharp EL–735 have this function; calculate bond price, yield to maturity, etc..
financial database	Only the Sharp EL–735 model has this function; it allows storage of financial information, lets the user recall the data items, and use them directly in financial calculations

As of 1998, the most widely traded currency is the US dollar trading at $315 billion daily. This is followed by the German mark at $122 billion and the Japanese yen at $86 billion.

Table 3.2.3 Details of other functions.

Special functions	Factorial	– b, c, d, e, f
	Random number	– b
	Combination	– b
	Permutation	– b
	Rounding key	– b, c
	auto scientific	
	Notation display	– a, b, c, d/e/f (only for positive exponents)
	Brackets	– b, c
	Last Answer feature	– b
	correcting entry error	– a, b, c, d, e, f
	format number separator (for numbers greater than one thousand)	
	comma	– a
	comma or period	– b, c
	apostrophe	– d, e
	none	– f
calculator case	Both TI models have hard plastic cases, HP 10B has a soft plastic pouch, Sharp and Casio calculators have a folding plastic case.	
auto power OFF	Except for the TI solar–powered model, all other financial calculator models have auto power OFF function whereby the calculator turns itself to OFF if not used after a = not applicable (solar–powered) b = 10 minutes c = 10 minutes d = 9–13 minutes e = several minutes f = 6 minutes	
power	TI BA 35 Solar is solar powered. TI BA II Plus, one lithium manganese battery; HP 10B, three 1.5 v alkaline or silver oxide button–cell batteries; Sharp EL–733A, two alkaline manganese batteries; Sharp EL–735, one lithium battery; Casio FC–100, one lithium battery.	
dim display	only the HP 10B model has display contrast to adjust the brightness of the display	

where a = TI BA–35 Solar, b = TI BA II Plus, c = HP 10B, d = Sharp EL–733A,
e = Sharp EL–735, f = Casio FC–100

According to the latest UN reports, Europeans are the largest consumers of ice cream. In 1997, their ice cream consumption totalled $11 billion US.

Table 3.2.4 Interest rates used for TVM problems

TI BA-35 Solar	TI BA II Plus	HP 10B	Sharp EL-733A	Sharp EL-735	Casio FC-100
in%	I/Yr	I/Yr	in%	in%	in%

where in% = periodic interest rate in percent and I/Yr = annual interest rate in percent

The relationship between (in) and (I/Yr) is given by equation 2.1.2 as

$$in = \frac{(I/Yr)}{100 \times (P/Yr)}$$

where (I/Yr) is the nominal interest per year in percent (%) and (P/Yr) is the frequency of interest payment per year.

Periodic interest rate (in%) is given by equation 2.1.3 as

$$in\% = in \times 100$$

Table 3.2.5 DCF range of values for CFi and Ni, and DCF interest data entry.

Financial Calculator Model	Cash Flow CF0 + CFi; Ni	Max cash flows per Ni = x	DCF interest data entry
TI BA-35 Solar	not applicable	not applicable	not applicable
TI BA II Plus	i = 24	x = 9,999	in%
HP 10B	i = 14	x = 99	I/Yr
Sharp EL-733A	i = 19	x = 99	in%
Sharp EL-735	i = 69 (if no memory space used for financial database)	x = 99	in%
Casio FC-100	i = 14	x = 99	in%

Gold has lost its status as the centerpiece of the world monetary system. Australia, the world's third-largest gold producer, has sold 68% of its gold reserves, or 167 tonnes. The selling price was $1.78 billion US. Other countries that had sold gold in the past five years since 1997 include Canada, Austria, and South Africa.

3.3 TEXAS INSTRUMENTS BA II PLUS

The Texas Instruments TI BA II Plus financial calculator comes with a durable plastic slide case, a quick reference card and a manual. Its main features are:

- powerful statistical functions with four regression options
- financial and business worksheets including TVM, Amortization, DCF, Bonds, Depreciation, Statistics, Interest Conversion, Date, Profit and Breakeven
- all common mathematical, trigonometric, and log functions
- advanced user interface with prompts to make data entry for calculations easy
- special functions such as factorial, random number, combinations and permutations, etc..

Aside from the business application memory or registers, there are 10 independent memories available.

Because of the prompting feature of the calculator, there are several display indicators in the display area. One of the most useful indicators is the asterisk (*). It is shown to indicate that the displayed value has been computed in a worksheet. If a value in the worksheet is changed, this invalidates the previously calculated value and the (*) is removed.

There is a Constant Memory™ feature that retains all worksheet values, settings, memory contents and all format settings. This feature is lost when the battery is replaced or discharged. The Automatic Power Down (APD™) feature turns off the calculator automatically when none of the keys are pressed after a period of about 10 minutes. Because of the Constant Memory feature however, the memory content, mode, and values entered are retained when the calculator is turned on again. The 'Last Answer' feature allows access to the last value calculated before turning power off to the calculator.

This is the only financial calculator of the six considered in this book that uses both parameters, payment per year (P/Yr) and interest compounding per year (C/Yr). These parameters take the place of APR and EFF keys available in other financial calculators for calculating adjusted nominal interest rate when P/Yr is not equal to C/Yr.

The Format for dates is interchangeable:

US format mm-dd-yy:	12-31-1996
European format dd-mm-yy:	31-12-1996

The display separators are interchangeable:

US and UK format:	1,000.00
European format:	1.000,00

Data Entry

Table 3.3.1 Important calculator set-up for TVM and DCF applications using TI BA II Plus.

	key (s)	calculator display	function
1.	2nd, Format , 2, ENTER	DEC = 2.00	access FORMAT settings and set DEC value of 2.00
2.	2nd, QUIT	0.00	QUIT current operation
3.	2nd, QUIT, 2nd, CLR TVM	0.00	QUIT and CLEAR TVM worksheet
4.	2nd, QUIT, CF, 2nd, CLR Work	CFO = 0.00	QUIT, access DCF worksheet and CLEAR DCF worksheet
5.	2nd, BGN, 2nd, SET, 2nd, QUIT	BGN or <blank> see note 3.	Toggles beginning- or end-of-period for annuity payments.

notes:

1. 2nd = accesses second function of a calculator key
2. , (comma) = separator between calculator keystroke inputs in the order shown
3. If calculator is set for beginning-of-period for annuity payments, BGN (beginning) is shown at the upper right corner of the display area; otherwise, if set for end-of-period for annuity payments, nothing is shown in the same area.

Before doing any of the sample calculations we will discuss, you need to check the following settings:

1. First check that the decimal is set to 2. To check, turn ON the calculator; if the display does not show 0.00, set to decimal 2. See Table 3.3.1.
2. For TVM analysis, reset memories by pressing: 2nd, QUIT, 2nd, CLR TVM (for reference, see Table 3.3.1). For DCF analysis, reset memories by pressing: CF, 2nd, CLR Work.
3. Check that annuity payments are correctly set; end-of-period or beginning-of-period. If the calculator display shows "BGN", the annuity payments are set to beginning-of-period; see Table 3.3.1. Ignore this if there are no annuity payments.

Table 3.3.2 Important calculator keys for TVM and DCF applications using TI BA II Plus.

key (s)	function
N	period (per)
I/Y	interest per year (I/Yr)
PV	present value (pr)
FV	future value (fu)
PMT	annuity payment value (an)
CPT, xyz	compute TVM parameter xyz = N, I/Y, PV, FV or PMT
2nd, P/Y, ↑ or ↓	access payment per year (P/Yr); compounding per year (C/Yr) accessed by up or down arrow key
2nd, Amort, ↑ or ↓	access amortization worksheet; periods P1 and P2 accessed by up or down arrow key; enter a value for P1 and P2 and press ENTER after each entry; calculator calculates BAL, PRN and INT after pressing ↑ or ↓
2nd, IConv	access interest conversion worksheet, convert between nominal interest and effective interest (when P/Yr ≠ C/Yr)
↑	up arrow key, to access other parameters in a worksheet
↓	down arrow key, to access other parameters in a worksheet
CF	to access cash flow worksheet; enter cash flow values CF0, Cnn and Fnn where nn = 1–24; use up or down arrow key, to access other parameters in the CF worksheet
NPV	accesses NPV calculation sheet; first enter periodic interest (in%) and with up or down arrow display NPV then press CPT
IRR	after pressing IRR, press CPT to calculate
+/–	change sign of displayed value

In 1937, Oldsmobile introduced the Automatic Safety Transmission, which eliminated the need for clutching and shifting gears. Its additional cost to the car is $100 US.

Sample Calculations from Section 2.1, Basics of Time Value of Money Analysis

From Table 2.1.10 Type I, Class A.1 financial problem. (P/Yr = C/Yr = 12).

per	I/Yr	pr	fu
104.32	8.00	-5,000.00	10,000.00

Table 3.3.3 Keystrokes to solve Table 2.1.10.

input keystrokes	comments	calculator display
(clear TVM)	see Table 3.3.1	0.00
2nd, P/Y, 12, ENTER	set P/Y = 12 (monthly payments)	P/Y = 12.00
↑ or ↓, 12, ENTER	set C/Y = 12(monthly interest compounding)	C/Y = 12.00
2nd, QUIT, 8, I/Y	enter I/Y	I/Y = 8.00
5000, +/–, PV	enter PV	PV = –5,000.00
10000, FV	enter FV	FV = 10,000.00
CPT, N	compute N (in months)	N = 104.32

From Table 2.1.15 Type II, Class B.1 financial problem. (P/Yr = C/Yr = 12).

per	per	I/Yr	pr	an
E	B			
61.02	60.52	8.00	5,000.00	-100.00

Table 3.3.4 Keystrokes to solve Table 2.1.15.

input keystrokes	comments	calculator display
(clear TVM, set END of period annuity payment)	see Table 3.3.1	0.00
2nd, P/Y, 12, ENTER	set P/Y = 12 (monthly payments)	P/Y = 12.00
↑ or ↓, 12, ENTER	set C/Y = 12 monthly interest compounding)	C/Y = 12.00
2nd, QUIT, 5000, PV	enter PV	PV = 5,000.00
8, I/Y	enter I/Y	I/Y = 8.00
100, +/–, PMT	enter PMT	PMT = –100.00
CPT, N	compute N (END of period)	N = 61.02
2nd, QUIT, (select BGN)	see Table 3.3.1	0.00
CPT, N	compute N (BGN of period)	N = 60.52

From Table 2.1.20 Type II, Class C.1 financial problem. (P/Yr = C/Yr = 12).

per E	per B	I/Yr	fu	an
76.88	76.48	8.00	20,000.00	–200.00

Table 3.3.5 Keystrokes to solve Table 2.1.20.

input keystrokes	comments	calculator display
(clear TVM, set END of period annuity payment)	see Table 3.3.1	0.00
2nd, P/Y, 12, ENTER	set P/Y = 12 (monthly payments)	P/Y = 12.00
↑ or ↓, 12, ENTER	set C/Y = 12 (monthly interest compounding)	C/Y = 12.00
2nd, QUIT, 8, I/Y	enter I/Y	I/Y = 8.00
20000, FV	enter FV	FV = 20,000.00
200, +/–, PMT	enter PMT	PMT = –200.00
CPT, N	compute N (END of period)	N = 76.88
2nd, QUIT, (select BGN)	see Table 3.3.1	0.00
CPT, N	compute N (BGN of period)	N = 76.48

From Table 2.1.25 Type III, Class D.1 financial problem. (P/Yr = C/Yr = 1).

per E	per B	I/Yr	pr	fu	an
24.18	23.57	8.00	–50,000.00	1,000,000.00	–10,000.00

Table 3.3.6 Keystrokes to solve Table 2.1.25.

input keystrokes	comments	calculator display
(clear TVM, set END of period annuity payment)	see Table 3.3.1	0.00
2nd, P/Y, 1, ENTER	set P/Y = 1 (annual payments)	P/Y = 1.00
↑ or ↓, 1, ENTER	set C/Y = 1 (yearly interest compounding)	C/Y = 1.00
2nd, QUIT, 50000, +/–, PV	enter PV	PV = –50,000.00
10000, +/–, PMT	enter PMT	PMT = –10,000.00
8, I/Y	enter I/Y	I/Y = 8.00
1000000, FV	enter FV	FV = 1,000,000.00
CPT, N	compute N (END of period)	N = 24.18
2nd, QUIT, (select BGN)	see Table 3.3.1	0.00
CPT, N	compute N (BGN of period)	N = 23.57

Sample Calculations from Section 2.2, Interest, Annuity, and Inflation

From Table 2.2.6 Future values of $1,000 for periods 1, 2, 3, 4, and 5 at 6% interest rate and annual compounding. (C/Yr = P/Yr = 1).

Annual interest rate	end of first year	end of second year	end of third year	end of fourth year	end of fifth year
6.00%	1,060.00	1,123.60	1,191.02	1,262.48	1,338.23

Table 3.3.7 Keystrokes to solve Table 2.2.6.

input keystrokes	comments	calculator display
(clear TVM)	see Table 3.3.1	0.00
2nd, P/Y, 1, ENTER	set P/Y = 1 (annual payments)	P/Y = 1.00
↑ or ↓, 1, ENTER	set C/Y = 1 (yearly interest compounding)	C/Y = 1.00
2nd, QUIT, 1, N	enter N	N = 1.00
6, I/Y	enter I/Y	I/Y = 6.00
1000, +/−, PV	enter PV	PV = −1,000.00
CPT, FV	compute FV	FV = 1,060.00
2nd, QUIT	quit	0.00
2, N	enter N	N = 2.00
CPT, FV	compute FV	FV = 1,123.60
2nd, QUIT	quit	0.00
3, N	enter N	N = 3.00
CPT, FV	compute FV	FV = 1,191.02
2nd, QUIT	quit	0.00
4, N	enter N	N = 4.00
CPT, FV	compute FV	FV = 1,262.48
2nd, QUIT	quit	0.00
5, N	enter N	N = 5.00
CPT, FV	compute FV	FV = 1,338.23

From Table 2.2.10 Effective rate of interest (Eff/Yr) and adjusted nominal interest rate ($(I/Yr)_{adj}$) for various compounding periods at (P/Yr) = 1.

(I/Yr)	C/Yr	(Eff/Yr)	(P/Yr)	$(I/Yr)_{adj}$
6.00	2.00	6.09	1.00	6.09

Table 3.3.8 Keystrokes to solve Table 2.2.10 for Eff/Yr and $(I/Yr)_{adj}$

input keystrokes	comments	calculator display
(clear TVM)	see Table 3.3.1	0.00
2nd, Iconv, 2nd, CLR Work	call up interest conversion worksheet and clear worksheet registers	NOM = 0.00
6, ENTER	enter nominal interest rate	NOM = 6.00
↑, 2, ENTER	enter compounding per year	C/Y = 2.00
↑, CPT	compute effective interest	EFF = 6.09
↑, ↑, 1, ENTER	enter P/Yr	C/Y = 1.00
↑, ↑, CPT	compute adjusted nominal interest rate	NOM = 6.09

For TVM applications, the TI BA II PLUS calculates the parameter, $(I/Yr)_{adj}$ internally using P/Yr and C/Yr.

From Table 2.2.14 Effective rate of interest calculations for Banks A, B, C, and D.

Bank	(I/Yr)	(C/Yr)	(Eff/Yr)
B	8.35	4.00	8.62

Table 3.3.9 Keystrokes to solve Table 2.2.14 for Eff/Yr.

input keystrokes	comments	calculator display
(clear TVM)	see Table 3.3.1	0.00
2nd, Iconv, 2nd, CLR Work	call up interest conversion worksheet and clear worksheet registers	NOM = 0.00
8.35, ENTER	enter nominal interest rate	NOM = 8.35
↑, 4, ENTER	enter compounding per year	C/Y = 4.00
↑, CPT	compute effective interest	EFF = 8.62

From Table 2.2.30 Future value of $0.01 annuity payment made at the end of each day for 30 days, at interest rate of 100% per day.
Type II, Class C.3 financial problem. (P/Yr = C/Yr = 365).

per	I/Yr	fu	an(E)
30.00	36,500.00	–10,737,418.23	0.01

Table 3.3.10 Keystrokes to solve Table 2.2.30.

input keystrokes	comments	calculator display
2nd, Format , 2, ENTER, 2nd, QUIT, 2nd, CLR TVM	set Decimal 2, clear TVM registers	0.00
2nd, BGN, 2nd, SET, 2nd, QUIT	if 'BGN' is shown in the calculator display, perform the indicated input keystrokes; see page 198 note 3	0.00
2nd, P/Y, 365, ENTER	set P/Y = 365 (daily payments)	P/Y = 365.00
↑ or ↓, 365, ENTER	set C/Y = 365 (daily interest compounding)	C/Y = 365.00
2nd, QUIT, 30, N	enter N	N = 30.00
36500, I/Y	enter I/Y	I/Y = 36,500.00
.01, PMT	enter PMT	PMT = 0.01
CPT, FV	compute FV	FV = –10,737,418.23

Sample Calculations from Section 2.3, Four Methods to Implement a Savings Plan

From Table 2.3.8 Present value for various cash flows with I/Yr = 6%.
Type I, Class A.3 financial problem. (P/Yr = 1, C/Yr = 12).

period (per)	cash flow amount (fu)	present value (pr)
2.00	–2,000.00	1,774.37

Table 3.3.11 Keystrokes to solve Table 2.3.8.

input keystrokes	comments	calculator display
(clear TVM)	see Table 3.3.1	0.00
2nd, P/Y, 1, ENTER	set P/Y = 1 (yearly payments)	P/Y = 1.00
↑ or ↓, 12, ENTER	set C/Y = 12 (monthly interest compounding)	C/Y = 12.00
2nd, QUIT, 6, I/Y	enter I/Y	I/Y = 6.00
2, N	enter N	N = 2.00
2000, +/–, FV	enter FV	FV= –2,000.00
CPT, PV	compute PV	PV= 1,774.37

Sample Calculations from Section 2.4, Loans and Mortgages

From Table 2.4.13 Amortization table – Distribution of $435.70 monthly payment ($22,537 loan at 6% interest rate and 5-year term with payments made at the end of each period). (P/Yr = C/Yr = 12).

per	principal	principal payment	interest payment	principal balance
1.00	22,537.00	-323.01	-112.69	22,213.99
2.00	22,213.99	-324.63	-111.07	21,889.36
3.00	21,889.36	-326.25	-109.45	21,563.11

Table 3.3.12 Keystrokes to solve Table 2.4.13.

input keystrokes	comments	calculator display
(clear TVM, set END of period annuity payment)	see Table 3.3.1	0.00
2nd, P/Y, 12, ENTER	set P/Y = 12 (monthly payments)	P/Y = 12.00
↑ or ↓, 12, ENTER	set C/Y = 12 (monthly interest compounding)	C/Y = 12.00
2nd, QUIT, 6, I/Y	enter I/Y	I/Y = 6.00
22537, PV	enter PV	PV = 22,537.00
60, N	enter N	N = 60.00
CPT, PMT	compute PMT (END of period)	PMT = -435.70
2nd, Amort, 1, ENTER	call up amortization worksheet and enter P1	P1 = 1.00
↓, 1, ENTER	in amortization worksheet, enter P2	P2 = 1.00
↓	calculate and display principal balance	BAL = 22,213.99
↓	calculate and display principal paid	PRN = -323.01
↓	calculate and display interest paid	INT = -112.69
↓, 2, ENTER	in amortization worksheet, enter P1	P1 = 2.00
↓, 2, ENTER	in amortization worksheet, enter P2	P2 = 2.00
↓	calculate and display principal balance	BAL = 21,889.36
↓	calculate and display principal paid	PRN = -324.63
↓	calculate and display interest paid	INT = -111.07
↓, 3, ENTER	in amortization worksheet, enter P1	P1 = 3.00
↓, 3, ENTER	in amortization worksheet, enter P2	P2 = 3.00
↓	calculate and display principal balance	BAL = 21,563.11
↓	calculate and display principal paid	PRN = -326.25
↓	calculate and display interest paid	INT = -109.45

From Table 2.4.14 Total principal and interest payments from periods 1–60 for $22,537 loan at 6% interest rate, 5-year term and $435.70 monthly payment. (P/Yr = C/Yr = 12).

per	principal	total principal payment	total interest payment	principal balance
1-60	22,537.00	-22,536.76	-3,605.24	0.24

Table 3.3.13 Keystrokes to solve Table 2.4.14.

input keystrokes	comments	calculator display
(clear TVM, set END of period annuity payment)	see Table 3.3.1	0.00
2nd, P/Y, 12, ENTER	set P/Y = 12 (monthly payments)	P/Y = 12.00
↑ or ↓, 12, ENTER	set C/Y = 12 (monthly interest compounding)	C/Y = 12.00
2nd, QUIT, 6, I/Y	enter I/Y	I/Y = 6.00
22537, PV	enter PV	PV = 22,537.00
60, N	enter N	N = 60.00
CPT, PMT	compute PMT (END of period)	PMT = -435.70
2nd, Amort, 1, ENTER	call up amortization worksheet and enter P1	P1 = 1.00
↓, 60, ENTER	in amortization worksheet and enter P2	P2 = 60.00
↓	calculate and display principal balance	BAL = 0.24
↓	calculate and display principal paid	PRN = -22,536.76
↓	calculate and display interest paid	INT = -3,605.24

From Table 2.4.21 Summary of 5 consecutive 5-year term mortgages of $95,000 amortized over 25 years with different interest rates at renewal. (P/Yr = C/Yr = 12).

per	I/Yr	monthly payment	principal balance	principal paid	interest paid	remaining amortization period
300.00	8.50	-764.97	88,147.32	-6,852.68	-39,045.52	240.00
240.00	8.00	-737.30	77,151.48	-10,995.84	-33,242.16	180.00
180.00	9.00	-782.52	61,773.70	-15,377.78	-31,573.42	120.00

Table 3.3.14 Keystrokes to solve Table 2.4.21.

input keystrokes	comments	calculator display
(clear TVM, set END of period annuity payment)	see Table 3.3.1	0.00
2nd, P/Y, 12, ENTER	set P/Y = 12 (monthly payments)	P/Y = 12.00
↑ or ↓, 12, ENTER	set C/Y = 12 (monthly interest compounding)	C/Y = 12.00
2nd, QUIT, 8.5, I/Y	enter I/Y	I/Y = 8.50
95000, PV	enter PV	PV = 95,000.00
300, N	enter N	N = 300.00
CPT, PMT	compute PMT (END of period)	PMT = –764.97
2nd, Amort, 1, ENTER	call up amortization worksheet and enter P1	P1 = 1.00
↓, 60, ENTER	in amortization worksheet, enter P2 (5 years)	P2 = 60.00
↓	calculate and display principal balance	BAL = 88,147.32
↓	calculate and display principal paid	PRN = –6,852.68
↓	calculate and display interest paid	INT = –39,045.52
2nd, QUIT, RCL, N, –, 60, =, N	quit, recall N, subtract 60 and store to N	N = 240.00
8, I/Y	enter I/Y	I/Y = 8.00
88147.32, PV	enter PV	PV = 88,147.32
CPT, PMT	compute PMT (END of period)	PMT = –737.30
2nd, Amort, 1, ENTER	call up amortization worksheet, enter P1	P1 = 1.00
↓, 60, ENTER	in amortization worksheet, enter P2 (5 years)	P2 = 60.00
↓	calculate and display principal balance	BAL = 77,151.48
↓	calculate and display principal paid	PRN = –10,995.84
↓	calculate and display interest paid	INT = –33,242.16
2nd, QUIT, RCL, N, –, 60, =, N	quit, recall N, subtract 60 and store to N	N = 180.00
9, I/Y	enter I/Y	I/Y = 9.00
77151.48, PV	enter PV	PV = 77,151.48
CPT, PMT	compute PMT (END of period)	PMT = –782.52
2nd, Amort, 1, ENTER	call up amortization worksheet and enter P1	P1 = 1.00
↓, 60, ENTER	in amortization worksheet and enter P2 (5 years)	P2 = 60.00
↓	calculate and display principal balance	BAL = 61,773.70
↓	calculate and display principal paid	PRN = –15,377.78
↓	calculate and display interest paid	INT = –31,573.42

From Table 2.4.22 Status of $95,000 mortgage at the end of 25-year term amortized for 25 years at 8.4% interest compounded monthly. (P/Yr = C/Yr = 12).

per	I/Yr	monthly payment	principal balance	principal paid	interest paid
300.00	8.4	−758.57	4.99	−94,995.01	−132,575.99

Table 3.3.15 Keystrokes to solve Table 2.4.22.

input keystrokes	comments	calculator display
(clear TVM, set END of period annuity payment)	see Table 3.3.1	0.00
2nd, P/Y, 12, ENTER	set P/Y = 12 (monthly payments)	P/Y = 12.00
↑ or ↓, 12, ENTER	set C/Y = 12 (monthly interest compounding)	C/Y = 12.00
2nd, QUIT, 8.4, I/Y	enter I/Y	I/Y = 8.40
95000, PV	enter PV	PV = 95,000.00
300, N	enter N	N = 300.00
CPT, PMT	compute PMT (END of period)	PMT = −758.57
2nd, Amort, 1, ENTER	call up amortization worksheet and enter P1	P1 = 1.00
↓, 300, ENTER	in amortization worksheet, enter P2 (25 years)	P2 = 300.00
↓	calculate and display principal balance	BAL = 4.99
↓	calculate and display principal paid	PRN = −94,995.01
↓	calculate and display interest paid	INT = −132,575.99

From Table 2.4.30 Monthly payment and interest saved for various interest compounding at 8% nominal interest rate, loan of $95,643.43 and 20-year amortization. Type II, Class B.4 financial problem. (P/Yr = 12).

C/Yr	per	pr	an	total cost	total interest	interest saved
12.00	240.00	95,643.43	−800.00	192,000.00	96,356.57	0.00
2.00	240.00	95,643.43	−792.27	190,144.80	94,501.37	1,855.20

Table 3.3.16 Keystrokes to solve Table 2.4.30.

input keystrokes	comments	calculator display
(clear TVM, set END of period annuity payment)	see Table 3.3.1	0.00
2nd, P/Y, 12, ENTER	set P/Y = 12 (monthly payments)	P/Y = 12.00
↑ or ↓, 2, ENTER	set C/Y = 2 (semi-annual interest compounding)	C/Y = 2.00
2nd, QUIT, 8, I/Y	enter I/Y	I/Y = 8.00
95643.43, PV	enter PV	PV = 95,643.43
240, N	enter N	N = 240.00
CPT, PMT	compute PMT (END of period)	PMT = –792.27
792.27, x, 12, x, 20, =	compute total cost	190,144.80
–, 95643.43, =	compute total interest	94,501.37
+/–, +, 96356.57, =	compute interest saved	1,855.20

Sample Calculations from Section 2.5, Planning for the Children's Education

From Table 2.5.16 Yearly payments at the beginning of each period when saving for Giuseppe's education fund is delayed. 8% interest rate compounded monthly with lump-sum payments of $0, $1,000, $5,000, and $10,000. Future value = $67,021.11. Type III, Class D.5 financial problem. (P/Yr = 1, C/Yr = 12).

year fund started	per	an(B) pr = 0.00	an(B) pr = -1,000.00	an(B) pr = -5,000.00	an(B) pr = -10,000.00
1999	12.00	-3,203.46	-3,079.03	-2,581.28	-1,959.10
2000	11.00	-3,658.75	-3,527.52	-3,002.60	-2,346.45

Table 3.3.17 Keystrokes to solve Table 2.5.16.

input keystrokes	comments	calculator display
(clear TVM, set BGN of period annuity payment)	see Table 3.3.1	0.00
2nd, P/Y, 1, ENTER	set P/Y = 1 (annual payments)	P/Y = 1.00
↑ or ↓, 12, ENTER	set C/Y = 12 (monthly interest compounding)	C/Y = 12.00
2nd, QUIT, 67021.11, FV	enter FV	FV = 67,021.11
8, I/Y	enter I/Y	I/Y = 8.00
0, PV	enter PV	PV = 0.00
12, N	enter N	N = 12.00
CPT, PMT	compute PMT (BGN of period)	PMT = –3,203.46
11, N	enter N	N = 11.00
CPT, PMT	compute PMT (BGN of period)	PMT = –3,658.75
1000, +/–, PV	enter PV	PV = –1,000.00
12, N	enter N	N = 12.00
CPT, PMT	compute PMT (BGN of period)	PMT = –3,079.03
11, N	enter N	N = 11.00
CPT, PMT	compute PMT (BGN of period)	PMT = –3,527.52
5000, +/–, PV	enter PV	PV = –5,000.00
12, N	enter N	N = 12.00
CPT, PMT	compute PMT (BGN of period)	PMT = –2,581.28
11, N	enter N	N = 11.00
CPT, PMT	compute PMT (BGN of period)	PMT = –3,002.60
10000, +/–, PV	enter PV	PV = –10,000.00
12, N	enter N	N = 12.00
CPT, PMT	compute PMT (BGN of period)	PMT = –1,959.10
11, N	enter N	N = 11.00
CPT, PMT	compute PMT (BGN of period)	PMT = –2,346.45

Sample Calculations from Section 2.6, Planning for Retirement

From Table 2.6.2 Total earnings at the end of age 65 for various starting salaries, ages and yearly increase. Type II, Class C.3 financial problem. (P/Yr = C/Yr = 1), use end-of-period payments.

	Age				Age			
	23	31	41	51	23	31	41	51
	per = 43	per = 35	per = 25	per = 15	per = 43	per = 35	per = 25	per = 15
Initial Salary	2% yearly increase				3% yearly increase			
40,000	2,686,379	1,999,779	1,281,212	691,737	3,419,356	2,418,483	1,458,371	743,957

Table 3.3.18 Keystrokes to solve Table 2.6.2.

input keystrokes	comments	calculator display
(clear TVM, set END of period annuity payment)	see Table 3.3.1	0.00
2nd, P/Y, 1, ENTER	set P/Y = 1 (yearly payments)	P/Y = 1.00
↑ or ↓, 1, ENTER	set C/Y = 1 (yearly interest compounding)	C/Y = 1.00
2nd, QUIT, 43, N	enter N	N = 43.00
2, I/Y	enter I/Y	I/Y = 2.00
40000, +/–, PMT	enter PMT	PMT = –40,000.00
CPT,FV	compute FV (END of period)	FV = 2,686,378.71
35, N	enter N	N = 35.00
CPT,FV	compute FV (END of period)	FV = 1,999,779.11
25, N	enter N	N = 25.00
CPT,FV	compute FV (END of period)	FV = 1,281,211.99
15, N	enter N	N = 15.00
CPT,FV	compute FV (END of period)	FV = 691,736.68
3, I/Y	enter I/Y	I/Y = 3.00
43, N	enter N	N = 43.00
CPT,FV	compute FV (END of period)	FV = 3,419,355.69
35, N	enter N	N = 35.00
CPT,FV	compute FV (END of period)	FV = 2,418,483.27

Continued, Table 3.3.18

25, N	enter N	N = 25.00
CPT,FV	compute FV (END of period)	FV = 1,458,370.57
15, N	enter N	N = 15.00
CPT,FV	compute FV (END of period)	FV = 743,956.56

From Table 2.6.4 Future values at the end of age 65 for various monthly savings amounts. Interest is compounded monthly. Monthly payments are made at the beginning of each period. Period = 43 x 12.
Type II, Class C.3 financial problem. (P/Yr = C/Yr = 12).

savings amount	total savings	future value at 6% interest	future value at 8% interest	future value at 10% interest
150.00	77,400	365,194	675,716	1,295,878

Table 3.3.19 Keystrokes to solve Table 2.6.4.

input keystrokes	comments	calculator display
(clear TVM, set BGN of period annuity payment)	see Table 3.3.1	0.00
2nd, P/Y, 12, ENTER	set P/Y = 12 (monthly payments)	P/Y = 12.00
↑ or ↓, 12, ENTER	set C/Y = 12 (monthly interest compounding)	C/Y = 12.00
2nd, QUIT, 43, x, 12, =, N	enter N	N = 516.00
6, I/Y	enter I/Y	I/Y = 6.00
150, +/−, PMT	enter PMT	PMT = −150.00
CPT,FV	compute FV (BGN of period)	FV = 365,194.03
8, I/Y	enter I/Y	I/Y = 8.00
CPT,FV	compute FV (BGN of period)	FV = 675,716.40
10, I/Y	enter I/Y	I/Y = 10.00
CPT,FV	compute FV (BGN of period)	FV = 1,295,878.40
RCL, N, x, 150, =	calculate total savings	77,400.00

From Table 2.6.23 Monthly payments to finance $3,000 and $4,000 monthly retirement income for 20 years if $10,000 retirement fund has already been started. Money earns 4%, 6%, and 8% interest, compounded monthly at 3% inflation compounded monthly for various years to retirement. Use beginning-of-period payments. (P/Yr = C/Yr = 12)

Years to retirement	$3,000 monthly retirement income	$4,000 monthly retirement income
	4%	8%
40.00	–1,347	–385

Table 3.3.20 Keystrokes to solve Table 2.6.23.

input keystrokes	comments	calculator display
(clear TVM, set BGN of period annuity payment)	see Table 3.3.1	0.00
2nd, P/Y, 12, ENTER	set P/Y = 12 (monthly payments)	P/Y = 12.00
↑ or ↓, 12, ENTER	set C/Y = 12 (monthly interest compounding)	C/Y = 12.00
2nd, QUIT, 4, I/Y	enter I/Y	I/Y = 4.00
20, x, 12, =, N	enter N (retirement period in months)	N = 240.00
3000, PMT	enter PMT	PMT = 3,000.00
CPT, PV	compute PV	PV = –496,715.79
0, PMT	set PMT register to 0 (zero)	PMT = 0.00
3, I/Y	store inflation rate to I/Y	I/Y = 3.00
40, x, 12, =, N	enter N (period to retirement in months)	N = 480.00
CPT, FV	compute FV	FV = 1,646,686.74
10000, +/–, PV	store lump-sum amount to PV	PV = –10,000.00
4, I/Y	store nominal rate to I/Y	I/Y = 4.00
CPT, PMT	compute PMT	PMT = –1,346.90
(clear TVM)	see Table 3.3.1 (BGN still selected)	0.00
8, I/Y	enter I/Y	I/Y = 8.00
20, x, 12, =, N	enter N (retirement period in months)	N = 240.00
4000, PMT	enter PMT	PMT = 4,000.00
CPT, PV	compute PV	PV = –481,405.28
0, PMT	set PMT register to 0 (zero)	PMT = 0.00
3, I/Y	store inflation rate to I/Y	I/Y = 3.00
40, x, 12, =, N	enter N (period to retirement in months)	N = 480.00
CPT, FV	compute FV	FV = 1,595,930.12
10000, +/–, PV	store lump-sum amount to PV	PV = –10,000.00
8, I/Y	store nominal rate to I/Y	I/Y = 8.00
CPT, PMT	compute PMT	PMT = –385.06

From Table 2.6.30 Monthly retirement payments in today's dollars for 20 years with existing $50,000 retirement fund. Money earns 4%, 6%, and 8% interest compounded monthly at 3% inflation compounded monthly for various years to retirement. Use beginning-of-period payments. (P/Yr = C/Yr = 12).

Years to retirement	–$1,000 monthly savings payment	–$2,000 monthly savings payment
	6%	8%
30	3,803	11,997

Table 3.3.21 Keystrokes to solve Table 2.6.30.

input keystrokes	comments	calculator display
(clear TVM, set BGN of period annuity payment)	see Table 3.3.1	0.00
2nd, P/Y, 12, ENTER	set P/Y = 12 (monthly payments)	P/Y = 12.00
↑ or ↓, 12, ENTER	set C/Y = 12 (monthly interest compounding)	C/Y = 12.00
2nd, QUIT, 6, I/Y	store nominal rate to I/Y	I/Y = 6.00
30, x, 12, =, N	enter N (period to retirement in months)	N = 360.00
1000, +/–, PMT	enter PMT	PMT = –1,000.00
50000, +/–, PV	store lump-sum amount to PV	PV = –50,000.00
CPT, FV	compute FV	FV = 1,310,666.38
0, PMT	set PMT register to 0 (zero)	PMT = 0.00
3, I/Y	store inflation rate to I/Y	I/Y = 3.00
CPT, PV	compute PV	PV = –533,476.01
20, x, 12, =, N	enter N (retirement period in months)	N = 240.00
0, FV	set FV register to 0 (zero)	FV = 0.00
6, I/Y	enter I/Y	I/Y = 6.00
CPT, PMT	compute PMT	PMT = 3,802.97
(clear TVM)	see Table 3.3.1 (BGN still selected)	0.00
8, I/Y	store nominal rate to I/Y	I/Y = 8.00
30, x, 12, =, N	enter N (period to retirement in months)	N = 360.00
2000, +/–, PMT	enter PMT	PMT = –2,000.00
50000, +/–, PV	store lump-sum amount to PV	PV = –50,000.00
CPT, FV	compute FV	FV = 3,547,376.84
0, PMT	set PMT register to 0 (zero)	PMT = 0.00
3, I/Y	store inflation rate to I/Y	I/Y = 3.00
CPT, PV	compute PV	PV = –1,443,876.54

Continued, Table 3.3.21

20, x, 12, =, N	enter N (retirement period in months)	N = 240.00
0, FV	set FV register to 0 (zero)	FV = 0.00
8, I/Y	enter I/Y	I/Y = 8.00
CPT, PMT	compute PMT	PMT = 11,997.18

Sample Calculations from Section 2.7, Investment Decision Making

In this subsection, DCF analysis will be performed.

From Table 2.7.2 Financial calculator data entry values for Example 1.
I/Yr = 20%, P/Yr = C/Yr = 12.

cash flow	frequency
CF0 = −10,000.00	
CF1 = −500.00	N1 = 1.00
CF2 = −3,000.00	N2 = 1.00
CF3 = 0.00	N3 = 15.00
CF4 = 20,000.00	N4 = 1.00

NPV = \$1,458.80, IRR = 27.22% (yearly rate, periodic interest rate or monthly rate is 2.27%).

Table 3.3.22 Keystrokes to solve Table 2.7.2.

input keystrokes	comments	calculator display
CF, 2nd, CLR Work	reset DCF Worksheet	CF0 = 0.00
10000, +/−, ENTER	enter amount for cash flow CF0	CF0 = −10,000.00
↓, 500, +/−, ENTER	enter amount for cash flow C01	C01 = −500.00
↓	accept frequency of cash flow group C01 = 1	F01 = 1.00
↓, 3000, +/−, ENTER	enter amount for cash flow C02	C02 = −3,000.00
↓	accept frequency of cash flow group C02 = 1	F02 = 1.00
↓	accept amount for cash flow C03 = 0	C03 = 0.00
↓, 15, ENTER	enter frequency of cash flow group C03	F03 = 15.00
↓, 20000, ENTER	enter amount for cash flow C04	C04 = 20,000.00
↓	accept frequency of cash flow group C04 = 1	F04 = 1.00
NPV, 20, ÷, 12, =, ENTER	enter periodic interest (monthly rate)	I = 1.67
↓, CPT	compute NPV	NPV = 1,458.80
IRR, CPT	compute IRR periodic rate (monthly)	IRR = 2.27
x, 12, =	compute yearly rate for IRR	IRR 27.22

From Table 2.7.3 Financial calculator data entry values for Example 2. I/Yr = 10%, P/Yr = C/Yr = 12.

cash flow	frequency
CF0 = 35,000	
CF1 = 35,000	N1 = 23
CF2 = 35,000 x 1.15 = 40,250	N2 = 24
CF3 = 40,250 x 1.15 = 46,288	N3 = 24
CF4 = 46,288 x 1.15 = 53,231	N4 = 24
CF5 = 53,231 x 1.15 = 61,216	N5 = 24

NPV = $3,407,611.54

Table 3.3.23 Keystrokes to solve Table 2.7.3.

input keystrokes	comments	calculator display
CF, 2nd, CLR Work	reset DCF Worksheet	CFO = 0.00
35000, ENTER	enter amount for cash flow CFO	CFO = 35,000.00
↓, 35000, ENTER	enter amount for cash flow C01	C01 = 35,000.00
↓, 23, ENTER	enter frequency of cash flow group C01	F01 = 23.00
↓, 40250, ENTER	enter amount for cash flow C02	C02 = 40,250.00
↓, 24, ENTER	enter frequency of cash flow group C02	F02 = 24.00
↓, 46288, ENTER	enter amount for cash flow C03	C03 = 46,288.00
↓, 24, ENTER	enter frequency of cash flow group C03	F03 = 24.00
↓, 53231, ENTER	enter amount for cash flow C04	C04 = 53,231.00
↓, 24, ENTER	enter frequency of cash flow group C04	F04 = 24.00
↓, 61216, ENTER	enter amount for cash flow C05	C05 = 61,216.00
↓, 24, ENTER	enter frequency of cash flow group C05	F05 = 24.00
NPV, 10, ÷, 12, =, ENTER	enter periodic interest (monthly rate)	I = 0.83
↓, CPT	compute NPV	NPV = 3,407,611.54

A $130 US investment by thirteen blue-collar workers turned into the biggest lottery win ever. A group of machinists from Ohio claimed the Powerball jackpot of $295.7 million US drawn last July 29, 1998. Instead of taking payments over 25 years, the group chose the single lump-sum option of about $161.5 million US, or $12.42 million each.

3.4

TEXAS INSTRUMENTS BA-35 SOLAR

Like the BA II Plus, the BA-35 Solar financial calculator comes with a durable plastic slide case, a quick reference card, and a manual. The 3" x 5" manual does not do justice to its powerful features and computing capabilities. It has financial, statistical, algebraic, and memory functions. A maximum of ten digits can be displayed in the LCD (liquid crystal display). The calculator can operate in three modes: statistical, financial, and profit margin mode. The number of decimal places displayed can be set.

This model is the only financial calculator I have come across that is powered by solar cells instead of batteries. I have not had any problems using the calculator at home in the evenings with artificial light. The calculator automatically turns off when the solar cells are no longer exposed to light.

This solar-powered model is the recent upgrade to the older BA-35 model, which was battery powered. The solar-powered model was enhanced with better amortization calculation user keystroke interface, and the ability to perform TVM analysis calculations using present value (pr), future value (fu) and annuity payment (an) simultaneously, as in Type III financial problems.

This model is also the least expensive financial calculator I have come across that supports the TVM analysis method, interest conversion, and loan amortization schedule.

Iridium Canada Communications is the major investor in a $6.5 billion project that will launch 66 low-Earth-orbit satellites starting late 1998. The objective is to provide mobile telephone service to any point in the world.

Data Entry

Table 3.4.1 Important calculator set-up for TVM applications using TI BA-35 Solar.

	key (s)	calculator display	function
1.	AC/ON, 2nd, FIX, 2	0.00	Clear TVM, set end-of-period annuity payments, and set decimal value of 2
2.	MODE (several times)	(FIN) 0.00	Access FINANCIAL functions
3.	2nd, BGN	Begin or <blank> see note 3.	Toggles beginning- or end-of-period for annuity payments.

notes:

1. 2nd = accesses second function of a calculator key
2. , (comma) = separator between calculator keystroke inputs in the order shown
3. If calculator is set for beginning-of-period for annuity payments, 'Begin' is shown at the bottom line of the display area; if set for end-of-period annuity payments, nothing is shown in this area.
4. The TI BA-35 Solar does not follow the conventions of cash flow diagrams used throughout this book, by which inflow is always a positive (+) amount and outflow is a negative (-) amount. Instead, for Type I, II and III financial problems, PV and FV are positive values on this calculator. In Type II and Type III financial problems, annuity payments are a negative value for savings applications, and a positive value for loan applications.
5. Interest rate used by the calculator for TVM calculations requires entry of periodic interest rate in percent (in%).
6. For (P/Yr) = (C/Yr), interest rate in% to be entered to the financial calculator is the periodic interest rate; (I/Yr)/(P/Yr).

Before doing any of the sample calculations we will discuss, you need to check the following settings:

1. Check that the calculator is set for FINANCIAL mode and the decimal is set to 2 (the display shows 0.00; if not see Table 3.4.1).
2. Reset TVM memories and set decimal value of 2 (for reference, see Table 3.4.1).
3. Check that annuity payments are correctly set; end-of-period or beginning-of-period. If the calculator display shows "Begin", the annuity payments are set to beginning-of-period; see Table 3.4.1. Ignore this if there are no annuity payments.

In 1997, the highest paid professional athlete was Evander Holyfield. He made $53 million US.

Table 3.4.2 Important calculator keys for TVM and DCF applications using TI BA–35 Solar.

key (s)	function
N	period (per)
%i	periodic interest
PV	present value (pr)
FV	future value (fu)
PMT	annuity payment value (an)
CPT, xyz	compute TVM parameter xyz = N, %i, PV, FV or PMT
I/P	calculate interest and principal balance of a single payment
P1/P2	select range of payments to calculate accumulated interest and principal
BAL	calculate remaining principal (loan balance) after a selected payment range
x, 2nd, EFF	convert x to EFF
y, 2nd, APR	convert y to APR
+/–	change sign of displayed value

Wastewater treatment systems are currently being installed on US Navy ships navigating the world's oceans. Soon, they will be required for all ships in the world, including cruise liners. The system, estimated to cost about $1 million for an average-sized vessel, would clean toilet and kitchen wastes before discharging them into the world's oceans. There are more than 5,000 major vessels across the world, 2,000 of which are NATO vessels.

Sample Calculations from Section 2.1, Basics of Time Value of Money Analysis

From Table 2.1.10 Type I, Class A.1 financial problem. (P/Yr = C/Yr = 12).

per	I/Yr	pr	fu
104.32	8.00	−5,000.00	10,000.00

Table 3.4.3 Keystrokes to solve Table 2.1.10.

input keystrokes	comments	calculator display
(clear TVM)	see Table 3.4.1	0.00
8, ÷, 12, =, %I	enter %I	0.67
5000, PV	enter PV	5,000.00
10000, FV	enter FV	10,000.00
CPT, N	compute N (in months)	104.32

From Table 2.1.15 Type II, Class B.1 financial problem. (P/Yr = C/Yr = 12).

per E	per B	I/Yr	pr	an
61.02	60.52	8.00	5,000.00	−100.00

Table 3.4.4 Keystrokes to solve Table 2.1.15.

input keystrokes	comments	calculator display
(clear TVM, set END of period annuity payment)	see Table 3.4.1	0.00
5000, PV	enter PV	5,000.00
8, ÷, 12, =, %I	enter %I	0.67
100, PMT	enter PMT	100.00
CPT, N	compute N (END of period)	61.02
2nd, BGN	select BEGIN of period	61.02
CPT, N	compute N (BGN of period)	60.52

From Table 2.1.20 Type II, Class C.1 financial problem. (P/Yr = C/Yr = 12).

per E	per B	I/Yr	fu	an
76.88	76.48	8.00	20,000.00	-200.00

Table 3.4.5 Keystrokes to solve Table 2.1.20.

input keystrokes	comments	calculator display
(clear TVM, set END of period annuity payment)	see Table 3.4.1	0.00
8, ÷, 12, =, %I	enter %I	0.67
20000, FV	enter FV	20,000.00
200, +/–, PMT	enter PMT	-200.00
CPT, N	compute N (END of period)	76.88
2nd, BGN	select BEGIN of period	76.88
CPT, N	compute N (BGN of period)	76.48

From Table 2.1.25 Type III, Class D.1 financial problem. (P/Yr = C/Yr = 1).

per E	per B	I/Yr	pr	fu	an
24.18	23.57	8.00	–50,000.00	1,000,000.00	–10,000.00

Table 3.4.6 Keystrokes to solve Table 2.1.25.

input keystrokes	comments	calculator display
(clear TVM, set END of period annuity payment)	see Table 3.4.1	0.00
50000, PV	enter PV	50,000.00
10000, +/–, PMT	enter PMT	–10,000.00
8, ÷, 1, =, %I	enter %I	8.00
1000000, FV	enter FV	1,000,000.00
CPT, N	compute N (END of period)	24.18
2nd, BGN	select BEGIN of period	24.18
CPT, N	compute N (BGN of period)	23.57

Sample Calculations from Section 2.2, Interest, Annuity, and Inflation

From Table 2.2.6 Future values of $1,000 for periods 1, 2, 3, 4, and 5 at 6% interest rate and annual compounding. (C/Yr = P/Yr = 1).

Annual interest rate	end of first year	end of second year	end of third year	end of fourth year	end of fifth year
6.00%	1,060.00	1,123.60	1,191.02	1,262.48	1,338.23

Table 3.4.7 Keystrokes to solve Table 2.2.6.

input keystrokes	comments	calculator display
(clear TVM)	see Table 3.4.1	0.00
1, N	enter N	1.00
6, 2nd, EFF, 1, =	calculate EFF	6.00
2nd, APR, 1, =, ÷, 1, =, %I	calculate adjusted APR (periodic rate – yearly)	6.00
1000, PV	enter PV	1,000.00
CPT, FV	compute FV	1,060.00
2, N	enter N	2.00
CPT, FV	compute FV	1,123.60
3, N	enter N	3.00
CPT, FV	compute FV	1,191.02
4, N	enter N	4.00
CPT, FV	compute FV	1,262.48
5, N	enter N	5.00
CPT, FV	compute FV	1,338.23

From Table 2.2.10 Effective rate of interest (Eff/Yr) and adjusted nominal interest rate ($(I/Yr)_{adj}$) for various compounding periods at (P/Yr) = 1.

(I/Yr)	C/Yr	(Eff/Yr)	(P/Yr)	$(I/Yr)_{adj}$
6.00	2.00	6.09	1.00	6.09

Table 3.4.8 Keystrokes to solve Table 2.2.10 for (Eff/Yr) and $(I/Yr)_{adj}$

input keystrokes	comments	calculator display
(clear TVM)	see Table 3.4.1	0.00
6, 2nd, EFF, 2, =	calculate EFF	6.09
2nd, APR, 1, =	calculate adjusted APR	6.09

From Table 2.2.14 Effective rate of interest calculations for Banks A, B, C, and D.

Bank	(I/Yr)	(C/Yr)	(Eff/Yr)
B	8.35	4.00	8.62

Table 3.4.9 Keystrokes to solve Table 2.2.14 for Eff/Yr.

input keystrokes	comments	calculator display
(clear TVM)	see Table 3.4.1	0.00
8.35, 2nd, EFF, 4, =	calculate EFF	8.62

From Table 2.2.30 Future value of $0.01 annuity payment made at the end of each day for 30 days, at interest rate of 100% per day.
Type II, Class C.3 financial problem. (P/Yr = C/Yr = 365).

per	I/Yr	fu	an(E)
30.00	36,500.00	−10,737,418.23	0.01

Table 3.4.10 Keystrokes to solve Table 2.2.30.

input keystrokes	comments	calculator display
(clear TVM, set END of period annuity payment)	see Table 3.4.1	0.00
30, N	enter N	30.00
36500, ÷, 365, =, %I	enter periodic interest rate (daily)	100.00
.01, PMT	enter PMT	0.01
CPT, FV	compute FV	−10,737,418.23

Sample Calculations from Section 2.3, Four Methods to Implement a Savings Plan

From Table 2.3.8 Present value for various cash flows with I/Yr = 6%. Type I, Class A.3 financial problem, (P/Yr = 1, C/Yr = 12).

period (per)	cash flow amount (fu)	present value (pr)
2.00	−2,000.00	1,774.37

Table 3.4.11 Keystrokes to solve Table 2.3.8.

input keystrokes	comments	calculator display
(clear TVM)	see Table 3.4.1	0.00
6, 2nd, EFF, 12, =	calculate EFF	6.17
2nd, APR, 1, =, ÷, 1, =, %I	calculate adjusted APR (periodic rate–monthly)	6.17
2, N	enter N	2.00
2000, FV	enter FV	2,000.00
CPT, PV	compute PV	1,774.37

Sample Calculations from Section 2.4, Loans and Mortgages

From Table 2.4.13 Amortization table – Distribution of $435.70 monthly payment ($22,537 loan at 6% interest rate and 5-year term with payments made at the end of each period). (P/Yr = C/Yr = 12).

per	principal	principal payment	interest payment	principal balance
1.00	22,537.00	−323.01	−112.69	22,213.99
2.00	22,213.99	−324.63	−111.07	21,889.36
3.00	21,889.36	−326.25	−109.45	21,563.11

Table 3.4.12 Keystrokes to solve Table 2.4.13.

input keystrokes	comments	calculator display
(clear TVM, set END of period annuity payment)	see Table 3.4.1	0.00
6, ÷, 12, =, %I	enter periodic interest rate (monthly)	0.50
22537, PV	enter PV	22,537.00
60, N	enter N	60.00
CPT, PMT	compute PMT (END of period)	435.70
1, P1/P2	call up amortization worksheet and enter P1	1.00
1, I/P	enter P2 and calculate interest paid	112.69
x←→y	calculate and display principal paid	323.02
1, BAL	calculate and display principal balance	22,213.98
2, P1/P2	in amortization worksheet enter P1	2.00
2, I/P	enter P2 and calculate interest paid	111.07
x←→y	calculate and display principal paid	324.63
2, BAL	calculate and display principal balance	21,889.35
3, P1/P2	in amortization worksheet enter P1	3.00
3, I/P	enter P2 and calculate interest paid	109.45
x←→y	calculate and display principal paid	326.26
3, BAL	calculate and display principal balance	21,563.09

From Table 2.4.14 Total principal and interest payments from periods 1–60 for $22,537 loan at 6% interest rate, 5-year term and $435.70 monthly payment. (P/Yr = C/Yr = 12).

per	principal	total principal payment	total interest payment	principal balance
1–60	22,537.00	–22,536.76	–3,605.24	0.24

Table 3.4.13 Keystrokes to solve Table 2.4.14.

input keystrokes	comments	calculator display
(clear TVM, set END of period annuity payment)	see Table 3.4.1	0.00
6, ÷, 12, =, %I	enter periodic interest rate (monthly)	0.50
22537, PV	enter PV	22,537.00

Continued, Table 3.4.13

60, N	enter N	60.00
CPT, PMT	compute PMT (END of period)	435.70
1, P1/P2	call up amortization worksheet and enter P1	1.00
60, I/P	enter P2 and calculate interest paid	3,605.20
x←→y	calculate and display principal paid	22,537.00
60, BAL	calculate and display principal balance	0.00

From Table 2.4.21 Summary of 5 consecutive 5-year term mortgages of $95,000 amortized over 25 years with different interest rates at renewal. (P/Yr = C/Yr = 12).

per	I/Yr	monthly payment	principal balance	principal paid	interest paid	remaining amortization period
300.00	8.50	-764.97	88,147.32	-6,852.68	-39,045.52	240.00
240.00	8.00	-737.30	77,151.48	-10,995.84	-33,242.16	180.00
180.00	9.00	-782.52	61,773.70	-15,377.78	-31,573.42	120.00

Table 3.4.14 Keystrokes to solve Table 2.4.21.

input keystrokes	comments	calculator display
(clear TVM, set END of period annuity payment)	see Table 3.4.1	0.00
8.5, ÷, 12, =, %I	enter periodic interest rate (monthly)	0.71
95000, PV	enter PV	95,000.00
300, N	enter N	300.00
CPT, PMT	compute PMT (END of period)	764.97
1, P1/P2	call up amortization worksheet and enter P1	1.00
60, I/P	enter P2 and calculate interest paid (after 5 years)	39,045.59
x←→y	calculate and display principal paid	6,852.36
60, BAL	calculate and display principal balance	88,147.64
RCL, N, –, 60, =, N	quit, recall N, subtract 60 and store to N	240.00
8, ÷, 12, =, %I	enter periodic interest rate (monthly)	0.67
88147.64, PV	enter PV	88,147.64
CPT, PMT	compute PMT (END of period)	737.30
1, P1/P2	call up amortization worksheet and enter P1	1.00
60, I/P	enter P2 and calculate interest paid (after 5 years)	33,242.23
x←→y	calculate and display principal paid	10,995.90

Continued, Table 3.4.14

60, BAL	calculate and display principal balance	77,151.74
RCL, N, –, 60, =, N	quit, recall N, subtract 60 and store to N	180.00
9, ÷, 12, =, %I	enter periodic interest rate (monthly)	0.75
77151.74, PV	enter PV	77,151.74
CPT, PMT	compute PMT (END of period)	782.52
1, P1/P2	call up amortization worksheet and enter P1	1.00
60,I/P	enter P2 and calculate interest paid (after 5 years)	31,573.51
x←→y	calculate and display principal paid	15,377.95
60, BAL	calculate and display principal balance	61,773.79

From Table 2.4.22 Status of $95,000 mortgage at the end of 25-year term amortized for 25 years at 8.4% interest compounded monthly. (P/Yr = C/Yr = 12).

per	I/Yr	monthly payment	principal balance	principal paid	interest paid
300.00	8.4	–758.57	4.99	–94,995.01	–132,575.99

Table 3.4.15 Keystrokes to solve Table 2.4.22.

input keystrokes	comments	calculator display
(clear TVM, set END of period annuity payment)	see Table 3.4.1	0.00
8.4 ÷, 12, =, %I	enter periodic interest rate (monthly)	0.70
95000, PV	enter PV	95,000.00
300, N	enter N	300.00
CPT, PMT	compute PMT (END of period)	758.57
1, P1/P2	call up amortization worksheet and enter P1	1.00
300, I/P	enter P2 and calculate interest paid (after 300 months)	132,572.32
x←→y	calculate and display principal paid	95,000.00
300, BAL	calculate and display principal balance	0.00

From Table 2.4.30 Monthly payment and interest saved for various interest compounding at 8% nominal interest rate, loan of $95,643.43 and 20-year amortization. Type II, Class B.4 financial problem. (P/Yr = 12).

C/Yr	per	pr	an	total cost	total interest	interest saved
12.00	240.00	95,643.43	–800.00	192,000.00	96,356.57	0.00
2.00	240.00	95,643.43	–792.27	190,144.80	94,501.37	1,855.20

Table 3.4.16 Keystrokes to solve Table 2.4.30.

input keystrokes	comments	calculator display
(clear TVM, set END of period annuity payment)	see Table 3.4.1	0.00
8, 2nd, EFF, 2, =	calculate EFF	8.16
2nd, APR, 12, =, ÷, 12, =, %I	calculate adjusted APR (periodic rate-yearly)	0.66
95643.43, PV	enter PV	95,643.43
240, N	enter N	240.00
CPT, PMT	compute PMT (END of period)	792.27
792.27, x, 12, x, 20, =	compute total cost	190,144.80
–, 95643.43, =	compute total interest	94,501.37
+/–, +, 96356.57, =	compute interest saved	1,855.20

Sample Calculations from Section 2.5, Planning for the Children's Education

From Table 2.5.16 Yearly payments at the beginning of each period when saving for Giuseppe's education fund is delayed. 8% interest rate compounded monthly with lump-sum payments of $0, $1,000, $5,000, and $10,000. Future value = $67,021.11. Type III, Class D.5 financial problem. (P/Yr = 1, C/Yr = 12).

year fund started	per	an(B) pr = 0.00	an(B) pr = –1,000.00	an(B) pr = –5,000.00	an(B) pr = –10,000.00
1999	12.00	–3,203.46	–3,079.03	–2,581.28	–1,959.10
2000	11.00	–3,658.75	–3,527.52	–3,002.60	–2,346.45

Table 3.4.17 Keystrokes to solve Table 2.5.16.

input keystrokes	comments	calculator display
(clear TVM, set BGN of period annuity payment)	see Table 3.4.1	0.00
67021.11, FV	enter FV	67,021.11
8, 2nd, EFF, 12, =	calculate EFF	8.30
2nd, APR, 1, =, ÷, 1, =, %I	calculate adjusted APR (periodic rate-yearly)	8.30
0, PV	enter PV	0.00

Continued, Table 3.4.17

12, N	enter N	12.00
CPT, PMT	compute PMT (BGN of period)	–3,203.46
11, N	enter N	11.00
CPT, PMT	compute PMT (BGN of period)	–3,658.75
1000, PV	enter PV	1,000.00
12, N	enter N	12.00
CPT, PMT	compute PMT (BGN of period)	–3,079.03
11, N	enter N	11.00
CPT, PMT	compute PMT (BGN of period)	–3,527.52
5000, PV	enter PV	5,000.00
12, N	enter N	12.00
CPT, PMT	compute PMT (BGN of period)	–2,581.28
11, N	enter N	11.00
CPT, PMT	compute PMT (BGN of period)	–3,002.60
10000, PV	enter PV	10,000.00
12, N	enter N	12.00
CPT, PMT	compute PMT (BGN of period)	–1,959.10
11, N	enter N	11.00
CPT, PMT	compute PMT (BGN of period)	–2,346.45

Sample Calculations from Section 2.6, Planning for Retirement

From Table 2.6.2 Total earnings at the end of age 65 for various starting salaries, ages and yearly increase. Type II, Class C.3 financial problem. (P/Yr = C/Yr = 1), use end-of-period payments.

	Age				Age			
	23	31	41	51	23	31	41	51
	per = 43	per = 35	per = 25	per = 15	per = 43	per = 35	per = 25	per = 15
Initial Salary	2% yearly increase				3% yearly increase			
40,000	2,686,379	1,999,779	1,281,212	691,737	3,419,356	2,418,483	1,458,371	743,957

Table 3.4.18 Keystrokes to solve Table 2.6.2.

input keystrokes	comments	calculator display
(clear TVM, set END of period annuity payment)	see Table 3.4.1	0.00
43, N	enter N	43.00
2, ÷, 1, =, %I	enter periodic interest rate (monthly)	2.00
40000, +/–, PMT	enter PMT	–40,000.00
CPT, FV	compute FV (END of period)	2,686,378.71
35, N	enter N	35.00
CPT, FV	compute FV (END of period)	1,999,779.11
25, N	enter N	25.00
CPT, FV	compute FV (END of period)	1,281,211.99
15, N	enter N	15.00
CPT, FV	compute FV (END of period)	691,736.68
3, ÷, 1, =, %I	enter periodic interest rate (monthly)	3.00
43, N	enter N	43.00
CPT, FV	compute FV (END of period)	3,419,355.69
35, N	enter N	35.00
CPT, FV	compute FV (END of period)	2,418,483.27
25, N	enter N	25.00
CPT, FV	compute FV (END of period)	1,458,370.57
15, N	enter N	15.00
CPT, FV	compute FV (END of period)	743,956.56

From Table 2.6.4 Future values at the end of age 65 for various monthly savings amounts. Interest is compounded monthly. Monthly payments are made at the beginning of each period. Period = 43 x 12.

Type II, Class C.3 financial problem. (P/Yr = C/Yr = 12).

savings amount	total savings	future value at 6% interest	future value at 8% interest	future value at 10% interest
150.00	77,400	365,194	675,716	1,295,878

Table 3.4.19 Keystrokes to solve Table 2.6.4.

input keystrokes	comments	calculator display
(clear TVM, set BGN of period annuity payment)	see Table 3.4.1	0.00
43, x, 12, =, N	enter N	516.00
6, ÷, 12, =, %I	enter periodic interest rate (monthly)	0.50
150, +/–, PMT	enter PMT	–150.00
CPT, FV	compute FV (BGN of period)	365,194.03
8, ÷, 12, =, %I	enter periodic interest rate (monthly)	0.67
CPT, FV	compute FV (BGN of period)	675,716.40
10, ÷, 12, =, %I	enter periodic interest rate (monthly)	0.83
CPT, FV	compute FV (BGN of period)	1,295,878.40
RCL, N, x, 150, =	calculate total savings	77,400.00

From Table 2.6.23 Monthly payments to finance $3,000 and $4,000 monthly retirement income for 20 years if $10,000 retirement fund has already been started. Money earns 4%, 6%, and 8% interest, compounded monthly at 3% inflation compounded monthly for various years to retirement. Use beginning-of-period payments. (P/Yr = C/Yr = 12).

Years to retirement	$3,000 monthly retirement income	$4,000 monthly retirement income
	4%	8%
40.00	–1,347	–385

Table 3.4.20 Keystrokes to solve Table 2.6.23.

input keystrokes	comments	calculator display
(clear TVM, set BGN of period annuity payment)	see Table 3.4.1	0.00
4, ÷, 12, =, %I	enter %I, periodic interest rate (monthly)	0.33
20, x, 12, =, N	enter N (retirement period in months)	240.00
3000, PMT	enter PMT	3,000.00
CPT, PV	compute PV	496,715.79

Continued, Table 3.4.20

0, PMT	set PMT register to 0 (zero)	0.00
3, ÷, 12, =, %I	enter periodic interest rate (monthly)	0.25
40, x, 12, =, N	enter N (period to retirement in months)	480.00
CPT, FV	compute FV	1,646,686.74
10000, PV	store lump-sum amount to PV	10,000.00
4, ÷, 12, =, %I	enter periodic interest rate (monthly)	0.33
CPT, PMT	compute PMT	–1,346.90
(clear TVM)	see Table 3.4.1	0.00
2nd, BGN	select BEGIN of period	0.00
8, ÷, 12, =, %I	enter %I, periodic interest rate (monthly)	0.67
20, x, 12, =, N	enter N (retirement period in months)	240.00
4000, PMT	enter PMT	4,000.00
CPT, PV	compute PV	481,405.28
0, PMT	set PMT register to 0 (zero)	0.00
3, ÷, 12, =, %I	enter periodic interest rate (monthly)	0.25
40, x, 12, =, N	enter N (period to retirement in months)	480.00
CPT, FV	compute FV	1,595,930.12
10000, PV	store lump-sum amount to PV	10,000.00
8, ÷, 12, =, %I	enter periodic interest rate (monthly)	0.67
CPT, PMT	compute PMT	–385.06

From Table 2.6.30 Monthly retirement payments in today's dollars for 20 years with existing $50,000 retirement fund. Money earns 4%, 6%, and 8% interest compounded monthly at 3% inflation compounded monthly for various years to retirement. Use beginning-of-period payments. (P/Yr = C/Yr = 12).

Years to retirement	–$1,000 monthly savings payment	–$2,000 monthly savings payment
	6%	8%
30	3,803	11,997

Table 3.4.21 Keystrokes to solve Table 2.6.30.

input keystrokes	comments	calculator display
(clear TVM, set BGN of period annuity payment)	see Table 3.4.1	0.00
6, ÷, 12, =, %I	enter periodic interest rate (monthly)	0.50
30, x, 12, =, N	enter N (period to retirement in months)	360.00
1000, +/–, PMT	enter PMT	–1,000.00
50000, PV	store lump–sum amount to PV	50,000.00
CPT, FV	compute FV	1,310,666.38
0, PMT	set PMT register to 0 (zero)	0.00
3, ÷, 12, =, %I	enter periodic interest rate (monthly)	0.25
CPT, PV	compute PV	533,476.01
20, x, 12, =, N	enter N (retirement period in months)	240.00
0, FV	set FV register to 0 (zero)	0.00
6, ÷, 12, =, %I	enter %I, periodic interest rate (monthly)	0.50
CPT, PMT	compute PMT	3,802.97
(clear TVM)	see Table 3.4.1	0.00
2nd, BGN	select BEGIN of period	0.00
8, ÷, 12, =, %I	enter periodic interest rate (monthly)	0.67
30, x, 12, =, N	enter N (period to retirement in months)	360.00
2000, +/–, PMT	enter PMT	–2,000.00
50000, PV	store lump–sum amount to PV	50,000.00
CPT, FV	compute FV	3,547,376.84
0, PMT	set PMT register to 0 (zero)	0.00
3, ÷, 12, =, %I	enter periodic interest rate (monthly)	0.25
CPT, PV	compute PV	1,443,876.55
20, x, 12, =, N	enter N (retirement period in months)	240.00
0, FV	set FV register to 0 (zero)	0.00
8, ÷, 12, =, %I	enter %I, periodic interest rate (monthly)	0.67
CPT, PMT	compute PMT	11,997.18

Sample Calculations from Section 2.7, Investment Decision Making

The Texas Instruments BA-35 Solar calculator does not have DCF functions.

In late 1998, Softbook Press, Inc., of Menlo Park marketed the first electronic book, called the E-book. A hand-held unit, it has a bright and touch-sensitive screen. It is used to download complete volumes of literature and nonfiction. It costs $299 US.

3.5
HEWLETT-PACKARD HP 10B

Excellence in engineering and manufacturing has produced this superior quality financial calculator. The design of the calculator is backed by extensive research on advanced materials, hostile effects of static electricity and harsh environment, and low power electronics. It comes with a soft, leather-feel pouch and an excellent manual. Some of its features include:

- powerful functions for one- and two-variable statistics
- applications to solve financial and business tasks using TVM, Amortization, DCF, Interest Conversion and Business Percentages;
- all common mathematical and log functions;
- special functions such as factorial, rounding, clearing entered digits, low battery symbol, self-test, adjusting display contrast and others

There are 10 business application registers, M (memory) register and 15 registers for storing numbers, cash flows and summary statistics.

The calculator has continuous memory. This means that if the calculator is turned off, the information in the registers is not affected. There is an automatic power down after about 10 minutes in which the calculator has not been used.

The period and comma can be interchanged.

US format:	1,000,000.00
International display:	1.000.000,00

In the 1967 movie Doctor Dolittle, *Rex Harrison initially backed out of playing the title role and was replaced by Christopher Plummer. Twentieth Century Fox, however, convinced Harrison to return and paid Plummer his fee of $300,000 US for doing nothing.*

Data Entry

Table 3.5.1 Important calculator set-up for TVM and DCF applications using HP 10B.

	key (s)	calculator display	function
1.	■, ./,	0.00 or 0,00	switch from US or International display
2.	■, CLEAR ALL	0.00	Clear all memory (Clear TVM)
3.	■, DISP, 2	0.00	Select 2 decimal places
4.	■, BEG/END	BEGIN or <blank> see note 3.	Toggles beginning– or end–of–period for annuity payments.

notes:

1. ■ = accesses second function of a calculator key
2. , (comma) = separator between calculator keystroke inputs in the order shown
3. If calculator is set for beginning-of-period for annuity payments, BEGIN is shown at the bottom line of the display area; otherwise, if set for end-of-period for annuity payments, nothing is shown in this area.
4. Clearing memory, (■, CLEAR ALL) does not reset the modes for P/Yr, Begin or End of annuity payments, and the display format.

Before doing any of the sample calculations we will discuss, you need to check the following settings:

1. First check that the decimal is set to 2 (to check, turn ON the calculator; if the display does not show 0.00, set to decimal 2, see Table 3.5.1).
2. Clear all memories (see Table 3.5.1).
3. Check that annuity payments are correctly set; end-of-period or beginning-of-period. If the calculator display shows "BEGIN", the annuity payments are set to beginning-of-period; see Table 3.5.1. Ignore this if there are no annuity payments.

One of the world's largest gold nuggets is the Evening Star. It weighs 16 kilograms and was found in Australia in 1992. It is expected to be sold for $360,000 US in a 1998 auction in Australia.

Table 3.5.2 Important calculator keys for TVM and DCF applications using HP 10B financial calculator.

key (s)	function
N	period (per), set or compute
I/YR	interest per year (I/Yr), set or compute
PV	present value (pr), set or compute
FV	future value (fu), set or compute
PMT	annuity payment value (an), set or compute
■, P/YR	Set Payment per Year
■, NOM%	calculate adjusted nominal interest rate, NOM %
■, EFF%	calculate effective interest rate, EFF %
■, AMORT	calculate amortization schedule
CFj	to access cash flow registers
■, Nj	to access cash flow frequency registers
■, NPV	calculate NPV
■, IRR/YR	calculate IRR/YR
+/–	change sign of displayed value

The Antonio Stradivari (1644-1737) family music shop in the Italian village of Cremona manufactured the much sought-after Stradivarius violin. The music shop has now started making electric guitars. The Strad that Jimi Hendrix allegedly played at Woodstock sold recently for $500,000 US.

Sample Calculations from Section 2.1, Basics of Time Value of Money Analysis

From Table 2.1.10 Type I, Class A.1 financial problem. (P/Yr = C/Yr = 12).

per	I/Yr	pr	fu
104.32	8.00	–5,000.00	10,000.00

Table 3.5.3 Keystrokes to solve Table 2.1.10.

input keystrokes	comments	calculator display
(clear TVM)	see Table 3.5.1	0.00
12, ■, P/YR	set P/YR = 12 (monthly payments)	12.00
8, I/YR	enter I/YR	8.00
5000, +/–, PV	enter PV	–5,000.00
10000, FV	enter FV	10,000.00
N	compute N (in months)	104.32

From Table 2.1.15 Type II, Class B.1 financial problem. (P/Yr = C/Yr = 12).

per E	per B	I/Yr	pr	an
61.02	60.52	8.00	5,000.00	–100.00

Table 3.5.4 Keystrokes to solve Table 2.1.15.

input keystrokes	comments	calculator display
(clear TVM, set END of period annuity payment)	see Table 3.5.1	0.00
12, ■, P/YR	set P/YR=12 (monthly payments)	12.00
5000, PV	enter PV	5,000.00
8, I/YR	enter I/YR	8.00
100, +/–, PMT	enter PMT	–100.00
N	compute N (END of period)	61.02
■, BEG/END	select BEGIN, see Table 3.5.1	61.02
N	compute N (BGN of period)	60.52

From Table 2.1.20 Type II, Class C.1 financial problem. (P/Yr = C/Yr = 12).

per E	per B	I/Yr	fu	an
76.88	76.48	8.00	20,000.00	-200.00

Table 3.5.5 Keystrokes to solve Table 2.1.20.

input keystrokes	comments	calculator display
(clear TVM, set END of period annuity payment)	see Table 3.5.1	0.00
12, ■, P/YR	set P/YR = 12 (monthly payments)	12.00
8, I/YR	enter I/YR	8.00
20000, FV	enter FV	20,000.00
200, +/–, PMT	enter PMT	–200.00
N	compute N (END of period)	76.88
■, BEG/END	select BEGIN, see Table 3.5.1	76.88
N	compute N (BGN of period)	76.48

From Table 2.1.25 Type III, Class D.1 financial problem. (P/Yr = C/Yr = 1).

per E	per B	I/Yr	pr	fu	an
24.18	23.57	8.00	–50,000.00	1,000,000.00	–10,000.00

Table 3.5.6 Keystrokes to solve Table 2.1.25.

input keystrokes	comments	calculator display
(clear TVM, set END of period annuity payment)	see Table 3.5.1	0.00
1, ■, P/YR	set P/YR = 1 (yearly payments)	1.00
50000, +/–, PV	enter PV	–50,000.00
10000, +/–, PMT	enter PMT	–10,000.00
8, I/YR	enter I/YR	8.00
1000000, FV	enter FV	1,000,000.00
N	compute N (END of period)	24.18
■, BEG/END	select BEGIN, see Table 3.5.1	24.18
N	compute N (BGN of period)	23.57

Sample Calculations from Section 2.2, Interest, Annuity, and Inflation

From Table 2.2.6 Future values of $1,000 for periods 1, 2, 3, 4, and 5 at 6% interest rate and annual compounding. (C/Yr = P/Yr = 1).

Annual interest rate	end of first year	end of second year	end of third year	end of fourth year	end of fifth year
6.00%	1,060.00	1,123.60	1,191.02	1,262.48	1,338.23

Table 3.5.7 Keystrokes to solve Table 2.2.6.

input keystrokes	comments	calculator display
(clear TVM)	see Table 3.5.1	0.00
1, N	enter N	1.00
1, ■, P/YR	set P/YR = 1 (yearly payments)	1.00
6, I/YR	enter I/YR	6.00
1000, +/–, PV	enter PV	–1,000.00
FV	compute FV	1,060.00
2, N	enter N	2.00
FV	compute FV	1,123.60
3, N	enter N	3.00
FV	compute FV	1,191.02
4, N	enter N	4.00
FV	compute FV	1,262.48
5, N	enter N	5.00
FV	compute FV	1,338.23

From Table 2.2.10 Effective rate of interest (Eff/Yr) and adjusted nominal interest rate ($(I/Yr)_{adj}$) for various compounding periods at (P/Yr) = 1.

(I/Yr)	C/Yr	(Eff/Yr)	(P/Yr)	$(I/Yr)_{adj}$
6.00	2.00	6.09	1.00	6.09

Table 3.5.8 Keystrokes to solve Table 2.2.10 for Eff/Yr and $(I/Yr)_{adj}$

input keystrokes	comments	calculator display
(clear TVM)	see Table 3.5.1	0.00
6, ■, NOM%, 2, ■, P/YR, ■, EFF%	enter Nominal % rate, enter compounding periods per year, calculate EFF %	6.09
1, ■, P/YR, ■, NOM%	enter payments per year, calculate adjusted NOM %	6.09

From Table 2.2.14 Effective rate of interest calculations for Banks A, B, C, and D.

Bank	(I/Yr)	(C/Yr)	(Eff/Yr)
B	8.35	4.00	8.62

Table 3.5.9 Keystrokes to solve Table 2.2.14 for Eff/Yr.

input keystrokes	comments	calculator display
(clear TVM, set END of period annuity payment)	see Table 3.5.1	0.00
8.35, ■, NOM%, 4, ■, P/YR, ■, EFF%	enter Nominal % rate, enter compounding periods per year, calculate EFF %	8.62

From Table 2.2.30 Future value of $0.01 annuity payment made at the end of each day for 30 days, at interest rate of 100% per day.

Type II, Class C.3 financial problem. (P/Yr = C/Yr = 365).

per	I/Yr	fu	an(E)
30.00	36,500.00	−10,737,418.23	0.01

Table 3.5.10 Keystrokes to solve Table 2.2.30.

input keystrokes	comments	calculator display
■, DISP, 2, ■, CLEAR ALL	set Decimal 2, clear TVM registers	0.00
■, BEG/END	if 'BEGIN' is shown in the calculator display, perform the indicated input keystrokes; see page 236 note 3	0.00
30, N	enter N	30.00
365, ■, P/YR	set P/YR = 365 (daily payments)	365.00
36500, I/YR	enter I/YR	36,500.00
.01, PMT	enter PMT	0.01
FV	compute FV	−10,737,418.23

Sample Calculations from Section 2.3, Four Methods to Implement a Savings Plan

From Table 2.3.8 Present value for various cash flows with I/Yr = 6%. Type I, Class A.3 financial problem, (P/Yr = 1, C/Yr = 12).

period (per)	cash flow amount (fu)	present value (pr)
2.00	-2,000.00	1,774.37

Table 3.5.11 Keystrokes to solve Table 2.3.8.

input keystrokes	comments	calculator display
(clear TVM)	see Table 3.5.1	0.00
6, ■, NOM%, 12, ■, P/YR, ■, EFF%	enter Nominal % rate, enter compounding periods per year, calculate EFF %	6.17
1, ■, P/YR, ■, NOM%	enter payments per year, calculate adjusted NOM %	6.17
2, N	enter N	2.00
2000, +/-, FV	enter FV	-2,000.00
PV	compute PV	1,774.37

Sample Calculations from Section 2.4, Loans and Mortgages

From Table 2.4.13 Amortization table – Distribution of $435.70 monthly payment ($22,537 loan at 6% interest rate and 5-year term with payments made at the end of each period). (P/Yr = C/Yr = 12).

per	principal	principal payment	interest payment	principal balance
1.00	22,537.00	-323.01	-112.69	22,213.99
2.00	22,213.99	-324.63	-111.07	21,889.36
3.00	21,889.36	-326.25	-109.45	21,563.11

Table 3.5.12 Keystrokes to solve Table 2.4.13.

input keystrokes	comments	calculator display
(clear TVM, set END of period annuity payment)	see Table 3.5.1	0.00
12, ■, P/YR	set P/YR = 12 (monthly payments)	12.00
6, I/YR	enter I/YR	6.00
22537, PV	enter PV	22,537.00
60, N	enter N	60.00
PMT	compute PMT (END of period)	–435.70
1, INPUT, 1, ■, AMORT	enter starting and ending amortization periods	PEr 1 – 1
=	calculate and display interest paid	Int, –112.69
=	calculate and display principal paid	Prin, –323.01
=	calculate and display principal balance	bAL, 22,213.99
■, AMORT	call next range of inputs	PEr 2 – 2
=	calculate and display interest paid	Int = –111.07
=	calculate and display principal paid	Prin, –324.63
=	calculate and display principal balance	bAL, 21,889.36
■, AMORT	call next range of inputs	PEr 3 – 3
=	calculate and display interest paid	Int, –109.45
=	calculate and display principal paid	Prin, –326.25
=	calculate and display principal balance	bAL, 21,563.11

From Table 2.4.14 Total principal and interest payments from periods 1–60 for \$22,537 loan at 6% interest rate, 5-year term and \$435.70 monthly payment. (P/Yr = C/Yr = 12).

per	principal	total principal payment	total interest payment	principal balance
1–60	22,537.00	–22,536.76	–3,605.24	0.24

Table 3.5.13 Keystrokes to solve Table 2.4.14.

input keystrokes	comments	calculator display
(clear TVM, set END of period annuity payment)	see Table 3.5.1	0.00
12, ■, P/YR	set P/YR = 12 (monthly payments)	12.00
6, I/YR	enter I/YR	6.00

Continued, Table 3.5.13

22537, PV	enter PV	22,537.00
60, N	enter N	60.00
PMT	compute PMT (END of period)	–435.70
1, INPUT, 60, ■, AMORT	enter starting and ending amortization periods	PEr 1 – 60
=	calculate and display interest paid	Int, –3,605.24
=	calculate and display principal paid	Prin, –22,536.76
=	calculate and display principal balance	bAL, 0.24

From Table 2.4.21 Summary of 5 consecutive 5-year term mortgages of $95,000 amortized over 25 years with different interest rates at renewal. (P/Yr = C/Yr = 12).

per	I/Yr	monthly payment	principal balance	principal paid	interest paid	remaining amortization period
300.00	8.50	–764.97	88,147.32	–6,852.68	–39,045.52	240.00
240.00	8.00	–737.30	77,151.48	–10,995.84	–33,242.16	180.00
180.00	9.00	–782.52	61,773.70	–15,377.78	–31,573.42	120.00

Table 3.5.14 Keystrokes to solve Table 2.4.21.

input keystrokes	comments	calculator display
(clear TVM, set END of period annuity payment)	see Table 3.5.1	0.00
12, ■, P/YR	set P/YR = 12 (monthly payments)	12.00
8.5, I/YR	enter I/YR	8.50
95000, PV	enter PV	95,000.00
300, N	enter N	300.00
PMT	compute PMT (END of period)	–764.97
1, INPUT, 60, ■, AMORT	enter starting and ending amortization periods	PEr 1 – 60
=	calculate and display interest paid	Int, –39,045.52
=	calculate and display principal paid	Prin, –6,852.68
=	calculate and display principal balance	bAL, 88,147.32
RCL, N, –, 60, =, N	quit, recall N, subtract 60 and store to N	240.00
8, I/YR	enter I/YR	8.00
88147.32, PV	enter PV	88,147.32

Continued, Table 3.5.14

PMT	compute PMT (END of period)	–737.30
1, INPUT, 60, ■, AMORT	enter starting and ending amortization periods	PEr 1 – 60
=	calculate and display interest paid	Int, –33,242.16
=	calculate and display principal paid	Prin, –10,995.84
=	calculate and display principal balance	bAL, 77,151.48
RCL, N, –, 60, =, N	quit, recall N, subtract 60 and store to N	180.00
9, I/YR	enter I/YR	9.00
77151.48, PV	enter PV	77,151.48
PMT	compute PMT (END of period)	–782.52
1, INPUT, 60, ■, AMORT	enter starting and ending amortization periods	PEr 1 – 60
=	calculate and display interest paid	Int, –31,573.42
=	calculate and display principal paid	Prin, –15,377.78
=	calculate and display principal balance	bAL, 61,773.70

From Table 2.4.22 Status of $95,000 mortgage at the end of 25-year term amortized for 25 years at 8.4% interest compounded monthly. (P/Yr = C/Yr = 12).

per	I/Yr	monthly payment	principal balance	principal paid	interest paid
300.00	8.4	–758.57	4.99	–94,995.01	–132,575.99

Table 3.5.15 Keystrokes to solve Table 2.4.22.

input keystrokes	comments	calculator display
(clear TVM, set END of period annuity payment)	see Table 3.5.1	0.00
12, ■, P/YR	set P/YR = 12 (monthly payments)	12.00
8.4, I/YR	enter I/YR	8.40
95000, PV	enter PV	95,000.00
300, N	enter N	300.00
PMT	compute PMT (END of period)	–758.57
1, INPUT, 300, ■, AMORT	enter starting and ending amortization periods	PEr 1 – 300
=	calculate and display interest paid	Int, –132,575.99
=	calculate and display principal paid	Prin, –94,995.01
=	calculate and display principal balance	bAL, 4.99

From Table 2.4.30 Monthly payment and interest saved for various interest compounding at 8% nominal interest rate, loan of $95,643.43 and 20-year amortization. Type II, Class B.4 financial problem. (P/Yr = 12).

C/Yr	per	pr	an	total cost	total interest	interest saved
12.00	240.00	95,643.43	−800.00	192,000.00	96,356.57	0.00
2.00	240.00	95,643.43	−792.27	190,144.80	94,501.37	1,855.20

Table 3.5.16 Keystrokes to solve Table 2.4.30.

input keystrokes	comments	calculator display
(clear TVM, set END of period annuity payment)	see Table 3.5.1	0.00
8, ■, NOM%, 2, ■, P/YR, ■, EFF%	enter Nominal % rate, enter compounding periods per year, calculate EFF %	8.16
12, ■, P/YR, ■, NOM%	enter payments per year, calculate adjusted NOM %	7.87
95643.43, PV	enter PV	95,643.43
240, N	enter N	240.00
PMT	compute PMT (END of period)	−792.27
792.27, x, 12, x, 20, =	compute total cost	190,144.80
−, 95643.43, =	compute total interest	94,501.37
+/−, +, 96356.57, =	compute interest saved	1,855.20

Sample Calculations from Section 2.5, Planning for the Children's Education

From Table 2.5.16 Yearly payments at the beginning of each period when saving for Giuseppe's education fund is delayed. 8% interest rate compounded monthly with lump-sum payments of $0, $1,000, $5,000, and $10,000. Future value = $67,021.11. Type III, Class D.5 financial problem. (P/Yr = 1, C/Yr = 12).

year fund started	per	an(B) pr = 0.00	an(B) pr = -1,000.00	an(B) pr = -5,000.00	an(B) pr = -10,000.00
1999	12.00	−3,203.46	−3,079.03	−2,581.28	−1,959.10
2000	11.00	−3,658.75	−3,527.52	−3,002.60	−2,346.45

Table 3.5.17 Keystrokes to solve Table 2.5.16.

input keystrokes	comments	calculator display
(clear TVM, set BEGIN of period annuity payment)	see Table 3.5.1	0.00
67021.11, FV	enter FV	67,021.11
8, ■, NOM%, 12, ■, P/YR, ■, EFF%	enter Nominal % rate, enter compounding periods per year, calculate EFF %	8.30
1, ■, P/YR, ■, NOM%	enter payments per year, calculate adjusted NOM %	8.30
0, PV	enter PV	0.00
12, N	enter N	12.00
PMT	compute PMT (BEGIN of period)	–3,203.46
11, N	enter N	11.00
PMT	compute PMT (BEGIN of period)	–3,658.75
1000, +/–, PV	enter PV	–1,000.00
12, N	enter N	12.00
PMT	compute PMT (BEGIN of period)	–3,079.03
11, N	enter N	11.00
PMT	compute PMT (BEGIN of period)	–3,527.52
5000, +/–, PV	enter PV	–5,000.00
12, N	enter N	12.00
PMT	compute PMT (BEGIN of period)	–2,581.28
11, N	enter N	11.00
PMT	compute PMT (BEGIN of period)	–3,002.60
10000, +/–, PV	enter PV	–10,000.00
12, N	enter N	12.00
PMT	compute PMT (BEGIN of period)	–1,959.10
11, N	enter N	11.00
PMT	compute PMT (BEGIN of period)	–2,346.45

Sample Calculations from Section 2.6, Planning for Retirement

From Table 2.6.2 Total earnings at the end of age 65 for various starting salaries, ages and yearly increase. Type II, Class C.3 financial problem. (P/Yr = C/Yr = 1), use end-of-period payments.

	Age				Age			
	23	31	41	51	23	31	41	51
	per = 43	per = 35	per = 25	per = 15	per = 43	per = 35	per = 25	per = 15
Initial Salary	2% yearly increase				3% yearly increase			
40,000	2,686,379	1,999,779	1,281,212	691,737	3,419,356	2,418,483	1,458,371	743,957

Table 3.5.18 Keystrokes to solve Table 2.6.2.

input keystrokes	comments	calculator display
(clear TVM, set END of period annuity payment)	see Table 3.5.1	0.00
43, N	enter N	43.00
1, ■, P/YR	set P/YR = 1 (yearly payments)	1.00
2, I/YR	enter I/YR	2.00
40000, +/–, PMT	enter PMT	–40,000.00
FV	compute FV (END of period)	2,686,378.71
35, N	enter N	35.00
FV	compute FV (END of period)	1,999,779.11
25, N	enter N	25.00
FV	compute FV (END of period)	1,281,211.99
15, N	enter N	15.00
FV	compute FV (END of period)	691,736.68
3, I/YR	enter I/YR	3.00
43, N	enter N	43.00
FV	compute FV (END of period)	3,419,355.69
35, N	enter N	35.00
FV	compute FV (END of period)	2,418,483.27
25, N	enter N	25.00
FV	compute FV (END of period)	1,458,370.57
15, N	enter N	15.00
FV	compute FV (END of period)	743,956.56

From Table 2.6.4 Future values at the end of age 65 for various monthly savings amounts. Interest is compounded monthly. Monthly payments are made at the beginning of each period. Period = 43 x 12.
Type II, Class C.3 financial problem. (P/Yr = C/Yr = 12).

savings amount	total savings	future value at 6% interest	future value at 8% interest	future value at 10% interest
150.00	77,400	365,194	675,716	1,295,878

Table 3.5.19 Keystrokes to solve Table 2.6.4.

input keystrokes	comments	calculator display
(clear TVM, set BGN of period annuity payment)	see Table 3.5.1	0.00
43, x, 12, =, N	enter N	516.00
12, ■, P/YR	set P/YR = 12 (monthly payments)	12.00
6, I/YR	enter I/YR	6.00
150, +/–, PMT	enter PMT	–150.00
FV	compute FV (BGN of period)	365,194.03
8, I/YR	enter I/YR	8.00
FV	compute FV (BGN of period)	675,716.40
10, I/YR	enter I/YR	10.00
FV	compute FV (BGN of period)	1,295,878.40
RCL, N, x, 150, =	calculate total savings	77,400.00

From Table 2.6.23 Monthly payments to finance $3,000 and $4,000 monthly retirement income for 20 years if $10,000 retirement fund has already been started. Money earns 4%, 6%, and 8% interest, compounded monthly at 3% inflation compounded monthly for various years to retirement. Use beginning-of-period payments. (P/Yr = C/Yr = 12).

Years to retirement	$3,000 monthly retirement income	$4,000 monthly retirement income
	4%	8%
40.00	–1,347	–385

Table 3.5.20 Keystrokes to solve Table 2.6.23.

input keystrokes	comments	calculator display
(clear TVM, set BEGIN of period annuity payment)	see Table 3.5.1	0.00
12, ■, P/YR	set P/YR = 12 (monthly payments)	12.00
4, I/YR	enter I/Y	4.00
20, x, 12, =, N	enter N (retirement period in months)	240.00
3000, PMT	enter PMT	3,000.00
PV	compute PV	–496,715.79
0, PMT	set PMT register to 0 (zero)	0.00
3, I/YR	store inflation rate to I/Y	3.00
40, x, 12, =, N	enter N (period to retirement in months)	480.00
FV	compute FV	1,646,686.74
10000, +/–, PV	store lump-sum amount to PV	–10,000.00
4, I/YR	store nominal rate to I/Y	4.00
PMT	compute PMT	–1,346.90
clear TVM	see Table 3.5.1 (BEGIN still selected)	0.00
8, I/YR	enter I/Y	8.00
20, x, 12, =, N	enter N (retirement period in months)	240.00
4000, PMT	enter PMT	4,000.00
PV	compute PV	–481,405.28
0, PMT	set PMT register to 0 (zero)	0.00
3, I/YR	store inflation rate to I/Y	3.00
40, x, 12, =, N	enter N (period to retirement in months)	480.00
FV	compute FV	1,595,930.12
10000, +/–, PV	store lump-sum amount to PV	–10,000.00
8, I/YR	store nominal rate to I/Y	8.00
PMT	compute PMT	–385.06

From Table 2.6.30 Monthly retirement payments in today's dollars for 20 years with existing $50,000 retirement fund. Money earns 4%, 6%, and 8% interest compounded monthly at 3% inflation compounded monthly for various years to retirement. Use beginning-of-period payments. (P/Yr = C/Yr = 12).

Years to retirement	–$1,000 monthly savings payment	–$2,000 monthly savings payment
	6%	8%
30	3,803	11,997

Table 3.5.21 Keystrokes to solve Table 2.6.30.

input keystrokes	comments	calculator display
(clear TVM, set BEGIN of period annuity payment)	see Table 3.5.1	0.00
12, ■, P/YR	set P/YR = 12 (monthly payments)	12.00
6, I/YR	store nominal rate to I/Y	6.00
30, x, 12, =, N	enter N (period to retirement in months)	360.00
1000, +/–, PMT	enter PMT	–1,000.00
50000, +/–, PV	store lump-sum amount to PV	–50,000.00
FV	compute FV	1,310,666.38
0, PMT	set PMT register to 0 (zero)	0.00
3, I/YR	store inflation rate to I/Y	3.00
PV	compute PV	–533,476.01
20, x, 12, =, N	enter N (retirement period in months)	240.00
0, FV	set FV register to 0 (zero)	0.00
6, I/YR	enter I/Y	6.00
PMT	compute PMT	3,802.97
clear TVM	see Table 3.5.1 (BEGIN still selected)	0.00
8, I/YR	store nominal rate to I/Y	8.00
30, x, 12, =, N	enter N (period to retirement in months)	360.00
2000, +/–, PMT	enter PMT	–2,000.00
50000, +/–, PV	store lump-sum amount to PV	–50,000.00
FV	compute FV	3,547,376.84
0, PMT	set PMT register to 0 (zero)	0.00
3, I/YR	store inflation rate to I/Y	3.00
PV	compute PV	–1,443,876.54

Continued, Table 3.5.21

20, x, 12, =, N	enter N (retirement period in months)	240.00
0, FV	set FV register to 0 (zero)	0.00
8, I/YR	enter I/Y	8.00
PMT	compute PMT	11,997.18

Sample Calculations from Section 2.7, Investment Decision Making

In this subsection, DCF analysis will be performed.

From Table 2.7.2 Financial calculator data entry values for Example 1. I/Yr = 20%, P/Yr = C/Yr = 12.

cash flow	frequency
CF0 = −10,000.00	
CF1 = −500.00	N1 = 1.00
CF2 = −3,000.00	N2 = 1.00
CF3 = 0.00	N3 = 15.00
CF4 = 20,000.00	N4 = 1.00

NPV = $1,458.80, IRR = 27.22% (yearly rate, periodic interest rate or monthly rate is 2.27%).

Table 3.5.22 Keystrokes to solve Table 2.7.2.

input keystrokes	comments	calculator display
■, CLEAR ALL	clear DCF memory	0.00
12, ■, P/YR	set P/YR = 12 (monthly payments)	12.00
10000, +/−, CFj	enter amount for cash flow CF0	CF0, −10,000.00
500, +/−, CFj	enter amount for cash flow C01	CF1, −500.00
1, ■, Nj	accept frequency of cash flow group C01 = 1	n1, 1.00
3000, +/−, CFj	enter amount for cash flow C02	CF2, −3,000.00
1, ■, Nj	accept frequency of cash flow group C02 = 1	n2, 1.00
0, CFj	accept amount for cash flow C03 = 0	CF3, 0.00
15, ■, Nj	enter frequency of cash flow group C03	n3, 15.00
20000, CFj	enter amount for cash flow C04	CF4, 20,000.00
1, ■, Nj	accept frequency of cash flow group C04 = 1	n4, 1.00
20, I/YR	store nominal rate to I/Y	20.00

Continued, Table 3.5.22

■, NPV	compute NPV	1,458.80
■, IRR/YR	compute IRR/YR	27.22
÷, 12, =	compute monthly rate for IRR	2.27

From Table 2.7.3 Financial calculator data entry values for Example 2. I/Yr = 10%, P/Yr = C/Yr = 12.

cash flow	frequency
CF0 = 35,000	
CF1 = 35,000	N1 = 23
CF2 = 35,000 x 1.15 = 40,250	N2 = 24
CF3 = 40,250 x 1.15 = 46,288	N3 = 24
CF4 = 46,288 x 1.15 = 53,231	N4 = 24
CF5 = 53,231 x 1.15 = 61,216	N5 = 24

NPV = $3,407,611.54

Table 3.5.23 Keystrokes to solve Table 2.7.3.

input keystrokes	comments	calculator display
■, CLEAR ALL	clear DCF memory	0.00
12, ■, P/YR	set P/YR = 12 (monthly payments)	12.00
35000, CFj	enter amount for cash flow CF0	CF0, 35,000.00
35000, CFj	enter amount for cash flow C01	CF1, 35,000.00
23, ■, Nj	enter frequency of cash flow group C01	n1, 23.00
40250, CFj	enter amount for cash flow C02	CF2, 40,250.00
24, ■, Nj	enter frequency of cash flow group C02	n2, 24.00
46288, CFj	enter amount for cash flow C03	CF3, 46,288.00
24, ■, Nj	enter frequency of cash flow group C03	n3, 24.00
53231, CFj	enter amount for cash flow C04	CF4, 53,231.00
24, ■, Nj	enter frequency of cash flow group C04	n4, 24.00
61216, CFj	enter amount for cash flow C05	CF5, 61,216.00
24, ■, Nj	enter frequency of cash flow group C05	n5, 24.00
10, I/YR	store nominal rate to I/Y	10.00
■, NPV	compute NPV	3,407,611.54

In 1963, the most costly painting was one by Rembrandt, "Aristotle Contemplating the Bust of Homer" at $2.3 million US. In 1998, Van Gogh's "Portrait du Dr Gachet" set a new record at $75 million US.

3.6
SHARP EL-733A, SHARP EL-735, AND CASIO FC-100

The following three calculators have similar keystrokes for TVM and DCF applications. The two models from Sharp; EL-733A and EL-735 and the CASIO FC-100 can perform TVM functions, including amortization calculations and DCF applications.

SHARP EL-733A

The Business/Financial Calculator Model EL-733A from Sharp comes with a plastic folding case and a manual.

The calculator has three operating modes: Normal, Financial and Statistical calculation mode. Aside from the business application memory or registers, there is one independent memory available, the M register.

The calculator has mathematical, logarithmic, exponential, one- and two-variable statistical and financial functions. For numbers 1,000 and over, digits are grouped by an apostrophe instead of a comma (US format) or period (European format). For example, the US format of 1,000,000.00 or its equivalent European format of 1.000.000,00 will be displayed by EL-733A as 1'000'000.00.

The Automatic Power Off feature will turn off the calculator after 9 to 13 minutes in which no calculation is performed. There is a RESET switch at the back of the calculator, which is used for the following cases:

- after battery replacement;
- to clear all memory contents;
- when an abnormal condition occurs and none of the keys are operative

There is a feature that saves the memory contents when the calculator is turned off, providing the mode has not been changed. This feature is lost when the batteries are replaced or discharged.

As of December 1997, the most expensive movie ever made is Titanic *at about $200 million US, surpassing Universal's* Waterworld, *which cost $175 million US.*

SHARP EL-735

The Business/Financial Calculator Model EL-735 from Sharp comes with a plastic folding case and a manual.

It has advanced functions compared to the Model EL-733A. These functions include DCF, days and date functions, bond calculations, and the financial database. The financial database allows storage of stock prices, exchange rates, and other financial information.

The manual describes the calculator as operating in two modes, financial and statistical. Arithmetic, logarithmic, and exponential functions are performed in the financial mode. Just like the EL-733A, the EL-735 model has one- and two-variable statistical and financial functions. For numbers 1,000 and over, digits are grouped by an apostrophe instead of a comma (US format) or period (European format).

The DCF memory shares the same location as the financial database. If the database is not used, up to 70 DCF memories are available. Aside from the business application memory or registers and registers for the financial database, there is also one independent memory available, the M register.

The Automatic Power Off feature will turn off the calculator after several minutes in which no calculation is performed. There is a RESET switch at the back of the calculator, which is used to delete all stored data, including memory and register contents.

There is a memory safeguard feature that saves the memory contents when the calculator is turned off. This feature is lost when the batteries are replaced or discharged.

CASIO FC-100

The CASIO Electronic Calculator FC-100 comes with a plastic folding case and a manual.

Although there are several MODE keys available to select the calculator display, number of days, financial, linear regression, standard deviation, and cash flow, there are basically two operating modes; the financial and statistical. Mathematical, logarithmic, and exponential functions are performed in the financial mode.

The calculator can perform day and date calculations. Its statistical functions include one-variable and two-variable functions. For numbers equal to or greater than 1,000, digits are not grouped. Thus, commas (US format), periods (European format) or apostrophes (Sharp format) are not used.

Aside from the business application memories or registers, there is one independent memory available, the M register, and there are 6 independent constant memories.

The Automatic Power Off feature will turn off the calculator after approximately 6 minutes in which no calculation is performed. The contents of the calculator memories are not erased when the power is turned OFF. This feature is lost, however, when the batteries are replaced or discharged.

Africa's most populous country is Nigeria. It earns $10 billion US annually from its oil.

Data Entry

Table 3.6.1 Important calculator set-up for TVM and DCF applications using SHARP EL–733A, EL–735 and CASIO FC–100.

	SHARP EL-733A	SHARP EL-735	CASIO FC-100	calculator display	function
1.	2nd F, TAB, 2	2nd F, TAB, 2	MODE, 5, 2	0.00	Select 2 decimal places
2.	2nd F, MODE (toggle)	2nd F, STAT (toggle)	MODE, 1 see note 6	0.00	select financial mode
3.	see note 2	see note 2	MODE, 4 see note 6	0.00	select cash flow mode
4.	2nd F, CA	2nd F, CA see note 5	SHIFT, FC	0.00	Clear all TVM and DCF memories
5.	BGN	2nd F, BGN/END	BGN	BGN or <blank> see note 4	Toggles beginning– or end–of–period for annuity payments.

notes:

1. For Sharp EL–733A and EL–735, "2nd F" accesses second function of a calculator key. For Casio FC–100, "SHIFT" accesses second function of a calculator key.
2. No special key required to enable cash flow analysis (DCF).
3. , (comma) = separator between calculator keystroke inputs in the order shown
4. If calculator is set for beginning–of–period for annuity payments, BGN is shown at the calculator display area; otherwise, if set for end–of–period for annuity payments, nothing is shown in the same area
5. For SHARP EL–735; 2nd F, CA clears TVM memories. DCF memories can be cleared only if there is cash flow data. If there is no data, the following keystrokes will not be applicable. To clear DCF memories, press RCL, CFi and then press V as many times as needed until the calculator display shows "CFi SEARCH". Then press: 2nd F, CA. Wait for calculator display "CA CFi? →ENT", then press ENT.
6. For CASIO FC–100, use financial mode for TVM calculations and cash flow mode for DCF calculations. Once a mode is set, it remains active until a different mode is selected.

Before doing any of the sample calculations we will discuss, you need to check the following settings:

1. Check that the calculator is selected for financial mode.

2. Check that the decimal is set to 2. To check for the SHARP models, turn ON the calculator; if the display does not show 0.00, set to decimal 2. (See Table 3.6.1) For CASIO model, press the equal sign (=), if set to decimal 2, the display will show 0.00.
3. Clear memory; see Table 3.6.1.
4. Check that annuity payments are correctly set; end-of-period or beginning-of-period. If the calculator display shows "BGN", the annuity payments are set to beginning-of-period; see Table 3.6.1. Ignore this if there are no annuity payments.

Table 3.6.2 Important calculator keys for TVM and DCF applications using SHARP EL-733A, EL-735 and CASIO FC-100.

SHARP EL-733A	SHARP EL-735	CASIO FC-100	function
n	n	n	period (per)
i	i	i%	periodic interest
PV	PV	PV	present value (pr)
FV	FV	FV	future value (fu)
PMT	PMT	PMT	annuity payment value (an)
COMP, xyz	COMP, xyz	COMP, xyz	compute TVM parameter xyz = n, i or i%, PV, FV or PMT
x, 2nd F, APR	x, 2nd F, APR	x, SHIFT, APR	convert x to adjusted nominal interest rate, NOM %
y, 2nd F, EFF	y, 2nd F, EFF	y, EFF	convert y to effective interest rate, EFF %
AMRT	AMRT	AMRT	calculate amortization schedule
CFi	CFi	CFj	to access cash flow registers
2nd F, Ni	2nd F, Ni	Nj	to access cash flow frequency registers
NPV	NPV	NPV	calculate NPV
IRR	IRR	IRR	calculate IRR
not applicable	V	not applicable	search down (only for Sharp EL-735)
+/-	+/-	+/-	change sign of displayed value

With the electric car becoming a reality, now comes the electric motorcycle. It is a cross between a motorcycle and a scooter. Called the Lectra, it weighs 340 pounds, runs up to 30 miles on a single charge, with a top speed of 45 mph. With zero emissions and almost no maintenance, it costs $3,995 US in 1998. The Lectra is manufactured and marketed by EMB, Inc. of Sebastopol, California.

Sample Calculations from Section 2.1, Basics of Time Value of Money Analysis

Note that except for Tables 3.6.22A and B and 3.6.23A and B, the column labeled "calculator display"' in the keystroke tables shows the US format (e.g., 1,234.45; 231,984.56). The three calculators use different formats to display the values. Refer to the discussion at the beginning of this section.

From Table 2.1.10 Type I, Class A.1 financial problem. (P/Yr = C/Yr = 12).

per	I/Yr	pr	fu
104.32	8.00	–5,000.00	10,000.00

Table 3.6.3 Keystrokes to solve Table 2.1.10.

SHARP EL-733A	SHARP EL-735	CASIO FC-100	comments	calculator display
(clear TVM)	(clear TVM)	(clear TVM)	see Table 3.6.1	0.00
8, ÷, 12, =, i	8, ÷, 12, =, i	8, ÷, 12, =, i%	enter I%	0.67
5000, +/–, PV	5000, +/–, PV	5000, +/–, PV	enter PV	-5,000.00
10000, FV	10000, FV	10000, FV	enter FV	10,000.00
COMP, n	COMP, n	COMP, n	compute N (in months)	104.32

From Table 2.1.15 Type II, Class B.1 financial problem. (P/Yr = C/Yr = 12).

per E	per B	I/Yr	pr	an
61.02	60.52	8.00	5,000.00	-100.00

Table 3.6.4 Keystrokes to solve Table 2.1.15.

SHARP EL-733A	SHARP EL-735	CASIO FC-100	comments	calculator display
(clear TVM, select END)	(clear TVM, select END)	(clear TVM, select END)	see Table 3.6.1	0.00
5000, PV	5000, PV	5000, PV	enter PV	5,000.00
8, ÷, 12, =, i	8, ÷, 12, =, i	8, ÷, 12, =, i%	enter I%	0.67
100, +/–, PMT	100, +/–, PMT	100, +/–, PMT	enter PMT	-100.00

Continued, Table 3.6.4

COMP, n	COMP, n	COMP, n	compute N (END of period)	61.02
BGN	2nd F, BGN/END	BGN	select BEGIN, see Table 3.6.1	61.02
COMP, n	COMP, n	COMP, n	compute N (BGN of period)	60.52

From Table 2.1.20 Type II, Class C.1 financial problem. (P/Yr = C/Yr = 12).

per E	per B	I/Yr	fu	an
76.88	76.48	8.00	20,000.00	-200.00

Table 3.6.5 Keystrokes to solve Table 2.1.20.

SHARP EL-733A	SHARP EL-735	CASIO FC-100	comments	calculator display
(clear TVM, select END)	(clear TVM, select END)	(clear TVM, select END)	see Table 3.6.1	0.00
8, ÷, 12, =, i	8, ÷, 12, =, i	8, ÷, 12, =, i%	enter I%	0.67
20000, FV	20000, FV	20000, FV	enter FV	20,000.00
200, +/–, PMT	200, +/–, PMT	200, +/–, PMT	enter PMT	-200.00
COMP, n	COMP, n	COMP, n	compute N (END of period)	76.88
BGN	2nd F, BGN/END	BGN	select BEGIN, see Table 3.6.1	76.88
COMP, n	COMP, n	COMP, n	compute N (BGN of period)	76.48

From Table 2.1.25 Type III, Class D.1 financial problem. (P/Yr = C/Yr = 1).

per E	per B	I/Yr	pr	fu	an
24.18	23.57	8.00	-50,000.00	1,000,000.00	-10,000.00

Table 3.6.6 Keystrokes to solve Table 2.1.25.

SHARP EL-733A	SHARP EL-735	CASIO FC-100	comments	calculator display
(clear TVM, select END)	(clear TVM, select END)	(clear TVM, select END)	see Table 3.6.1	0.00
50000, +/–, PV	50000, +/–, PV	50000, +/–, PV	enter PV	-50,000.00

Continued, Table 3.6.6

10000, +/–, PMT	10000, +/–, PMT	10000, +/–, PMT	enter PMT	–10,000.00
8, ÷, 1, =, i	8, ÷, 1, =, i	8, ÷, 1, =, i%	enter I%	8.00
1000000, FV	1000000, FV	1000000, FV	enter FV	1,000,000.00
COMP, n	COMP, n	COMP, n	compute N (END of period)	24.18
BGN	2nd F, BGN/END	BGN	select BEGIN, see Table 3.6.1	24.18
COMP, n	COMP, n	COMP, n	compute N (BGN of period)	23.57

Sample Calculations from Section 2.2, Interest, Annuity, and Inflation

From Table 2.2.6 Future values of $1,000 for periods 1, 2, 3, 4, and 5 at 6% interest rate and annual compounding. (C/Yr = P/Yr = 1).

Annual interest rate	end of first year	end of second year	end of third year	end of fourth year	end of fifth year
6.00%	1,060.00	1,123.60	1,191.02	1,262.48	1,338.23

Table 3.6.7 Keystrokes to solve Table 2.2.6.

SHARP EL-733A	SHARP EL-735	CASIO FC-100	comments	calculator display
(clear TVM)	(clear TVM)	(clear TVM)	see Table 3.6.1	0.00
1, n	1, n	1, n	enter N	1.00
6, ÷, 1, =, i	6, ÷, 1, =, i	6, ÷, 1, =, i%	enter I%	6.00
1000, +/–, PV	1000, +/–, PV	1000, +/–, PV	enter PV	–1,000.00
COMP, FV	COMP, FV	COMP, FV	compute FV	1,060.00
2, n	2, n	2, n	enter N	2.00
COMP, FV	COMP, FV	COMP, FV	compute FV	1,123.60
3, n	3, n	3, n	enter N	3.00
COMP, FV	COMP, FV	COMP, FV	compute FV	1,191.02
4, n	4, n	4, n	enter N	4.00
COMP, FV	COMP, FV	COMP, FV	compute FV	1,262.48
5, n	5, n	5, n	enter N	5.00
COMP, FV	COMP, FV	COMP, FV	compute FV	1,338.23

From Table 2.2.10 Effective rate of interest (Eff/Yr) and adjusted nominal interest rate ($(I/Yr)_{adj}$) for various compounding periods at (P/Yr) = 1.

(I/Yr)	C/Yr	(Eff/Yr)	(P/Yr)	$(I/Yr)_{adj}$
6.00	2.00	6.09	1.00	6.09

Table 3.6.8 Keystrokes to solve Table 2.2.10 for (Eff/Yr) and $(I/Yr)_{adj}$

SHARP EL-733A	SHARP EL-735	CASIO FC-100	comments	calculator display
2, 2nd F, EFF, 6, =, X→M	2, 2nd F, EFF, 6, =, X→M	2, EFF, 6, =, Min	enter compounding periods per year, enter Nominal % rate, calculate EFF %	6.09
1, 2nd F, APR, RM, =	1, 2nd F, APR, RM, =	1, SHIFT, APR, MR, =	enter payments per year, calculate adjusted NOM %	6.09

From Table 2.2.14 Effective rate of interest calculations for Banks A, B, C, and D.

Bank	(I/Yr)	(C/Yr)	(Eff/Yr)
B	8.35	4.00	8.62

Table 3.6.9 Keystrokes to solve Table 2.2.14 for Eff/Yr.

SHARP EL-733A	SHARP EL-735	CASIO FC-100	comments	calculator display
4, 2nd F, EFF, 8.35, =	4, 2nd F, EFF, 8.35, =	4, EFF, 8.35, =	enter compounding periods per year, enter Nominal % rate, calculate EFF %	8.62

From Table 2.2.30 Future value of $0.01 annuity payment made at the end of each day for 30 days, at interest rate of 100% per day.

Type II, Class C.3 financial problem. (P/Yr = C/Yr = 365).

per	I/Yr	fu	an(E)
30.00	36,500.00	−10,737,418.23	0.01

Table 3.6.10 Keystrokes to solve Table 2.2.30.

SHARP EL-733A	SHARP EL-735	CASIO FC-100	comments	calculator display
(clear TVM, select END)	(clear TVM, select END)	(clear TVM, select END)	see Table 3.6.1	0.00
30, n	30, n	30, n	enter N	30.00
36500, ÷, 365, =, i	36500, ÷, 365, =, i	36500, ÷, 365, =, i%	enter I%	100.00
.01, PMT	.01, PMT	.01, PMT	enter PMT	0.01
COMP, FV	COMP, FV	COMP, FV	compute FV	–10,737,418.23

Sample Calculations from Section 2.3, Four Methods to Implement a Savings Plan

From Table 2.3.8 Present value for various cash flows with I/Yr = 6%. Type I, Class A.3 financial problem, (P/Yr = 1, C/Yr = 12).

period (per)	cash flow amount (fu)	present value (pr)
2.00	–2,000.00	1,774.37

Table 3.6.11 Keystrokes to solve Table 2.3.8.

SHARP EL-733A	SHARP EL-735	CASIO FC-100	comments	calculator display
(clear TVM)	(clear TVM)	(clear TVM)	see Table 3.6.1	0.00
12, 2nd F, EFF, 6, =, X→M	12, 2nd F, EFF, 6, =, X→M	12, EFF, 6, =, Min	enter compounding periods per year, enter Nominal % rate, calculate EFF %	6.17
1, 2nd F, APR, RM, =, i	1, 2nd F, APR, RM, =, i	1, SHIFT, APR, MR, =, i%	enter payments per year, calculate adjusted NOM %	6.17
2, n	2, n	2, n	enter N	2.00
2000, +/–, FV	2000, +/–, FV	2000, +/–, FV	enter FV	–2,000.00
COMP, PV	COMP, PV	COMP, PV	compute PV	1,774.37

Sample Calculations from Section 2.4, Loans and Mortgages

From Table 2.4.13 Amortization table – Distribution of $435.70 monthly payment ($22,537 loan at 6% interest rate and 5-year term with payments made at the end of each period). (P/Yr = C/Yr = 12).

per	principal	principal payment	interest payment	principal balance
1.00	22,537.00	−323.01	−112.69	22,213.99
2.00	22,213.99	−324.63	−111.07	21,889.36
3.00	21,889.36	−326.25	−109.45	21,563.11

Table 3.6.12 Keystrokes to solve Table 2.4.13.

SHARP EL-733A	SHARP EL-735	CASIO FC-100	comments	calculator display
(clear TVM, select END)	(clear TVM, select END)	(clear TVM, select END)	see Table 3.6.1	0.00
6, ÷, 12, =, i	6, ÷, 12, =, i	6, ÷, 12, =, i%	enter I%	0.50
22537, PV	22537, PV	22537, PV	enter PV	22,537.00
60, n	60, n	60, n	enter N	60.00
COMP, PMT	COMP, PMT	COMP, PMT	compute PMT (END of period)	−435.70
1, AMRT	1, AMRT	1, AMRT	calculate and display principal paid for first payment	−323.02
AMRT	AMRT	AMRT	calculate and display interest paid for first payment	−112.69
AMRT	AMRT	AMRT	calculate and display principal balance after first payment	22,213.98
2, AMRT	2, AMRT	2, AMRT	calculate and display principal paid for second payment	−324.63
AMRT	AMRT	AMRT	calculate and display interest paid for second payment	−111.07
AMRT	AMRT	AMRT	calculate and display principal balance after second payment	21,889.35
3, AMRT	3, AMRT	3, AMRT	calculate and display principal paid for third payment	−326.26
AMRT	AMRT	AMRT	calculate and display interest paid for third payment	−109.45
AMRT	AMRT	AMRT	calculate and display principal balance after third payment	21,563.09

From Table 2.4.14 Total principal and interest payments from periods 1–60 for $22,537 loan at 6% interest rate, 5-year term and $435.70 monthly payment. (P/Yr = C/Yr = 12).

per	principal	total principal payment	total interest payment	principal balance
1–60	22,537.00	–22,536.76	–3,605.24	0.24

Table 3.6.13 Keystrokes to solve Table 2.4.14.

SHARP EL-733A	SHARP EL-735	CASIO FC-100	comments	calculator display
(clear TVM, select END)	(clear TVM, select END)	(clear TVM, select END)	see Table 3.6.1	0.00
6, ÷, 12, =, i	6, ÷, 12, =, i	6, ÷, 12, =, i%	enter I%	0.50
22537, PV	22537, PV	22537, PV	enter PV	22,537.00
60, n	60, n	60, n	enter N	60.00
COMP, PMT	COMP, PMT	COMP, PMT	compute PMT (END of period)	–435.70
1, P1/P2, 60, P1/P2, ACC	1, P1/P2, 60, P1/P2, ACC	60, ACC	calculate and display principal paid after 60th payment	–22,537.00
ACC	ACC	ACC	calculate and display interest paid for 60th payment	–3,605.20
60, AMRT, AMRT, AMRT	60, AMRT, AMRT, AMRT	60, AMRT, AMRT, AMRT	calculate and display principal balance after 60th payment	0.00

From Table 2.4.21 Summary of 5 consecutive 5-year term mortgages of $95,000 amortized over 25 years with different interest rates at renewal. (P/Yr = C/Yr = 12).

per	I/Yr	monthly payment	principal balance	principal paid	interest paid	remaining amortization period
300.00	8.50	–764.97	88,147.32	–6,852.68	–39,045.52	240.00
240.00	8.00	–737.30	77,151.48	–10,995.84	–33,242.16	180.00
180.00	9.00	–782.52	61,773.70	–15,377.78	–31,573.42	120.00

Table 3.6.14 Keystrokes to solve Table 2.4.21.

SHARP EL-733A	SHARP EL-735	CASIO FC-100	comments	calculator display
(clear TVM, select END)	(clear TVM, select END)	(clear TVM, select END)	see Table 3.6.1	0.00
8.5, ÷, 12, =, i	8.5, ÷, 12, =, i	8.5, ÷, 12, =, i%	enter I%	0.71
95000, PV	95000, PV	95000, PV	enter PV	95,000.00
300, n	300, n	300, n	enter N	300.00
COMP, PMT	COMP, PMT	COMP, PMT	compute PMT (END of period)	–764.97
1, P1/P2, 60, P1/P2, ACC	1, P1/P2, 60, P1/P2, ACC	60, ACC	calculate and display principal paid after 60th payment	–6,852.36
ACC	ACC	ACC	calculate and display interest paid for 60th payment	–39,045.59
60, AMRT, AMRT, AMRT	60, AMRT, AMRT, AMRT	60, AMRT, AMRT, AMRT	calculate and display principal balance after 60th payment	88,147.64
2nd F, RCL, n, –, 60, =, n	RCL, n, –, 60, =, n	RCL, n, –, 60, =, n	recall N, subtract 60 and store to N	240.00
8, ÷, 12, =, i	8, ÷, 12, =, i	8, ÷, 12, =, i%	enter I%	0.67
88147.64, PV	88147.64, PV	88147.64, PV	enter PV	88,147.64
COMP, PMT	COMP, PMT	COMP, PMT	compute PMT (END of period)	–737.30
1, P1/P2, 60, P1/P2, ACC	1, P1/P2, 60, P1/P2, ACC	60, ACC	calculate and display principal paid after 60th payment	–10,995.90
ACC	ACC	ACC	calculate and display interest paid after 60th payment	–33,242.23
60, AMRT, AMRT, AMRT	60, AMRT, AMRT, AMRT	60, AMRT, AMRT, AMRT	calculate and display principal balance after 60th payment	77,151.74
2nd F, RCL, n, –, 60, =, n	RCL, n, –, 60, =, n	RCL, N, –, 60, =, n	recall N, subtract 60 and store to N	180.00
9, ÷, 12, =, i	9, ÷, 12, =, i	9, ÷, 12, =, i%	enter I%	0.75
77151.74, PV	77151.74, PV	77151.74, PV	enter PV	77,151.74
COMP, PMT	COMP, PMT	COMP, PMT	compute PMT (END of period)	–782.52
1, P1/P2, 60, P1/P2, ACC	1, P1/P2, 60, P1/P2, ACC	60, ACC	calculate and display principal paid after 60th payment	–15,377.95
ACC	ACC	ACC	calculate and display interest paid after 60th payment	–31,573.51
60, AMRT, AMRT, AMRT	60, AMRT, AMRT, AMRT	60, AMRT, AMRT, AMRT	calculate and display principal balance after 60th payment	61,773.79

From Table 2.4.22 Status of $95,000 mortgage at the end of 25-year term amortized for 25 years at 8.4% interest compounded monthly. (P/Yr = C/Yr = 12).

per	I/Yr	monthly payment	principal balance	principal paid	interest paid
300.00	8.4	−758.57	4.99	−94,995.01	−132,575.99

Table 3.6.15 Keystrokes to solve Table 2.4.22.

SHARP EL-733A	SHARP EL-735	CASIO FC-100	comments	calculator display
(clear TVM, select END)	(clear TVM, select END)	(clear TVM, select END)	see Table 3.6.1	0.00
8.4, ÷, 12, =, i	8.4, ÷, 12, =, i	8.4, ÷, 12, =, i%	enter I%	0.70
95000, PV	95000, PV	95000, PV	enter PV	95,000.00
300, n	300, n	300, n	enter N	300.00
COMP, PMT	COMP, PMT	COMP, PMT	compute PMT (END of period)	−758.57
1, P1/P2, 300, P1/P2, ACC	1, P1/P2, 300, P1/P2, ACC	300, ACC	calculate and display principal paid after 300th payment	−95,000.00
ACC	ACC	ACC	calculate and display interest paid after 300th payment	−132,572.32
300, AMRT, AMRT, AMRT	300, AMRT, AMRT, AMRT	300, AMRT, AMRT, AMRT	calculate and display principal balance after 60th payment	0.00

From Table 2.4.30 Monthly payment and interest saved for various interest compounding at 8% nominal interest rate, loan of $95,643.43 and 20-year amortization. Type II, Class B.4 financial problem. (P/Yr = 12).

C/Yr	per	pr	an	total cost	total interest	interest saved
12.00	240.00	95,643.43	−800.00	192,000.00	96,356.57	0.00
2.00	240.00	95,643.43	−792.27	190,144.80	94,501.37	1,855.20

Table 3.6.16 Keystrokes to solve Table 2.4.30.

SHARP EL-733A	SHARP EL-735	CASIO FC-100	comments	calculator display
(clear TVM, select END)	(clear TVM, select END)	(clear TVM, select END)	see Table 3.6.1	0.00
2, 2nd F, EFF, 8, =, X→M	2, 2nd F, EFF, 8, =, X→M	2, EFF, 8, =, Min	enter compounding periods per year, enter Nominal % rate, calculate EFF %	8.16
12, 2nd F, APR, RM, =, ÷, 12, =, i	12, 2nd F, APR, RM, =, ÷, 12, =, i	12, SHIFT, APR, MR, =, ÷, 12, =, i%	enter payments per year, calculate adjusted NOM %	0.66
95643.43, PV	95643.43, PV	95643.43, PV	enter PV	95,643.43
240, n	240, n	240, n	enter N	240.00
COMP, PMT	COMP, PMT	COMP, PMT	compute PMT (END of period)	–792.27
792.27, x, 12, x, 20, =	792.27, x, 12, x, 20, =	792.27, x, 12, x, 20, =	compute total cost	190,144.80
–, 95643.43, =	–, 95643.43, =	–, 95643.43, =	compute total interest	94,501.37
+/–, +, 96356.57, =	+/–, +, 96356.57, =	+/–, +, 96356.57, =	compute interest saved	1,855.20

Sample Calculations from Section 2.5, Planning for the Children's Education

From Table 2.5.16 Yearly payments at the beginning of each period when saving for Giuseppe's education fund is delayed. 8% interest rate compounded monthly with lump-sum payments of \$0, \$1,000, \$5,000, and \$10,000. Future value = \$67,021.11. Type III, Class D.5 financial problem. (P/Yr = 1, C/Yr = 12).

year fund started	per	an(B) pr = 0.00	an(B) pr = -1,000.00	an(B) pr = -5,000.00	an(B) pr = -10,000.00
1999	12.00	–3,203.46	–3,079.03	–2,581.28	–1,959.10
2000	11.00	–3,658.75	–3,527.52	–3,002.60	–2,346.45

Table 3.6.17 Keystrokes to solve Table 2.5.16.

SHARP EL-733A	SHARP EL-735	CASIO FC-100	comments	calculator display
(clear TVM, select BGN)	(clear TVM, select BGN)	(clear TVM, select BGN)	see Table 3.6.1	0.00
67021.11, FV	67021.11, FV	67021.11, FV	enter FV	67,021.11
12, 2nd F, EFF, 8, =, X→M	12, 2nd F, EFF, 8, =, X→M	12, EFF, 8, =, Min	enter compounding periods per year, enter Nominal % rate, calculate EFF %	8.30
1, 2nd F, APR, RM, =, ÷, 1, =, i	1, 2nd F, APR, RM, =, ÷, 1, =, i	1, SHIFT, APR, MR, =, ÷, 1, =, i%	enter payments per year, calculate adjusted NOM %	8.30
0, PV	0, PV	0, PV	enter PV	0.00
12, n	12, n	12, n	enter N	12.00
COMP, PMT	COMP, PMT	COMP, PMT	compute PMT (BGN of period)	–3,203.46
11, n	11, n	11, n	enter N	11.00
COMP, PMT	COMP, PMT	COMP, PMT	compute PMT (BGN of period)	–3,658.75
1000, +/–, PV	1000, +/–, PV	1000, +/–, PV	enter PV	–1,000.00
12, n	12, n	12, n	enter N	12.00
COMP, PMT	COMP, PMT	COMP, PMT	compute PMT (BGN of period)	–3,079.03
11, n	11, n	11, n	enter N	11.00
COMP, PMT	COMP, PMT	COMP, PMT	compute PMT (BGN of period)	–3,527.52
5000, +/–, PV	5000, +/–, PV	5000, +/–, PV	enter PV	–5,000.00
12, n	12, n	12, n	enter N	12.00
COMP, PMT	COMP, PMT	COMP, PMT	compute PMT (BGN of period)	–2,581.28
11, n	11, n	11, n	enter N	11.00
COMP, PMT	COMP, PMT	COMP, PMT	compute PMT (BGN of period)	–3,002.60
10000, +/–, PV	10000, +/–, PV	10000, +/–, PV	enter PV	–10,000.00
12, n	12, n	12, n	enter N	12.00
COMP, PMT	COMP, PMT	COMP, PMT	compute PMT (BGN of period)	–1,959.10
11, n	11, n	11, n	enter N	11.00
COMP, PMT	COMP, PMT	COMP, PMT	compute PMT (BGN of period)	–2,346.45

Sample Calculations from Section 2.6, Planning for Retirement

From Table 2.6.2 Total earnings at the end of age 65 for various starting salaries, ages and yearly increase. Type II, Class C.3 financial problem. (P/Yr = C/Yr = 1), use end–of–period payments.

	Age				Age			
	23	31	41	51	23	31	41	51
	per = 43	per = 35	per = 25	per = 15	per = 43	per = 35	per = 25	per = 15
Initial Salary	2% yearly increase				3% yearly increase			
40,000	2,686,379	1,999,779	1,281,212	691,737	3,419,356	2,418,483	1,458,371	743,957

Table 3.6.18 Keystrokes to solve Table 2.6.2.

SHARP EL-733A	SHARP EL-735	CASIO FC-100	comments	calculator display
(clear TVM, select END)	(clear TVM, select END)	(clear TVM, select END)	see Table 3.6.1	0.00
43, n	43, n	43, n	enter N	43.00
2, ÷, 1, =, i	2, ÷, 1, =, i	2, ÷, 1, =, i%	enter I%	2.00
40000, +/–, PMT	40000, +/–, PMT	40000, +/–, PMT	enter PMT	–40,000.00
COMP, FV	COMP, FV	COMP, FV	compute FV (END of period)	2,686,378.71
35, n	35, n	35, n	enter N	35.00
COMP, FV	COMP, FV	COMP, FV	compute FV (END of period)	1,999,779.11
25, n	25, n	25, n	enter N	25.00
COMP, FV	COMP, FV	COMP, FV	compute FV (END of period)	1,281,211.99
15, n	15, n	15, n	enter N	15.00
COMP, FV	COMP, FV	COMP, FV	compute FV (END of period)	691,736.68
3, ÷, 1, =, i	3, ÷, 1, =, i	3, ÷, 1, =, i%	enter I%	3.00
43, n	43, n	43, n	enter N	43.00
COMP, FV	COMP, FV	COMP, FV	compute FV (END of period)	3,419,355.69
35, n	35, n	35, n	enter N	35.00
COMP, FV	COMP, FV	COMP, FV	compute FV (END of period)	2,418,483.27
25, n	25, n	25, n	enter N	25.00
COMP, FV	COMP, FV	COMP, FV	compute FV (END of period)	1,458,370.57
15, n	15, n	15, n	enter N	15.00
COMP, FV	COMP, FV	COMP, FV	compute FV (END of period)	743,956.56

From Table 2.6.4 Future values at the end of age 65 for various monthly savings amounts. Interest is compounded monthly. Monthly payments are made at the beginning of each period. Period = 43 x 12.
Type II, Class C.3 financial problem. (P/Yr = C/Yr = 12).

savings amount	total savings	future value at 6% interest	future value at 8% interest	future value at 10% interest
150.00	77,400	365,194	675,716	1,295,878

Table 3.6.19 Keystrokes to solve Table 2.6.4.

SHARP EL-733A	SHARP EL-735	CASIO FC-100	comments	calculator display
(clear TVM, select BGN)	(clear TVM, select BGN)	(clear TVM, select BGN)	see Table 3.6.1	0.00
43, x, 12, =, n	43, x, 12, =, n	43, x, 12, =, n	enter N	516.00
6, ÷, 12, =, i	6, ÷, 12, =, i	6, ÷, 12, =, i%	enter I%	0.50
150, +/–, PMT	150, +/–, PMT	150, +/–, PMT	enter PMT	–150.00
COMP, FV	COMP, FV	COMP, FV	compute FV (BGN of period)	365,194.03
8, ÷, 12, =, i	8, ÷, 12, =, i	8, ÷, 12, =, i%	enter I%	0.67
COMP, FV	COMP, FV	COMP, FV	compute FV (BGN of period)	675,716.40
10, ÷, 12, =, i	10, ÷, 12, =, i	10, ÷, 12, =, i%	enter I%	0.83
COMP, FV	COMP, FV	COMP, FV	compute FV (BGN of period)	1,295,878.40
2nd F, RCL, n, x, 150, =	RCL, n, x, 150, =	RCL, n, x, 150, =	calculate total savings	77,400.00

From Table 2.6.23 Monthly payments to finance $3,000 and $4,000 monthly retirement income for 20 years if $10,000 retirement fund has already been started. Money earns 4%, 6%, and 8% interest, compounded monthly at 3% inflation compounded monthly for various years to retirement. Use beginning-of-period payments. (P/Yr = C/Yr = 12).

Years to retirement	$3,000 monthly retirement income	$4,000 monthly retirement income
	4%	8%
40.00	–1,3437	–385

Table 3.6.20 Keystrokes to solve Table 2.6.23.

SHARP EL-733A	SHARP EL-735	CASIO FC-100	comments	calculator display
(clear TVM, select BGN)	(clear TVM, select BGN)	(clear TVM, select BGN)	see Table 3.6.1	0.00
4, ÷, 12, =, i	4, ÷, 12, =, i	4, ÷, 12, =, i%	enter I%	0.33
20, x, 12, =, n	20, x, 12, =, n	20, x, 12, =, n	enter N (retirement period in months)	240.00
3000, PMT	3000, PMT	3000, PMT	enter PMT	3,000.00
COMP, PV	COMP, PV	COMP, PV	compute PV	–496,715.79
0, PMT	0, PMT	0, PMT	set PMT register to 0 (zero)	0.00
3, ÷, 12, =, i	3, ÷, 12, =, i	3, ÷, 12, =, i%	enter I%	0.25
40, x, 12, =, n	40, x, 12, =, n	40, x, 12, =, n	enter N (period to retirement in months)	480.00
COMP, FV	COMP, FV	COMP, FV	compute FV	1,646,686.74
10000, +/–, PV	10000, +/–, PV	10000, +/–, PV	store lump-sum amount to PV	–10,000.00
4, ÷, 12, =, i	4, ÷, 12, =, i	4, ÷, 12, =, i%	enter I%	0.33
COMP, PMT	COMP, PMT	COMP, PMT	compute PMT	–1,346.90
(clear TVM)	(clear TVM)	(clear TVM)	see Table 3.6.1 (BGN still selected)	0.00
8, ÷, 12, =, i	8, ÷, 12, =, i	8, ÷, 12, =, i%	enter I/Y	0.67
20, x, 12, =, n	20, x, 12, =, n	20, x, 12, =, n	enter N (retirement period in months)	240.00
4000, PMT	4000, PMT	4000, PMT	enter PMT	4,000.00
COMP, PV	COMP, PV	COMP, PV	compute PV	–481,405.28
0, PMT	0, PMT	0, PMT	set PMT register to 0 (zero)	0.00
3, ÷, 12, =, i	3, ÷, 12, =, i	3, ÷, 12, =, i%	enter I%	0.25
40, x, 12, =, n	40, x, 12, =, n	40, x, 12, =, n	enter N (period to retirement in months)	480.00
COMP, FV	COMP, FV	COMP, FV	compute FV	1,595,930.12
10000, +/–, PV	10000, +/–, PV	10000, +/–, PV	store lump-sum amount to PV	–10,000.00
8, ÷, 12, =, i	8, ÷, 12, =, i	8, ÷, 12, =, i%	enter I%	0.67
COMP, PMT	COMP, PMT	COMP, PMT	compute PMT	–385.06

From Table 2.6.30 Monthly retirement payments in today's dollars for 20 years with existing $50,000 retirement fund. Money earns 4%, 6%, and 8% interest compounded monthly; 3% inflation compounded monthly; various years to retirement. Use beginning–of–period payments. (P/Yr = C/Yr = 12).

Years to retirement	-$1,000 monthly savings payment	-$2,000 monthly savings payment
	6%	8%
30	3,803	11,997

Table 3.6.21 Keystrokes to solve Table 2.6.30.

SHARP EL–733A	SHARP EL–735	CASIO FC–100	comments	calculator display
(clear TVM, select BGN)	(clear TVM, select BGN)	(clear TVM, select BGN)	see Table 3.6.1	0.00
6, ÷, 12, =, i	6, ÷, 12, =, i	6, ÷, 12, =, i%	enter I%	0.50
30, x, 12, =, n	30, x, 12, =, n	30, x, 12, =, n	enter N (period to retirement in months)	360.00
1000, +/–, PMT	1000, +/–, PMT	1000, +/–, PMT	enter PMT	–1,000.00
50000, +/–, PV	50000, +/–, PV	50000, +/–, PV	store lump–sum amount to PV	–50,000.00
COMP, FV	COMP, FV	COMP, FV	compute FV	1,310,666.38
0, PMT	0, PMT	0, PMT	set PMT register to 0 (zero)	0.00
3, ÷, 12, =, i	3, ÷, 12, =, i	3, ÷, 12, =, i%	enter I%	0.25
COMP, PV	COMP, PV	COMP, PV	compute PV	–533,476.01
20, x, 12, =, n	20, x, 12, =, n	20, x, 12, =, n	enter N (retirement period in months)	240.00
0, FV	0, FV	0, FV	set FV register to 0 (zero)	0.00
6, ÷, 12, =, i	6, ÷, 12, =, i	6, ÷, 12, =, i	enter I/Y	0.50
COMP, PMT	COMP, PMT	COMP, PMT	compute PMT	3,802.97
(clear TVM)	(clear TVM)	(clear TVM)	see Table 3.6.1 (BGN still selected)	0.00
8, ÷, 12, =, i	8, ÷, 12, =, i	8, ÷, 12, =, i%	enter I%	0.67
30, x, 12, =, n	30, x, 12, =, n	30, x, 12, =, n	enter N (period to retirement in months)	360.00
2000, +/–, PMT	2000, +/–, PMT	2000, +/–, PMT	enter PMT	–2,000.00
50000, +/–, PV	50000, +/–, PV	50000, +/–, PV	store lump–sum amount to PV	–50,000.00
COMP, FV	COMP, FV	COMP, FV	compute FV	3,547,376.83
0, PMT	0, PMT	0, PMT	set PMT register to 0 (zero)	0.00
3, ÷, 12, =, i	3, ÷, 12, =, i	3, ÷, 12, =, i%	enter I%	0.25

Continued, Table 3.6.21

COMP, PV	COMP, PV	COMP, PV	compute PV	–1,443,876.54
20, x, 12, =, n	20, x, 12, =, n	20, x, 12, =, n	enter N (retirement period in months)	240.00
0, FV	0, FV	0, FV	set FV register to 0 (zero)	0.00
8, ÷, 12, =, i	8, ÷, 12, =, i	8, ÷, 12, =, i%	enter I/Y	0.67
COMP, PMT	COMP, PMT	COMP, PMT	compute PMT	11,997.18

Sample Calculations from Section 2.7, Investment Decision Making

In this subsection, DCF analysis will be performed.

From Table 2.7.2 Financial calculator data entry values for Example 1. I/Yr = 20%, P/Yr = C/Yr = 12.

cash flow	frequency
CF0 = –10,000.00	
CF1 = –500.00	N1 = 1.00
CF2 = –3,000.00	N2 = 1.00
CF3 = 0.00	N3 = 15.00
CF4 = 20,000.00	N4 = 1.00

NPV = $1,458.80, IRR = 27.22% (yearly rate; periodic interest rate or monthly rate is 2.27%).

Table 3.6.22A Keystrokes to solve Table 2.7.2.

SHARP EL-733A	SHARP EL-735	comments	calculator display
2nd F, CA	RCL, CFi, 2nd F, CA, ENT	clear DCF Memories, see Table 3.6.1	0.00
1, 2nd F, Ni	1, 2nd F, Ni	enter frequency of cash flow CF0	1.00
10000, +/–, CFi	10000, +/–, CFi	enter amount for cash flow CF0	–10'000.00
1, 2nd F, Ni	1, 2nd F, Ni	enter frequency of cash flow group C01	1.00
500, +/–, CFi	500, +/–, CFi	enter amount for cash flow C01	–500.00
1, 2nd F, Ni	1, 2nd F, Ni	enter frequency of cash flow group C02	1.00
3000, +/–, CFi	3000, +/–, CFi	enter amount for cash flow C02	–3'000.00

Continued, Table 3.6.22A

15, 2nd F, Ni	15, 2nd F, Ni	enter frequency of cash flow group C03	15.00
0, CFi	0, CFi	enter amount for cash flow C03	0.00
1, 2nd F, Ni	1, 2nd F, Ni	enter frequency of cash flow group C04	1.00
20000, CFi	20000, CFi	enter amount for cash flow C04	20'000.00
20, ÷, 12, =, i	20, ÷, 12, =, i	store nominal rate to I%	1.67
NPV	NPV	compute NPV	1'458.80
IRR	IRR	compute periodic rate, IRR	2.27
x, 12, =	x, 12, =	compute yearly rate, IRR/YR	27.22

Table 3.6.22B Keystrokes to solve Table 2.7.2.

CASIO FC–100	comments	calculator display
SHIFT, FC	clear DCF memories, see Table 3.6.1	0.00
MODE, 4	select Cash Flow mode	0.00
10000, +/–, CFj	enter amount for cash flow CF0	–10000.00
500, +/–, CFj	enter amount for cash flow C01	–500.00
1, Nj	enter frequency of cash flow group C01	1.00
3000, +/–, CFj	enter amount for cash flow C02	–3000.00
1, Nj	enter frequency of cash flow group C02	1.00
0, CFj	enter amount for cash flow C03	0.00
15, Nj	enter frequency of cash flow group C03	15.00
20000, CFj	enter amount for cash flow C04	20000.00
1, Nj	enter frequency of cash flow group C04	1.00
20, ÷, 12, =, i%	store nominal rate to I%	1.67
NPV	compute NPV	1458.80
IRR	compute periodic rate, IRR	2.27
x, 12, =	compute yearly rate, IRR/YR	27.22

From Table 2.7.3 Financial calculator data entry values for Example 2.
I/Yr = 10%, P/Yr = C/Yr = 12

cash flow	frequency
CF0 = 35,000	
CF1 = 35,000	N1 = 23
CF2 = 35,000 x 1.15 = 40,250	N2 = 24
CF3 = 40,250 x 1.15 = 46,288	N3 = 24
CF4 = 46,288 x 1.15 = 53,231	N4 = 24
CF5 = 53,231 x 1.15 = 61,216	N5 = 24

NPV = $3,407,611.54

Table 3.6.23A Keystrokes to solve Table 2.7.3.

SHARP EL-733A	SHARP EL-735	comments	calculator display
2nd F, CA	RCL, CFi, 2nd F, CA, ENT	clear DCF Memories, see Table 3.6.1	0.00
1, 2nd F, Ni	1, 2nd F, Ni	enter frequency of cash flow CF0	1.00
35000, CFi	35000, CFi	enter amount for cash flow CF0	35'000.00
23, 2nd F, Ni	23, 2nd F, Ni	enter frequency of cash flow group C01	23.00
35000, CFi	35000, CFi	enter amount for cash flow C01	35'000.00
24, 2nd F, Ni	24, 2nd F, Ni	enter frequency of cash flow group C02	24.00
40250, CFi	40250, CFi	enter amount for cash flow C02	40'250.00
24, 2nd F, Ni	24, 2nd F, Ni	enter frequency of cash flow group C03	24.00
46288, CFi	46288, CFi	enter amount for cash flow C03	46'288.00
24, 2nd F, Ni	24, 2nd F, Ni	enter frequency of cash flow group C04	24.00
53231, CFi	53231, CFi	enter amount for cash flow C04	53'231.00
24, 2nd F, Ni	24, 2nd F, Ni	enter frequency of cash flow group C05	24.00
61216, CFi	61216, CFi	enter amount for cash flow C05	61'216.00
10, ÷, 12, =, i	10, ÷, 12, =, i	store nominal rate to I%	0.83
NPV	NPV	compute NPV	3'407'611.54

Table 3.6.23B Keystrokes to solve Table 2.7.3.

CASIO FC–100	comments	calculator display
SHIFT, FC	clear DCF memories, see Table 3.6.1	0.00
MODE, 4	select Cash Flow mode	0.00
35000, CFj	enter amount for cash flow CF0	35000.00
35000, CFj	enter amount for cash flow C01	35000.00
23, Nj	enter frequency of cash flow group C01	23.00
40250, CFj	enter amount for cash flow C02	40250.00
24, Nj	enter frequency of cash flow group C02	24.00
46288, CFj	enter amount for cash flow C03	46288.00
24, Nj	enter frequency of cash flow group C03	24.00
53231, CFj	enter amount for cash flow C04	53231.00
24, Nj	enter frequency of cash flow group C04	24.00
61216, CFj	enter amount for cash flow C05	61216.00
24, Nj	enter frequency of cash flow group C05	24.00
10, ÷, 12, =, i%	store nominal rate to I%	0.83
NPV	compute NPV	3407611.54

The $13 billion US company in Round Rock, Texas founded in 1984 by a 19-year old freshman from University of Texas (he dropped out in his second year) is Dell Computer Corp. In 1998, at age 33, Michael Dell is the youngest and longest-serving chief of a big computer company. His company sells computers directly to customers and has outsold IBM and Compaq.

PART 3
SUPPORTING MATERIALS

4

RULES OF THUMB

What he doth, he doth by rule of thumb, and not by art.

Sir William Hope (1692), *The Fencing Master*

Throughout this book, I have endeavored to show how easy it is to perform the basic math of personal finances. We covered calculations relating to single payments and series of payments, with practical applications ranging from interest rates, loans, and mortgages to planning for the children's education and retirement and investment decision making. These calculations are all simple with a financial calculator. But sometimes you don't have the financial calculator handy. You can quickly estimate some TVM parameters using the useful short-cut rules we'll cover in this chapter.

SINGLE PAYMENT RULES

In this sub-section we will look at the following time value of money (TVM) variables: period (per), interest rate (I/Yr), present value (pr) and future value (fu). Typical applications relate to investments at a given annual rate of interest.

The Rule of 72

> Rule of 72: To estimate the number of years it will take to double your initial investment, divide 72 by the annual interest rate.

That is:

per = 72/(I/Yr) *equation (4.1)*

For example, if your initial investment is $1,000, how long will it take for the investment to double in value if the interest rate is 9% per year? Using equation 4.1,

per = 72/9 = 8 years

Simple! But why does it work? Let's work it out using the financial calculator. Our problem is as follows:

present value (pr) = \$100
future value (fu) = \$200

Calculate period (per) for 5% to 15% interest rate per year (I/Yr). Then, calculate the product of per x (I/Yr). Table 4.1 below shows the results. Note that the results will be the same if the present and future values were \$1 and \$2 respectively, or \$1,000,000 and \$2,000,000 respectively.

Table 4.1 For pr = \$100, fu = \$200, calculate period (per) for interest rates (I/Yr) of 5% to 15% and per x (I/Yr).
Type I, Class A.1 financial problem. (P/Yr = C/Yr = 1).

per	I/Yr	pr	fu	per x (I/Yr)
14.21	5.0	-100.00	200.00	71.03
11.90	6.0	-100.00	200.00	71.37
10.24	7.0	-100.00	200.00	71.71
9.01	8.0	-100.00	200.00	72.05
8.04	9.0	-100.00	200.00	72.39
7.27	10.0	-100.00	200.00	72.73
6.64	11.0	-100.00	200.00	73.06
6.12	12.0	-100.00	200.00	73.40
5.67	13.0	-100.00	200.00	73.73
5.29	14.0	-100.00	200.00	74.06
4.96	15.0	-100.00	200.00	74.39

The last column calculates to an average value of 72.72, or use 72. Thus,

per = 72/(I/Yr), as in equation 4.1

The 12 Apollo astronauts who landed on the moon from 1969 to 1972 brought home 842 lbs of lunar rock. Considering that the Apollo program cost \$40 billion US, the moon rocks therefore cost about \$3 million US per ounce.

The Rule of 42

Now that we know how the rule of 72 came about, we can extend the technique. Let us find a rule that will estimate how long an investment will generate half of its original value given the annual rate of interest. Similarly as done above, assume:

present value (pr)	= $100
future value(fu)	= $150

Calculate period for 5% to 15% interest rate per year. Then, calculate the product of per x (I/Yr). The table below shows the results. Again, note that the results will be the same if the present and future values are $1 and $1.50 respectively, or $1,000,000 and $1,500,000 respectively.

Table 4.2 For pr = $100, fu = $150, calculate period (per) for interest rates (I/Yr) of 5% to 15% and per x (I/Yr).
Type I, Class A.1 financial problem. (P/Yr = C/Yr = 1).

per	I/Yr	pr	fu	per x (I/Yr)
8.31	5.0	-100.00	150.00	41.55
6.96	6.0	-100.00	150.00	41.75
5.99	7.0	-100.00	150.00	41.95
5.27	8.0	-100.00	150.00	42.15
4.70	9.0	-100.00	150.00	42.34
4.25	10.0	-100.00	150.00	42.54
3.89	11.0	-100.00	150.00	42.74
3.58	12.0	-100.00	150.00	42.93
3.32	13.0	-100.00	150.00	43.13
3.09	14.0	-100.00	150.00	43.32
2.90	15.0	-100.00	150.00	43.52

The last column calculates to an average value of 42.54, or use 42. Thus,

per = 42/(I/Yr) *equation (4.2)*

Rule of 42: To estimate the number of years it will take for your initial investment to generate half its original value, divide 42 by the annual interest rate.

George Cohon of McDonald's Canada is donating $1 million CDN royalties from his new book to McDonald's charities. If the goal is reached, Ray Kroc's widow has promised to match it. Ray Kroc was the founder of McDonald's.

The Rule of 115

Finally, let us find the rule to estimate the number of years it will take to triple our initial investment given the annual rate of interest. Our problem therefore is as follows:

present value (pr) = \$100
future value (fu) = \$300

Calculate period for 5% to 15% interest rate per year. Then, calculate the product of per x (I/Yr). The table below shows the results.

Table 4.3 For pr = \$100, fu = \$300, calculate period (per) for interest rates (I/Yr) of 5% to 15% and per x (I/Yr).
Type I, Class A.1 financial problem. (P/Yr = C/Yr = 1).

per	I/Yr	pr	fu	per x (I/Yr)
22.52	5.0	-100.00	300.00	112.59
18.85	6.0	-100.00	300.00	113.13
16.24	7.0	-100.00	300.00	113.66
14.27	8.0	-100.00	300.00	114.20
12.75	9.0	-100.00	300.00	114.73
11.53	10.0	-100.00	300.00	115.27
10.53	11.0	-100.00	300.00	115.80
9.69	12.0	-100.00	300.00	116.33
8.99	13.0	-100.00	300.00	116.86
8.38	14.0	-100.00	300.00	117.38
7.86	15.0	-100.00	300.00	117.91

The last column calculates to an average value of 115.26, which we can round to 115. Thus,

per = 115/(I/Yr) *equation (4.3)*

Rule of 115: To estimate the number of years it will take to triple your initial investment, divide 115 by the annual interest rate.

Apart from being a successful inventor, Thomas Edison was also a filmmaker. His film studio, "Black Maria," was completed on February 1, 1893 at a cost of about \$640. Here he made short films for use in his Kinetoscope, a peep-show machine for amusement arcades.

Your own Rules

There is no reason why you cannot come up with your own rules by following the same techniques as shown in the previous three rules.

Table 4.4 Summary for Single Payment Rules

Given the annual interest rate (I/Yr), estimate the number of years (per):	equation to use
to double the initial investment	per = 72/(I/Yr) (equation 4.1) – Rule of 72
for initial investment to generate half of its original value	per = 42/(I/Yr) (equation 4.2) – Rule of 42
to triple the initial investment	per = 115/(I/Yr) (equation 4.3) – Rule of 115

SERIES OF PAYMENT RULES

Mortgages and Loans

In this sub-section we will look at the following time value of money (TVM) variables: period (per), annual interest rate (I/Yr), present value (pr) and annuity or periodic payment (an). Typical application is loan or mortgage, where the amount of the monthly payments depends on the interest rate and period.

Mortgages

For first-time homebuyers, it is particularly useful to estimate how much mortgage they can afford given an annual rate of interest (I/Yr), mortgage amortization period (per) and the monthly or annuity payments (an).

A very useful rule is the following:

> For every $10,000 mortgage with an amortization period of 20 years and interest rate of 10%, the monthly payment is about $100.

Thus, for the same 20-year amortization period and 10% interest rate, the monthly payment for $20,000 mortgage is about $200; for $50,000, it is about $500; for $100,000, it is about $1,000; for $150,000 it is about $1,500; etc..

With this rule, first-time home buyers will be able to estimate the mortgage they can afford without going through the detailed calculations. Real estate agents and bank mortgage officers can also help prospective home buyers estimate the monthly mortgage payments.

Let us use the financial calculator to see the exact monthly payments for an amortization period of 20 years, with 10% interest rate at different mortgage amounts.

Table 4.5 Monthly payments at the end of every period for various mortgage amounts at 20-years amortization and 10% interest rate.
Type II, Class B.4 financial problem. (P/Yr = C/Yr = 12).

per	I/Yr	pr	an(E)	an (from rule)
20 x 12	10.00	10,000.00	-96.50	100.00
20 x 12	10.00	20,000.00	-193.00	200.00
20 x 12	10.00	50,000.00	-482.51	500.00
20 x 12	10.00	100,000.00	-965.02	1000.00
20 x 12	10.00	150,000.00	-1,447.53	1,500.00
20 x 12	10.00	200,000.00	-1,930.04	2,000.00

Let us investigate other rules by considering the same 10% interest rate and estimating the monthly mortgage payments for amortization periods of 15 and 25 years.

Thus for a 10% interest rate:

Table 4.6 Monthly payments at the end of every period for various mortgage amounts at 15 and 25 years amortization and 10% interest rate.
Type II, Class B.4 financial problem. (P/Yr = C/Yr = 12).

			15-year amortization		25-year amortization	
I/Yr	pr	an (from rule)	per	an(E)	per	an(E)
10.00	10,000.00	100.00	15 x 12	-107.46	25 x 12	-90.87
10.00	20,000.00	200.00	15 x 12	-214.92	25 x 12	-181.74
10.00	50,000.00	500.00	15 x 12	-537.30	25 x 12	-454.35
10.00	100,000.00	1,000.00	15 x 12	-1,074.61	25 x 12	-908.70
10.00	150,000.00	1,500.00	15 x 12	-1,611.91	25 x 12	-1,363.05
10.00	200,000.00	2,000.00	15 x 12	-2,149.21	25 x 12	-1,817.40

Let us calculate the difference between the actual monthly payment for 15-, 20- and 25-year amortization and payments from the rule.

By end of 1994, the Metropolitan Life Insurance Co. of New York City has insurance in force to the tune of $1.27 trillion US.

Table 4.7 Summary table for difference between actual monthly payments for 15-, 20-, and 25-year amortization and monthly payments from the rule.

Principal	15-year amort.	20-year amort.	25-year amort.
10,000.00	7.46	-3.50	-9.13
20,000.00	14.92	-7.00	-18.26
50,000.00	37.30	-17.49	-45.65
100,000.00	74.61	-34.98	-91.30
150,000.00	111.91	-52.47	-136.95
200,000.00	149.21	-69.96	-182.60

Note that the 20-year amortization matches the rule's prediction most closely. The rule overestimates monthly payment values as indicated by the negative values in the "20-year amort." column in the above table; but still provides a good working estimate. The rule underestimates the monthly payment values for 15-year amortization (as shown by the positive values in the above table) and overestimates the 25-year amortization. Thus, the rule stated above can be rewritten as:

> For every $10,000 mortgage with an amortization period of 15, 20, or 25 years and interest rate of 10%, the monthly payment is about $100;

Note however, that the monthly payment is underestimated for the 15-year amortization and overestimated for the 20-year and especially, the 25-year amortization.

Loans

Loans are differentiated from mortgages by their shorter periods, typically three, four, or five years. Loans may be taken out for home improvement, purchasing a vehicle, financing business or education, or many other purposes.

For a 10% interest rate,

Table 4.8 Present and periodic payment values at the end of every period for a 10% loan at 36-, 48- and 60-month periods.
Type II financial problem. (P/Yr = C/Yr = 12).

	Period = 3 yrs	Period = 4 yrs	Period = 5 yrs
Periodic payment	-100.00	-100.00	-100.00
Present value	3,099.12	3,942.82	4,706.54
Present value	3,000.00	4,000.00	5,000.00
Periodic payment	-96.80	-101.45	-106.24

Thus, from the above tables, we can derive the following rules:

> For a loan period of 3 years, every $3,000 loan can be repaid by monthly payments of about $100, if the interest rate is 10%.
>
> For a loan period of 4 years, every $4,000 loan can be repaid by monthly payments of about $100, if the interest rate is 10%.
>
> For a loan period of 5 years, every $5,000 loan can be repaid by monthly payments of about $100, if the interest rate is 10%.

From the above rules, one can estimate the monthly payment for a $12,000 loan at 10% interest rate and a period of 4 years. If it takes about $100 monthly to repay a $4,000 loan at 10% and period of 4 years, the monthly payment for $12,000 is approximately $300 ($12,000 x $100/$4,000). The actual value calculated on a financial calculator is $304.35 for end-of-period annuity payments.

Similarly, let's try estimating the monthly payment for a $10,000 loan at 10% interest rate and 5-year period: the above rule estimates $100 monthly payment for a $5,000 loan. For a $10,000 loan, the monthly payment is about $200 ($10,000 x $100/$5,000). The actual value is $212.47 for end-of-period annuity payments.

A $12,000 loan at 10% interest rate and 3 year period will require a monthly payment of $400 ($12,000 x $100/$3,000). The actual value is $387.21 for end-of-period annuity payments.

SAVINGS PLANS

In this sub-section we will look at the following time value of money (TVM) variables: period (per), annual interest rate (I/Yr), future value (fu) and annuity or periodic payment (an). A typical application is setting aside monthly savings toward a future financial goal. It would be useful to be able to quickly estimate the future value of the periodic monthly payments for a given annual interest rate and period.

Table 4.9 Future and periodic payment values at the end of every period at 10% for 36-, 48- and 60-month periods.
Type II financial problem. (P/Yr = C/Yr = 12).

	Period = 5 years	Period = 10 years	Period = 15 years
Periodic payment	−100.00	−100.00	−100.00
Future value	7,743.70	20,484.50	41,447.03
Future value	8,000.00	20,000.00	40,000.00
Periodic payment	−103.31	−97.63	−96.51

Thus, from the above tables, we can derive the following rules:

For a period of 5 years, every $100 monthly payment to a savings plan will have a future value of $8,000 if the interest rate is 10%.

For a period of 10 years, every $100 monthly payment to a savings plan will have a future value of $20,000 if the interest rate is 10%.

For a period of 15 years, every $100 monthly payment to a savings plan will have a future value of $40,000 if the interest rate is 10%.

Using the above rules, we can estimate the future value of a monthly payment of $150 towards a savings plan that pays 10% interest for a 5-year period. The future value is $12,000 ($150 x $8,000/$100). The real value obtained using a financial calculator is $11,615.56 for end-of-period annuity payments.

Let's take another example. Suppose the monthly payment is $250 towards a savings plan that pays 10% interest for a 10-year period, what is the future value? The future value is $50,000 ($250 x $20,000/$100). The real value obtained using a financial calculator is $51,211.24 for end-of-period annuity payments.

Finally, estimate the future value of monthly payments of $300 towards a savings plan that pays 10% interest over a 15-year period. The estimated future value using the rule is $120,000 ($300 x $40,000/$100). The real value obtained using a financial calculator is $124,341.10 for end-of-period annuity payments.

Miss Ellen Church was the world's first flight stewardess. She welcomed her first 11 passengers aboard a United Airlines on May 15, 1930. Early flight stewardesses were required to be registered nurses aged 25 or under. Their monthly salary was $125 US.

5

GLOSSARY

He shall be a god to me, who can rightly divide and define.

Ralph Waldo Emerson

Amortize	to liquidate or extinguish a debt, mortgage, or other obligation by periodic payments to the creditor
Amortization table	table of calculated values that shows, for each payment period, the interest paid, principal paid, and the principal balance; table can also show these three values over a range of payment periods
Annually	in financial context, a frequency of one payment in one year (P/Yr = 1) or a frequency of one interest compounding in one year (C/Yr = 1)
Annuity	equal payments payable at regular intervals for a fixed period
Annuity payment	time-value-of-money parameter that specifies the series of equal payments in a financial transaction
Balloon payment	payment made at the end of the loan term for the residual balance to completely extinguish the loan
Bi-weekly	in financial context, a frequency of 26 payments in one year (P/Yr = 26) or a frequency of 26 interest compoundings in one year (C/Yr = 26)
Beginning-of-period payment (see also end-of-period payment)	annuity payment made at the start of each period
Cash Flow Diagram	a plotting technique that assists in visualizing financial problems

Compounding	computing compound interest
Compound interest	interest paid on the principal and accrued interest
Currency	money, which is used as a medium of exchange and which has the quality of being accepted widely
Daily	in financial context, a frequency of 365 payments in one year (P/Yr = 365) or a frequency of 365 interest compoundings in one year (C/Yr = 365)
Deflation	decrease in the level of consumer prices or increase in the purchasing power of money
Discounted cash flow analysis (DCF)	financial analysis method used to evaluate an investment to see if it meets profit objectives
Effective interest rate	real rate of interest charged, based on frequency of compounding interest
End-of-period payment (see also beginning -of-period payment)	annuity payment made at the end of each period
Future Value	time-value-of-money parameter that specifies the future value of the financial transaction
Inflation	increase in the level of consumer prices or decrease in the purchasing power of money
Interest	charge for the use of money
Internal rate of return (IRR)	one of the parameters calculated by the DCF method; this is the rate of return at which NPV (net present value) = 0, the rate at which the investor's objective is exactly met
Interest compounding frequency	for a given financial transaction, how often the interest compounding is to be made; quoted as number of interest compoundings per year (C/Yr)
Interest rate	time-value-of-money parameter that specifies the rate of charge for the use of money, usually quoted as nominal rate in percentage per year (I/Yr)
Lease	a contract granting the use of property for a given period in exchange for a specified rent; payments are usually made at the beginning of each period
Loan	sum of money lent at interest

Lump-sum payment	a single sum of money for a complete payment obligation
Money	any article or substance used as medium of exchange
Monthly	in financial context, a frequency of 12 payments in one year (P/Yr = 12) or a frequency of 12 interest compoundings in one year (C/Yr = 12)
Mortgage	pledge of property to a creditor as security for performance of obligation such as repayment of money
Mortgagee	a person to whom property is mortgaged
Mortgagor	a person who mortgages property
Net present value (NPV)	One of the parameters calculated by the DCF method. An investment is worth pursuing if NPV calculates to a positive value; at NPV = 0, the investor's objective is exactly met.
Nominal interest rate	specified, stated, or named interest rate in a financial transaction
Ordinary annuity	series of regular, equal payments made at the end of each period
Payment period	time-value-of-money parameter that specifies the term or total length of the financial transaction
Payment frequency	for a given financial transaction, how often the payment is to be made; quoted as number of payments per year (P/Yr)
Periodic interest rate	parameter that specifies the interest rate to be charged per period, calculated as (I/Yr)/(P/Yr) as a decimal, or multiplied by 100 for percent
Present value	time-value-of-money parameter which specifies the present or current value of the financial transaction
Principal	capital sum in a financial transaction - distinguished from interest
Quarterly	in financial context, a frequency of 4 payments in one year (P/Yr = 4) or a frequency of 4 interest compoundings in one year (C/Yr = 4)

Rapid payment	mortgage interest reduction method whereby a total of 13 monthly payments are made in one year
Recession	extended decline in business activity
Rent	payment specified by a contract at regular intervals for the use of property; payments are usually made at the beginning of each period
Semi-annually	in financial context, a frequency of two payments in one year (P/Yr = 2) or a frequency of two interest compoundings in one year (C/Yr = 2)
Semi-monthly	in financial context, a frequency of 24 payments in one year (P/Yr = 24) or a frequency of 24 interest compoundings in one year (C/Yr = 24)
Savings plan	a lump-sum or a schedule of payments to accumulate the required future value
Simple interest	interest calculation as a percentage of the principal
Time value of money analysis (TVM)	financial analysis method based on the fact that a dollar today is worth more than a dollar in the future
Weekly	in financial context, a frequency of 52 payments in one year (P/Yr = 52) or a frequency of 52 interest compoundings in one year (C/Yr = 52)
Wrap-around mortgage	a mortgage that combines mortgage refinancing and borrowing against real estate equity
Yearly (see Annually)	in financial context, a frequency of one payment in one year (P/Yr = 1) or a frequency of one interest compounding in one year (C/Yr = 1)

An unemployed engineer, Charles Darrow, copyrighted the board game Monopoly in 1935. It was manufactured by the Parker Brothers toy company, which then produced about 20,000 Monopoly sets per week. Darrow, whose game was sold in thirty countries and translated into twenty languages, became a millionaire.

6
BIBLIOGRAPHY

Nothing is said nowadays that has not been said before.

Terence (BC 186-159), Roman comic dramatist and author

Applegarth, Ginger. *The Money Diet: Reaping the Rewards of Financial Fitness*. New York: Penguin Books USA Inc., 1995.

Beige, Carl E., with appendix by Gennifer Sussman. *Inflation is a Social Malady*. Montreal: British–North American Committee, 1979.

Burns, Peggy. *Money*. New York: Thomson Learning, 1995.

Casey, Douglas. *Crisis Investing for the Rest of the '90s*. New York: Carol Publishing Group, 1993.

Cohen, Bruce, with Alyssa Diamond. *The Money Adviser*. Toronto: Stoddart Publishing Co. Limited, 1995.

De Rooy, Jacob. *Economic Literacy: What Everyone Needs to Know about Money and Markets*. New York: Crown Publishers, Inc., 1995.

Frischke, Bernhard A. *Inflation: It's Your Bag!* Toronto: Simon & Pierre Publishing Company Limited, 1976.

Gray, Douglas A. *Mortgage Payment Tables Made Easy*. Toronto: McGraw–Hill Ryerson Limited, 1995.

Heilbroner, Robert and Lester Thurow. *Economics Explained*. New York: Simon & Schuster Inc., 1994.

Homer, Sidney. *A History of Interest Rates 2000 BC to the Present*. 2nd ed. New Jersey: Rutgers University Press 1977.

Howell, Michael J. *Winning Scholarships*. Toronto: University of Toronto Press, 1992.

LeClair, Robert T., Stephan R. Leimberg and Herbert Chasman. *Money and Retirement: How to Plan for Lifetime Financial Security*. Reading, MA: Addison-Wesley Publishing Company, 1982.

Maestro, Betsy. *The Story of Money*. New York: Houghton Mifflin Company, 1993.

Moynes, Riley. *The Money Coach: Your Game Plan for Growth, Tax Relief and Security*. Toronto: Copp Clark Pitman Ltd. and Ashlar House Publishing & Promotions, 1992.

Perry, John H. (ed.) *Chemical Engineer's Handbook*. 4th ed., McGraw-Hill Handbook, 1963.

Prud'homme, Marc. "What is the 'Current' Annual Rate of Inflation?" *The Consumer Price Index*, August 1992, Statistics Canada Cat. No. 62-001.

Quinn, Jane Bryant. *Making the Most of Your Money*. New York: Simon & Schuster, 1997.

Stowers, James E., with Jack Jonathan. *Yes You Can ... Achieve Financial Independence*. Kansas City: Andrews and McMeel, 1994.

Van Caspel, Venita. *Money Dynamics for the New Economy*. New York: Simon and Schuster, 1986.

Watters, Graydon G. *Financial Pursuit*. 2nd ed. Toronto: FKI Financial Knowledge Inc., 1994.

Wessels, Walter J. *Economics*. 2nd ed. New York: Barron's Educational Series, Inc., 1993.

BA II Plus Business Calculator Guidebook. Texas Instruments Canada Limited.

Bank of Montreal, RRSP Personal Check-up Planner. 1990.

Canadian Bankers Association Booklet on Saving for Your Children's Education. Toronto, Ontario, Canada, 1998.

Economic Reference Tables. Ottawa: Department of Finance Canada, 1995.

EL-733A Business/Financial Calculator Operation and Application Manual. Sharp Corporation.

EL-735 Business/Financial Calculator Instruction Guide and Application Manual. Sharp Corporation.

FC-100 Owner's Manual. Casio Computer Co. Ltd.

The Grolier Multi-Media Encyclopedia, 1995 ed.

HP 10B Business Calculator Owner's Manual. 6th ed. Oregon: Hewlett-Packard Co., 1994.

Market Research Handbook 1993–1994, Statistics Canada Cat. No. 63-224.

Microsoft Bookshelf Basics, CD-ROM, 1997 ed.

The New Encyclopaedia Britannica, 1992 ed.

Notre Dame Magazine.

Student Business Analyst Owner's Manual. Texas Instruments Canada Limited.

For an additional $800 US to the sticker price of your new GM car, an OnStar agent can tell you within 100 yards where you are by pressing a button on the installed cell phone. The system can remotely unlock your doors if you lock your keys inside the car. The system can also beep the horn and flash the lights of your car if you can't remember where you parked.

7

APPENDICES

From the end spring the new beginnings.

Pliny the Elder (AD 23-79), Roman scholar and author

7.1

IMPORTANCE OF TVM ANALYSIS, WITH YEARLY UPDATES

The example to be discussed in this section will show the importance of yearly updates for any personal finance application problem. In all financial problems, calculations are done as if the interest rate were constant for the entire period. Over a long period — say, 15, 20, or 25 years — the calculations can lead to overestimates or underestimates, because, in reality, the interest rate changes daily. To provide better estimates for long-term applications such as saving for the children's education and for retirement, you should redo the calculations at least once a year using the current interest rates and updated TVM parameter values.

Let us discuss an example in which Michael puts down $100,000 today towards an interest-bearing account earning, initially, 7% a year. The account is automatically renewed yearly at its anniversary date at the prevailing interest rate. He plans to keep this investment for 20 years. Michael should recalculate the estimated future value of his investment each year and consider whether he needs to top it up with additional funds. See Table 7.1.1.

Similarly, if you're saving for your children's education or for retirement, you may have to modify your savings strategy to attain the financial goal. If you used the lump-sum method, you might want to add or remove funds; if you used the series-of-payment method, you might need to increase or decrease the regular monthly payments.

In Table 7.1.1, using 7% as interest rate for the entire 20-year term results in a final value of $386,968.45. At the end of the first year, Michael reworks his calculations using a term of 19 years, and the actual amount of $107,000.00, which includes the sum of $7,000 earned by the original $100,000 investment at 7% after one year. But the current interest is now 7.5%, so Michael uses this figure. He is cheered to see that the future value is now more than $35,000 higher than his initial estimate. Should he take some money out of his account? Well, it might be wiser to wait and see what interest rates do over the following years.

If Michael performs the calculation at the end of each year using the updated values, he ends up calculating better estimates for the future value of his initial investment. The closer he is to the end of the term, the better his calculated estimates will be.

The column on the far right labeled "'actual fu value (at end of each period)" shows future values from calculations performed at the end of every year (per = 1) using the indicated interest rate. It starts off with $107,000.00, which came from the sum of the initial investment of $100,000.00 and the interest $7,000 earned after one year. This value is used as the present value (pr) for the next period down in the column "predicted future value calculation."

Table 7.1.1 Yearly update of future value calculations for $100,000, from periods of 20 years to 1 year at various interest rates. (P/Yr = C/Yr = 1).

Predicted future value calculation				actual fu value (at end of each period)
per	I/yr	pr	fu	fu (with per = 1)
20	7.00	−100,000.00	386,968.45	107,000.00
19	7.50	−107,000.00	422,809.37	115,025.00
18	7.00	−115,025.00	388,776.71	123,076.75
17	6.50	−123,076.75	359,020.59	131,076.74
16	6.00	−131,076.74	332,981.02	138,941.34
15	7.00	−138,941.34	383,343.54	148,667.23
14	6.50	−148,667.23	359,012.66	158,330.60
13	6.00	−158,330.60	337,707.81	167,830.44
12	6.00	−167,830.44	337,707.82	177,900.27
11	6.50	−177,900.27	355,649.57	189,463.79
10	6.00	−189,463.79	339,300.79	200,831.62
9	6.50	−200,831.62	353,979.87	213,885.68
8	7.00	−213,885.68	367,495.42	228,857.68
7	5.00	−228,857.68	322,025.74	240,300.56
6	3.00	−240,300.56	286,931.44	247,509.58
5	4.00	−247,509.58	301,133.25	257,409.96
4	5.00	−257,409.96	312,883.42	270,280.46
3	7.00	−270,280.46	331,105.19	289,200.09
2	6.00	−289,200.09	324,945.22	306,552.10
1	6.00	−306,552.10	324,945.23	324,945.23

The International Space Station (ISS) is a joint effort by US, Russia, Japan, Canada, Brazil, and 11 European countries: Belgium, Denmark, France, Germany, Italy, The Netherlands, Norway, Spain, Sweden, Switzerland, and UK. The objective is to build the $63 billion space station by the year 2004. It is estimated it will require 44 space flights to build the ISS.

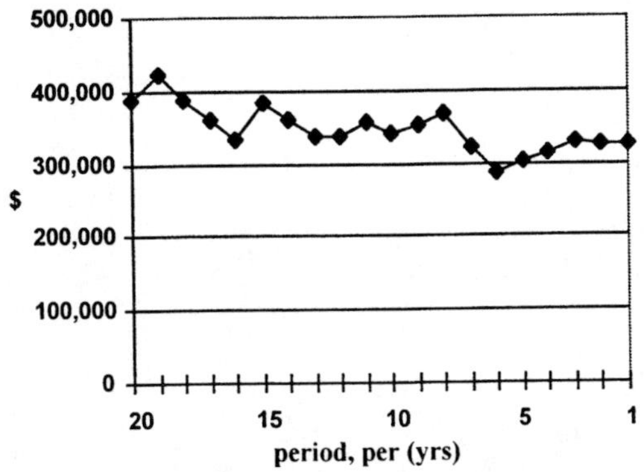

Figure 7.1 Future value of $100,000 with yearly updates at various interest rates

As shown in the above table, the final true value of the investment is $324,945.23 - quite different from the initial estimate of $386,968.45. In this example, interest rates fell over the term of the investment, and therefore predicted future value was overestimated. As the estimated future value is used for decision making — for example, deciding whether to add more money to the savings plan — it is very important to have the best possible estimate of future value. Updating calculations yearly and adjusting savings strategies as required is useful for both TVM and DCF analysis.

One thousand tons of heavy water, or deuterium, costs about $300 million US. Physicists borrowed this much heavy water for an experiment called the Sudbury Neutrino Observatory. The experiment is an attempt to solve some of the mysteries of particle physics and understand the makeup of the universe.

7.2
WORKSHEETS

This section will provide blank templates, which can assist you in solving your own personal finance problems. Each of the five application topics will be covered: implementing a savings plan, loans and mortgages, saving for the children's education, saving for retirement, and investment decision making.

The worksheets are similar to the tables that we used for various examples in the book. Except for the first row of cells in each table, all the others are blank. The first row shows TVM parameters for an example financial problem. For the blank ones, each row can be used for a specific problem. You will have to provide the values for the unshaded fields. The shaded field is for the unknown variable you are calculating. The main reference to this section are the application Sections 2.3 to 2.7.

At this point, it should be apparent that TVM analysis can be applied to either savings or loan problems. For example, consider the template shown in Table 7.2. This template can be used to solve either a savings or a loan problem.

Example:

Savings Problem. *You would like to accumulate a savings fund after a period (per) by putting down some money with a present value (pr) and by making regular annuity payments (an) into an interest-bearing account. What interest rate should you expect in order to accumulate the required future value (fu)?*

Loan Problem. *You opted for vehicle lease financing by your local car dealership for a period (per); the brand new car has a present value (pr) and a monthly lease payment of (an); the lease includes an option to buy the car at the end of the term with a future value (fu) which you have to pay the dealer. What is the interest rate being charged?*

In 1998, one ad page in the Cosmopolitan magazine costs $99,500 US.

Table 7.2 Type III, Class D.2 financial problem. Can be used for savings or loan applications. Use end-of-period annuity payments. (P/Yr = 1, C/Yr = 12).

per	(I/Yr) or (in%)	pr	fu	an(E)
10.00	6.85 (I/Yr)	-500.00	10,000.00	-650.00

The top row in Table 7.2 has been filled out for one particular financial problem so you can practice solving the problem using the financial calculator. Interest rate is the unknown variable. The blank rows in Table 7.2 are used for what-if analysis. That is, the first blank row can be used for the base case and the others can be used to investigate how by slightly changing the value of one or more parameters, the result of the unknown parameter is affected.

Depending on the financial calculator you are using, you have to enter the periodic interest rate in per cent (in%) or the annual interest rate (I/Yr). Refer to Table 3.2.4. The relationships between (I/Yr), (in) and (in%) are shown in equations 2.1.2 and 2.1.3. Where the payment per year (P/Yr) is not the same as the compounding interest per year (C/Yr), if you are using a financial calculator other than the Texas Instrument BA II Plus, you will need to calculate the effective interest and then the adjusted nominal interest rate. Refer to the section on interest in Section 2.2 for sample calculations.

I suggest that you photocopy these worksheets.

SAVINGS PLAN IMPLEMENTATION

Implementing a savings plan can involve Type I, II, III TVM (time value of money) problems and Type IV DCF (discounted cash flow) problems.

Single Payment (Type I Class A)

Table 7.2.1 - Used to calculate how long a period (per) it will take for a present value (pr) to accumulate to a savings amount future value (fu), given the rate of interest.
Table 7.2.2 - Used to calculate the interest rate for a given period (per) such that the present value (pr) will accumulate to a savings future value (fu).
Table 7.2.3 - Used to calculate the present value (pr) given the period (per) and the interest rate so that it will accumulate to the required savings amount future value (fu).
Table 7.2.4 - Used to calculate the savings amount future value (fu), given the period (per), savings amount present value (pr), and the interest rate.

Series of Payment (Type II Class C)

Note that the templates provided involve annuity payments, which could be made at the beginning or at the end of each period. Thus, for each unknown parameter, two fields are shaded; one is for beginning-of-period payments and the other is for end-of-period payments.

Table 7.2.5 - Used to calculate how long a period (per) it will take for a series of payment (an) amount to equal the savings amount future value (fu), given the rate of interest.

Table 7.2.6 - Used to calculate the interest rate such that the savings amount future value (fu) is equivalent to the annuity payments (an) at a given period (per).

Table 7.2.7 - Used to calculate the equivalent savings amount future value (fu) given the period (per), the annuity payment (an), and the interest rate.

Table 7.2.8 - Used to calculate the annuity payment (an) at the given period (per), savings amount future value (fu), and the interest rate.

Combination of Single Payment and Series of Payment (Type III Class D)

As the templates below involve annuity payments, there will be two shaded fields per unknown variable. One is for beginning-of-period payment and the other is for end-of-period payment.

Table 7.2.9 – Used to calculate how long a period (per) it will take for a lump-sum payment (pr) and a series of annuity payments (an) to equal the savings amount future value (fu), given the rate of interest.

Table 7.2.10 – Used to calculate the interest rate such that the lump-sum payment (pr) and annuity payments (an) at a given period (per) equals the savings amount future value (fu).

Table 7.2.11 – Used to calculate how large a lump-sum payment (pr) is required in combination with the annuity payment (an) at a given period (per) and interest rate to equal the savings amount future value (fu).

Table 7.2.12 – Used to calculate the savings amount future value (fu) given the lump-sum payment (pr) and annuity payments (an) at period (per) and interest rate.

Table 7.2.13 – Used to calculate the annuity payment (an) that, when combined with the lump-sum payment (pr), is equivalent to the savings amount future value (fu) given the period (per) and interest rate.

Discounted Cash Flow (Type IV)

To calculate the savings amount future value (fu), given the lump-sum and series of annuity payments; CF0, CFi where i = 1, 2, …., i at corresponding payment frequency Ni, where i = 1, 2, …, i at a given interest rate; first calculate the Net Present Value of the payments using the DCF method. Use Table 7.2.14. Then using Table 7.2.15, calculate the net future value (fu) given the period (per), present value (pr from the NPV) and the interest rate.

Table 7.2.1 Type I, Class A.1 financial problem.
(Sample problem, use P/Yr = C/Yr = 12).

per	(I/Yr) or (in%)	pr	fu
104.32	8.00 (I/Yr)	-5,000.00	10,000.00

Table 7.2.2 Type I, Class A.2 financial problem.
(Sample problem, use P/Yr = C/Yr = 12).

per	(I/Yr) or (in%)	pr	fu
100.00	8.35 (I/Yr)	-5,000.00	10,000.00

Table 7.2.3 Type I, Class A.3 financial problem.
(Sample problem, use P/Yr = C/Yr = 12).

per	(I/Yr) or (in%)	pr	fu
100.00	8.00 (I/Yr)	-5,145.54	10,000.00

Table 7.2.4 Type I, Class A.4 financial problem.
(Sample problem, use P/Yr = C/Yr = 12).

per	(I/Yr) or (in%)	pr	fu
100.00	8.00 (I/Yr)	–5,000.00	9,717.15

Table 7.2.5 Type II, Class C.1 financial problem.
(Sample problem, use P/Yr = C/Yr = 12).

per	per	(I/Yr) or (in%)	fu	an
E	B			
76.88	76.48	8.00 (I/Yr)	20,000.00	–200.00

Table 7.2.6 Type II, Class C.2 financial problem.
(Sample problem, use P/Yr = C/Yr = 12).

per	(I/Yr) or (in%)	(I/Yr) or (in%)	fu	an
	E	B		
60.00	19.38 (I/Yr)	18.82 (I/Yr)	20,000.00	–200.00

Table 7.2.7 Type II, Class C.3 financial problem.
(Sample problem, use P/Yr = C/Yr = 12).

per	(I/Yr) or (in%)	fu	fu	an
		E	B	
50.00	8.00 (I/Yr)	17,733.13	17,851.35	–300.00

Table 7.2.8 Type II, Class C.4 financial problem.
(Sample problem, use P/Yr = C/Yr = 12).

per	(I/Yr) or (in)	fu	an	an
			E	B
50.00	8.00 (I/Yr)	20,000.00	–338.35	–336.11

Table 7.2.9 Type III, Class D.1 financial problem.
(Sample problem, use P/Yr = C/Yr = 1).

per	per	(I/Yr) or (in%)	pr	fu	an
E	B				
24.18	23.57	8.00 (I/Yr)	–50,000.00	1,000,000.00	–10,000.00

Table 7.2.10 Type III, Class D.2 financial problem.
(Sample problem, use P/Yr = C/Yr = 1).

per	(I/Yr) or (in%)	(I/Yr) or (in%)	pr	fu	an
	E	B			
20.00	10.68 (I/Yr)	10.24 (I/Yr)	–50,000.00	1,000,000.00	–10,000.00

Table 7.2.11 Type III, Class D.3 financial problem.
(Sample problem, use P/Yr = C/Yr = 1).

per	(I/Yr) or (in%)	pr	pr	fu	an
		E	B		
20.00	8.00 (I/Yr)	–116,366.73	–108,512.22	1,000,000.00	–10,000.00

Table 7.2.12 Type III, Class D.4 financial problem.
(Sample problem, use P/Yr = C/Yr = 1).

per	(I/Yr) or (in%)	pr	fu	fu	an
			E	B	
20.00	8.00 (I/Yr)	–50,000.00	690,667.50	727,277.07	–10,000.00

Table 7.2.13 Type III, Class D.5 financial problem.
(Sample problem, use P/Yr = C/Yr = 1).

per	(I/Yr) or (in%)	pr	fu	an(E)	an(B)
				E	B
20.00	8.00 (I/Yr)	−50,000	1,000,000.00	−16,759.60	−15,518.15

Table 7.2.14 DCF problem

cash flow	frequency
CF0 = −900.00	
CF1 = 0.00	N1 = 1.00
CF2 = −500.00	N2 = 1.00
CF3 = 0.00	N3 = 3.00
CF4 = −300.00	N4 = 2.00
CF5 = 0.00	N5 = 6.00
CF6 = −1,000.00	N6 = 1.00
CF7 = 0.00	N7 = 5.00
CF8 = −1,000.00	N8 = 1.00
CF. =	N. =
CF. =	N. =
CFi =	Ni =
(in%) = 9.5/12	NPV = −3,711.78

cash flow	frequency
CF0 =	
CF1 =	N1 =
CF2 =	N2 =
CF3 =	N3 =
CF4 =	N4 =
CF5 =	N5 =
CF6 =	N6 =
CF7 =	N7 =
CF8 =	N8 =
CF. =	N. =
CF. =	N. =
CFi =	Ni =
(in%) =	NPV =

Continued, Table 7.2.14

cash flow	frequency
CF0 =	
CF1 =	N1 =
CF2 =	N2 =
CF3 =	N3 =
CF4 =	N4 =
CF5 =	N5 =
CF6 =	N6 =
CF7 =	N7 =
CF8 =	N8 =
CF. =	N. =
CF. =	N. =
CFi =	Ni =
(in%) =	NPV =

cash flow	frequency
CF0 =	
CF1 =	N1 =
CF2 =	N2 =
CF3 =	N3 =
CF4 =	N4 =
CF5 =	N5 =
CF6 =	N6 =
CF7 =	N7 =
CF8 =	N8 =
CF. =	N. =
CF. =	N. =
CFi =	Ni =
(in%) =	NPV =

Table 7.2.15 Type I, Class A.4 financial problem.
(Sample problem, use P/Yr = C/Yr = 12).

per	(I/Yr) or (in%)	pr	fu
20.00	9.5 (I/Yr)	-3,711.78	4,345.85

LOANS AND MORTGAGES

Note that the following templates involve annuity payments. Loans and mortgages usually involve Type II Class B problems with annuity payments made at the end of each period. Special cases such as balloon financing involve Type III Class D problems. Note that for Canadian mortgages, the interest compounding per year, C/Yr is 2, or semi-annually.

Table 7.2.16 – Used to calculate how long a period (per) it will take for a series of annuity payments (an) to pay off the loan or mortgage amount (pr) given the rate of interest.

Table 7.2.17 – Used to calculate the interest rate for a series of annuity payments (an) to pay off the loan or mortgage amount (pr) at a given period (per). Annuity payments are usually on a monthly or yearly frequency. This table can be used for both frequencies. The period (per) and (in%) should reflect the correct values for each.

Table 7.2.18 – Used to calculate the mortgage or loan amount (pr) one can afford given the period (per), the annuity payment (an), and the interest rate.

Table 7.2.19 – Used to calculate the annuity payment (an) for a given period (per), mortgage or loan amount (pr), and the interest rate.

Table 7.2.20 – Used to calculate the amortization table after solving a Type II Class B problem.

Table 7.2.21 – Used to calculate the amortization table after solving a Type II Class B problem for any range of amortization period.

Table 7.2.16 Type II, Class B.1 financial problem.
(Sample problem, use P/Yr = C/Yr = 12).

per	(I/Yr) or (in%)	pr	an(E)
61.02	8.00 (I/Yr)	5,000.00	-100.00

Table 7.2.17 Type II, Class B.2 financial problem.
(Sample problem, use P/Yr = C/Yr = 12).

per	(I/Yr) or (in%)	pr	an(E)
36.00	5.06 (I/Yr)	5,000.00	–150.00

Table 7.2.18 Type II, Class B.3 financial problem.
(Sample problem, use P/Yr = C/Yr = 12).

per	(I/Yr) or (in%)	pr	an(E)
48.00	6.00 (I/Yr)	4,258.03	–100.00

Table 7.2.19 Type II, Class B.4 financial problem.
(Sample problem, use P/Yr = C/Yr = 12).

per	(I/Yr) or (in%)	pr	an(E)
48.00	6.00 (I/Yr)	10,000.00	–234.85

Table 7.2.20 Amortization table - Distribution of annuity payment made at the end of each period. (Example, distribution of $435.70 monthly payment for $22,537 loan at 6% interest rate and 5-year term with payments made at the end of each period. Sample problem, use P/Yr = C/Yr = 12).

per	principal	principal payment	interest payment	principal balance
1.00	22,537.00	-323.01	-112.69	22,213.99
1				
2				
3				
4				
5				
6				
7				
8				
9				
10				
.				
.				
n				

Table 7.2.21 Total principal and interest payments for a range of period. (Example, total principal and interest payments from periods 1-60 for $22,537 loan at 6% interest rate, 5-year term and $435.70 monthly payment. Sample problem, use P/Yr = C/Yr = 12).

per	principal	total principal payment	total interest payment	principal balance
1-60	22,537.00	-22,536.76	-3,605.24	0.24

CHILDREN'S EDUCATION

In this sub-section, the templates in the order presented will lead to calculating the lump-sum payment, annuity payment, or a combination of both to finance the education of your child.

An example problem is used for Tables 7.2.22 – 7.2.26. The first row for each of these tables shows the TVM parameters to solve the example problem.

Recall in Section 2.5, we covered an example problem where the effect of inflation on the calculations was considered. The following templates are patterned after this example. They should be used in the order presented.

Table 7.2.22 – Used to calculate the present value (pr) of the education fund given:

per	=	years in university or college
I/Yr or in%	=	nominal interest rate
an(B)	=	yearly education cost at beginning of each period
pr	=	?, calculate present value

The calculated present value is the total education fund that would be required if the child were to start university *today*. However, since the child will be starting university several years from now, you need to calculate the fund's *future* value. The next calculation should take into account the inflation rate. The period to be used is the years until the child starts university. Therefore, to calculate the future value, use Table 7.2.23.

per	=	period until start of post-secondary education
I/Yr or in%	=	rate of inflation
pr	=	present value calculated from Table 7.2.22
fu	=	?, calculate future value

The calculated future value from Table 7.2.23 will then be used to estimate the lump-sum payment, annuity payment (yearly or monthly) or a combination of both in order to accumulate the future value. Use Table 7.2.24. Note that the (I/Yr) or (in%) to be used is the nominal interest rate that money earns, since inflation has already been taken into account in the calculated future value.

per	=	period until start of post-secondary education
I/Yr or in%	=	nominal interest rate
fu	=	future value calculated from Table 7.2.23
pr	=	?, calculate present value of lump-sum payment

Note that for annuity payment calculation, the same Table 7.2.25 can be used to calculate monthly or yearly payments. Appropriate values should be used for period (per) and (in%).

per	=	period until start of post-secondary education
I/Yr or in%	=	nominal interest rate
fu	=	future value calculated from Table 7.2.23
an	=	?, calculate annuity payment; an (E) or an(B)

If a savings fund has already been started, the problem becomes a Type III Class D.5 problem. To calculate the annuity payment, use Table 7.2.26.

per	=	period until start of post-secondary education
I/Yr or in%	=	nominal interest rate
pr	=	present value of existing education fund
fu	=	future value calculated from Table 7.2.23
an	=	?, calculate annuity payment; an (E) or an(B)

For planning purposes, you may want to repeat the above calculations using a shorter period to show what would happen if you delay implementing the savings plan. The smaller value for the period will result in a larger lump-sum payment and larger annuity payments to attain the required future value of the education fund.

Example,

You would like to start an education fund for your daughter and would like to know your options in saving for the education fund. The child will be attending university 10 years from now and you would like to prepare an education fund for the child's four years in university. It currently costs $12,000.00 per year to put a student through university, including tuition, board, lodging, and pocket money. If the rate of inflation is 3% and money earns interest at the rate of 8% both compounded monthly, what is the lump-sum payment that needs to be set aside now (Table 7.2.24)? What is the payment required at the beginning of each month (Table 7.2.25)? What is the monthly beginning-of-period payment if the savings plan has already been started and the current amount is $5,000.00 (Table 7.2.26)?

Table 7.2.22 Present value calculation. Type II, Class B.3 financial problem. (Sample problem, use P/Yr = 1, C/Yr = 12).

per	(I/Yr) or (in%)	pr	an(B)
4.00	8.00 (I/Yr)	42,758.55	-12,000.00

Table 7.2.23 Future value calculation. Type I, Class A.4 financial problem. (Sample problem, use P/Yr = 1, C/Yr = 12).

per	(I/Yr) or (in%)	pr	fu
10.00	3.00 (I/Yr)	–42,758.55	57,696.40

Table 7.2.24 Lump-sum calculation. Type I, Class A.3 financial problem. (Sample problem, use P/Yr = 1, C/Yr = 12).

per	(I/Yr) or (in%)	pr	fu
10.00	8.00 (I/Yr)	–25,993.58	57,696.40

Table 7.2.25 Type II, Class C.4 financial problem. (Sample problem, use P/Yr = C/Yr = 12).

per	(I/Yr) or (in%)	fu	an
120.00	8.00 (I/Yr)	57,696.40	–313.29 (an(B))

Table 7.2.26 Type III, Class D.5 financial problem.
(Sample problem, use P/Yr = C/Yr = 12).

per	(I/Yr) or (in%)	pr	fu	an
120.00	8.00 (I/Yr)	-5,000.00	57,696.40	-253.02 (an(B))

RETIREMENT

As in the previous subsection, you can use these templates, in the order presented, to calculate the lump-sum payment, annuity payment or a combination of both to finance your retirement.

An example problem is used for Tables 7.2.27 – 7.2.31. The first row for each of these tables shows the TVM parameters to solve the problem. Another example is used for Tables 7.2.32 – 7.2.34.

The first step is to determine, in today's dollars, your required monthly or yearly retirement income. The retirement income is the annuity payment amount (an). Next, decide how long a retirement period you wish to fund. This is the period (per). If annuity is on a monthly basis, the period should be the total number of months. If the annuity is on a yearly basis, the period should be the total number of years. The interest rate to be used is the rate at which money earns interest. Use Table 7.2.27. Depending on the financial calculator you are using, you will need to enter either (I/Yr) or (in%). See Section 3.2, Table 3.2.4 for reference.

Table 7.2.27 – Used to calculate the present value (pr) of the retirement fund given:

per	=	retirement period
I/Yr or in%	=	nominal interest rate
an	=	annuity payment retirement income
pr	=	?, calculate present value

The next step is to calculate the future value (fu) of the retirement fund when you start retirement. The interest rate to be used is the rate of inflation. Use Table 7.2.28.

per	=	period until start of retirement
I/Yr or in%	=	rate of inflation
pr	=	present value calculated from Table 7.2.27
fu	=	?, calculate future value

Using the calculated future value, you can determine the required lump-sum payment, yearly, and monthly payments to accumulate the required retirement fund. Table 7.2.29 is used to calculate the lump-sum payment. Table 7.2.30 is used to calculate annuity payment (either monthly or yearly). The interest rate to be used is the nominal rate, the rate at which money earns interest. Thus, for Table 7.2.29,

per	=	period until start of retirement
I/Yr or in%	=	nominal interest rate
fu	=	future value calculated from Table 7.2.28
pr	=	?, calculate present value of lump-sum payment

Table 7.2.30 is used to calculate annuity payment (monthly or yearly). The interest rate to be used is the nominal rate, the rate at which money earns interest.

per	=	period until start of retirement
I/Yr or in%	=	nominal interest rate
fu	=	future value calculated from Table 7.2.28
an	=	?, calculate annuity payment; an(E) or an(B)

If a retirement savings fund has already been started you need to include the present value of this fund in calculating the annuity payments. The TVM problem becomes a Type III Class D.5 problem. Use Table 7.2.31.

Table 7.2.31 – Used to calculate the annuity payment (an) given:

per	=	period until start of retirement
I/Yr or in%	=	nominal interest rate
pr	=	present value of existing retirement fund
fu	=	future value calculated from Table 7.2.28
an	=	?, calculate annuity payment; an(E) or an(B)

This is what I can afford to save

The question you answered using the preceding templates was, "How much should I save if I require this much retirement income?" We started by identifying the retirement income required, then we calculated the lump-sum or annuity payments needed to accumulate a fund sufficient to provide that income. Now let's look at the problem from the other side.

You have already started a retirement fund, either with a lump-sum payment and/or with annuity payments. You want to find out what is the annuity retirement payment in today's dollars that you can expect during your retirement years.

This time you are saying in effect, "This is what I can afford to save; how much retirement income can I expect?"

The first step is to calculate the future value of the retirement fund. Use Table 7.2.32.

per	=	period until start of retirement
I/Yr or in%	=	nominal interest rate
pr	=	present value of existing retirement fund
an	=	annuity payment towards retirement fund; an(E) or an(B)
fu	=	?, calculate future value

The next step is to calculate the present value (pr) of the retirement fund when you start retirement. Use Table 7.2.33.

per = period until start of retirement
I/Yr or in% = rate of inflation
fu = future value calculated from Table 7.2.32
pr = ?, calculate present value

Finally, the last step is to calculate the annuity payments during your retirement years. Calculate the annuity payment (an) given the retirement period (per), the present value calculated from Table 7.2.33, and the nominal interest rate. Use Table 7.2.34.

per = retirement period
I/Yr or in% = nominal interest rate
pr = present value of retirement fund calculated from Table 7.2.33
an = ?, calculate annuity payment; an(E) or an(B)

Example, (first approach: calculating payments given required retirement income)

You would like to prepare for retirement by setting up a fund from which you can draw income during your retirement years. You would like to retire 35 years from now and you would like the fund to provide $3,000 monthly retirement income for 20 years. If the inflation rate is 3% and money earns 8%, what is the lump-sum payment that needs to be set aside now (Table 7.2.29)? What is the monthly payment required at the beginning of each month (Table 7.2.30) if interest is compounded monthly? What is the monthly payment for beginning-of-period payment if the retirement savings plan has already been started and the current amount is $10,000.00 (Table 7.2.31)?

Table 7.2.27 Present value calculation. Type II, Class B.3 financial problem. (Sample problem, use P/Yr = C/Yr = 12).

per	(I/Yr) or (in%)	pr	an(B)
240.00	8.00 (I/Yr)	-361,053.96	3,000.00

Table 7.2.28 Future value calculation. Type I, Class A.4 financial problem. (Sample problem, use P/Yr = 1, C/Yr = 12).

per	(I/Yr) or (in%)	pr	fu
35.00	3.00 (I/Yr)	–361,053.96	1,030,415.20

Table 7.2.29 Lump-sum calculation. Type I, Class A.3 financial problem. (Sample problem, use P/Yr = 1, C/Yr = 12).

per	(I/Yr) or (in%)	pr	fu
35.00	8.00 (I/Yr)	–63,244.56	1,030,415.20

Table 7.2.30 Type II, Class C.4 financial problem. (Sample problem, use P/Yr = C/Y r = 12).

per	(I/Yr) or (in%)	fu	an
420.00	8.00 (I/Yr)	1,030,415.20	–446.23 (an(B))

Table 7.2.31 Type III, Class D.5 financial problem. (Sample problem, use beginning-of-period payments. P/Yr = C/Yr = 12).

per	(I/Yr) or (in%)	pr	fu	an
420.00	8.00 (I/Yr)	–10,000.00	1,030,415.20	–375.67 (an(B))

Example, (second approach: calculating retirement income from given payments)

You have already started a retirement savings account. It is currently worth $50,000.00 and you expect to be able to make monthly payments of $500.00 at the beginning of each month until you retire. You expect to retire in 30 years. How much monthly retirement income can you expect for 20 years if inflation is 3% and money earns interest at 8% (Table 7.2.34)? Assume interest compounding is monthly.

Table 7.2.32 Type III, Class D.4 financial problem.
(Sample problem, use P/Yr = C/Yr = 12).

per	(I/Yr) or (in%)	pr	fu	an
360.00	8.00 (I/Yr)	-50,000.00	1,296,934.07	-500.00 (an(B))

Table 7.2.33 Type I, Class A.3 financial problem.
(Sample problem, use P/Yr = C/Yr = 12).

per	(I/Yr) or (in%)	pr	fu
360.00	3.00 (I/Yr)	-527,886.60	1,296,934.07

Table 7.2.34 Type II, Class B.4 financial problem.
(Sample problem, use P/Yr = C/Yr = 12).

per	(I/Yr) or (in%)	pr	an
240.00	8.00 (I/Yr)	-527,886.60	4,386.21 (an(B))

INVESTMENT DECISION MAKING

Discounted Cash Flow (Type IV)

Refer to Section 2.7 for several examples of how to use the DCF method for investment decision making. See also Table 7.2.14 for an example calculation.

Cash flows — whether lump-sum payments or series of annuity payments (including $0) — with their corresponding frequencies, should be entered in the financial calculator. Two parameters are calculated using the DCF method. One is the NPV or net present value and the other is IRR, or internal rate of return. The calculation for NPV requires the periodic interest rate (in%) to be entered in the calculator except for HP 10B which requires entry of nominal interest rate (I/YR). The calculated IRR is the rate at which the investor's objective is exactly met, or NPV = 0. Refer to the discussion on problems with IRR calculation in Section 2.7.

Table 7.2.35 DCF problem

cash flow	frequency
CF0 =	
CF1 =	N1 =
CF2 =	N2 =
CF3 =	N3 =
CF4 =	N4 =
CF5 =	N5 =
CF6 =	N6 =
CF7 =	N7 =
CF8 =	N8 =
CF. =	N. =
CF. =	N. =
CFi =	Ni =
(in%) =	NPV =
	IRR =

cash flow	frequency
CF0 =	
CF1 =	N1 =
CF2 =	N2 =
CF3 =	N3 =
CF4 =	N4 =
CF5 =	N5 =
CF6 =	N6 =
CF7 =	N7 =
CF8 =	N8 =
CF. =	N. =
CF. =	N. =
CFi =	Ni =
(in%) =	NPV =
	IRR =

Continued, Table 7.2.35

cash flow	frequency
CF0 =	
CF1 =	N1 =
CF2 =	N2 =
CF3 =	N3 =
CF4 =	N4 =
CF5 =	N5 =
CF6 =	N6 =
CF7 =	N7 =
CF8 =	N8 =
CF. =	N. =
CF. =	N. =
CFi =	Ni =
(in%) =	NPV =
	IRR =

cash flow	frequency
CF0 =	
CF1 =	N1 =
CF2 =	N2 =
CF3 =	N3 =
CF4 =	N4 =
CF5 =	N5 =
CF6 =	N6 =
CF7 =	N7 =
CF8 =	N8 =
CF. =	N. =
CF. =	N. =
CFi =	Ni =
(in%) =	NPV =
	IRR =

7.3
ANSWERS TO SHORT QUIZ ON PERSONAL FINANCE LITERACY

1. The single most important concept that allows any item to be accepted as money is the special quality of acceptability. We have faith in it, we believe in it. People will accept any form of money because they know others will.

2. False. Since 1971, the world's monetary system has consisted of national fiat currencies linked by floating exchange rates set in the market. Today, currencies of most countries are no longer backed by gold reserves.

3. The five basic parameters involved when analyzing financial problems are Period (per), Interest Rate (I/Yr, in, or in%), Present Value (pr), Future Value (fu) and Annuity payments (an).

4. The four basic types of financial problems are: Type I - single lump-sum payment problems, Type II - series of equal payment problems, Type III - combination of single lump-sum and series of equal payment problems, and Type IV - combination of several lump-sum and several series of equal payment problems.

5. Present value (pr) and future value (fu).

6. False. Interest can be compounded at a frequency different from the loan payment frequency. An excellent example is the Canadian mortgage, where payments are made monthly and interest is compounded semi-annually.

7. False. Interest on Canadian mortgages is compounded semi-annually.

For 12 days' work in the 1978 film Superman, *Marlon Brando was paid $3.7 million US plus $15 million in royalties. This was about $1.5 million US per day.*

8. False. The real rate of return that the borrower is expecting for lending you money is just one of the components of the interest rate. The other two components are the rate of return to cover for inflation and the rate of return to cover for default or delinquent loans.

9. True. The effective interest is generally higher than the nominal interest rate, except for the case where (C/Yr) = 1; in that case, nominal interest rate (I/Yr) = effective interest (Eff/Yr).

10. False. For TVM and DCF applications, *annuity* payments refer to series of payments made at regular periods: daily, weekly, monthly, semi-annually, etc..

11. True. Annuity payments cannot be made at irregular periods for TVM applications. Annuity payments are made at regular intervals; either at the beginning or at the end of each period.

12. False. The last Great Inflation, which spanned more than 20 years started in the mid-1960s. In the US, it received initial stimulus from the spending spree which resulted from the Vietnam War.

13. The other measure of inflation is the rate of decrease of the value of money. For example, $1 US in 1900 was worth $0.06 in 1993. It is however, more common to measure inflation by how much the price of goods increases over time.

14. False. One merely needs a financial calculator, which is very affordable, in order to generate an amortization table. Most TVM calculations use exponential and natural logarithmic functions and some calculations require the iterative procedure. The user need not worry about these functions, which are built in to the financial calculator.

15. First, calculate the future value of $5,000 for the two periods 40 and 30 years, at 8% per year compounded yearly. The difference of the two future values is the amount of money you will lose if you delay the investment. For the period 40 years, the future value (fu) = $108,622.61. For period 30 years, the future value (fu) = $50,313.28. The difference therefore is $58,309.33.

16. False. As financial calculators have built-in financial functions, they can solve financial problems with great ease. Scientific calculators can also solve the same problems, but are very cumbersome and impractical to use in this way.

MRI or Magnetic Resonance Imaging is a diagnostic tool used in the medical field to provide detailed images of organs and structures within the body without radiation exposure or invasive procedures. The required magnetic fields come from expensive helium-cooled superconducting magnets, which makes the machines cost between $1 to $2 million US.

17. True. Although all financial calculators will solve the same financial problems, the data entry for interest rate is different. Some use the nominal interest rate (I/Yr) while others use the periodic interest in percent (in%). There is one calculator that uses solar cells for power while all the others use batteries. Some are capable of performing discounted cash flow (DCF) analysis while others are not. There are other capabilities that are available in some calculators but are not available in others. Tables 3.2.1-3.2.5 compare the six financial calculators covered in this book.

18. The rule of 72 came about by solving a Type I, Class A.1 financial problem. The period (per) is calculated for various interest rates (for example 5% to 15%) at a fixed present value (say, (pr) = $100) and a fixed future value (of twice that amount (fu) = -$200). Then, for each calculation, determine (per) x (I/Yr). The average value for (per) x (I/Yr) is approximately equal to 72. Therefore, the rule can be derived: To estimate how long it will take to double your initial investment, divide 72 by the annual interest rate.

19. $100.

20. Time value of money (TVM) problems involve financial problems that can include only one lump-sum payment and only one series of annuity payments. Discounted cash flow (DCF) problems, on the other hand, can include several lump-sum payments and several series of annuity payments, including annuity payments of $0.

21. NPV (net present value) and IRR (internal rate of return). An investment is worth pursuing if NPV calculates to a positive value for the required rate of return. A value of zero (0) for NPV indicates the investment revenue target is exactly met for the required rate of return. IRR is the rate of return required so that NPV = 0.

22. 1) the lump-sum payment method, 2) the annuity payment method, 3) the combination of lump-sum and annuity payment method; and 4) the discounted cash flow (DCF) method, which involves calculating NPV and then calculating the Net Future Value.

23. The lump-sum payment method. This method requires the lowest total investment of money for the same future value of the savings fund. It is the interest-earning power of the lump-sum payment over time that makes this possible. This is what is meant by the *time value of money*.

24. Beginning-of-period annuity payments made on a less frequent basis.

25. The US government deliberately sent the economy into a deep recession. This policy did control inflation, but was not a popular policy for the political incumbents as none were prepared to risk the political consequences of such a cure.

According to the United States Office of Consumer Affairs, by the year 2000, travel and tourism will be the largest industry in the United States.

26. Yes, DCF is a specialized application of TVM. In fact, NPV, which is one of the parameters calculated by the DCF method, can be solved by successive applications of the TVM method on Type I Class A.3 problems. Summing up the individual present values that were calculated by the TVM method gives the identical NPV to that calculated by DCF. It will require trial and error to calculate IRR using TVM analysis. One will need to find I/Yr so that NPV = 0.

27. There may be as many solutions for IRR as there are sign changes. However, for NPV, there is one and only one answer for every cash flow problem.

28. False. When solving TVM and DCF problems using a financial calculator, entering the signs of the cash flow values is important. A positive cash flow indicates cash received while a negative cash flow indicates cash paid out. The Texas Instruments BA-35 financial calculator follows different conventions. See note 4 under Table 3.4.1.

29. The final answer is $441.17 per month. Step 1 is to calculate the present value of the required monthly retirement income in today's dollars (Type II, Class B.3 financial problem; see Table 7.3.1). Step 2 is to calculate the future value of the present value calculated in Step 1 with inflation taken into account (see Table 7.3.2). Finally, the last step is to calculate the annuity payment (see Table 7.3.3).

Table 7.3.1 Step 1, Present value of $3,000 monthly retirement income taking into account 2% inflation compounded monthly; money earns 8% interest, compounded monthly. Payments are made at the beginning of each period. Type II, Class B.3 financial problem. (P/Yr = C/Yr = 12).

per	I/Yr	pr	an(B)
300.00	8.00	-391,284.86	3,000.00

Table 7.3.2 Step 2, Future value of $467,948.97 due to 2% inflation compounded monthly.
Type I, Class A.4 financial problem. (P/Yr = 1, C/Yr = 12).

per	I/Yr	pr	fu
12.00	2.00	-391,284.86	497,321.18

The Edison Lamp Works manufactured the first electric light bulbs in October 1880. They were manufactured by hand, undergoing up to 200 stages of the manufacturing process. This brought up the cost of each bulb to $2.50 each.

Table 7.3.3 Step 3, Monthly payments (an) made at end of each period required to accumulate $497,321.18 in 12 years, at 8% interest compounded monthly. Type III, Class D.5 financial problem. (P/Yr = C/Yr = 12).

per	I/Yr	pr	fu	an(B)
144.00	8.00	−150,000.00	497,321.18	−441.17

Thus, the answer is $441.17.

30. For a $95,000 mortgage amortized over 20 years at 9% interest rate compounded semi-annually, the monthly payment is $844.73.

Table 7.3.4 Type II, Class B.4 financial problem. (P/Yr = 12, C/Yr = 2).

per	(I/Yr)	pr	an(E)
20 x 12	9.00	95,000.00	−844.73

At the end of five years, the mortgage principal balance is calculated using the amortization function of the financial calculator. The answer is $84,092.99.

Table 7.3.5 Total principal and interest paid and principal balance after five years.

per	principal	total principal payment	total interest payment	principal balance
1–60	95,000.00	−10,907.01	−39,776.79	84,092.99

Note that, as was shown in Chapter 3, not all financial calculators gave the same final value. See Table 2.4.14 and corresponding Chapter 3 tables.

The new term is for 15 years amortization with 10% interest. The new monthly payment is $893.29.

Table 7.3.6 Type II, Class B.4 financial problem. (P/Yr = 12, C/Yr = 2).

per	(I/Yr)	pr	an(E)
15 x 12	10.00	84,092.99	−893.29

Microsoft's annual revenue is $13 billion US (1997).

At the above payment schedule, the total payments (principal + interest) = $893.29 x 15 x 12 = $160,792.20. Therefore, total interest = $160,792.20 – $84,092.99 = $76,699.21. If the monthly payment is increased by $50 to $943.29, the payment period will be shorter than 15 years and therefore less interest to pay. Let us calculate the period required to pay off the principal with $943.29 monthly payment.

Table 7.3.7 Type II, Class B.1 financial problem. (P/Yr = 12, C/Yr = 2)

per	(I/Yr)	pr	an(E)
160.06	10.00	84,092.99	-943.29

Thus, total payments (principal + interest) = $943.29 x 160.06 = $150,983.00. Therefore, total interest = $150,983.00 – $84,092.99 = $66,890.01. Total interest savings therefore is $76,699.21 – $66,890.01 = $9,809.20.

Another way of reducing the interest is to reduce the amortization period. If instead of 15 years, the amortization is 10 years, the new monthly payment is $1,101.90.

Table 7.3.8 Type II, Class B.4 financial problem. (P/Yr = 12, C/Yr = 2)

per	(I/Yr)	pr	an(E)
10 x 12	10.00	84,092.99	-1,101.90

The total payments = $1,101.90 x 120 = $132,228.00. Total interest = $132,228.00 – $84,092.99 = $48,135.01. Therefore, total interest savings compared to the regular 15-year amortization = $76,699.21 – $48,135.01 = $28,564.20.

Another way to reduce interest is to reduce the principal by $5,000 to $79,092.99. At 10% interest and 15-year amortization, the monthly payment is $840.18.

Table 7.3.9 Type II, Class B.4 financial problem. (P/Yr = 12, C/Yr = 2)

per	(I/Yr)	pr	an(E)
15 x 12	10.00	79,092.99	-840.18

The total payments = $840.18 x 15 x 12 = $151,232.40. Total interest = $151,232.40 – $79,092.99 = $72,139.41. Therefore, total interest savings compared to the regular 15-year amortization = $76,699.21 – $72,139.41 = $4,559.80.

Ted Turner announced in 1997 that he was donating $1 billion US to the charities of the United Nations.

31. Answer: $324.56.

Table 7.3.10 Step 1. Type II, Class B.3 financial problem.
P/Yr = 1, C/Yr = 12.

per	I/Yr	pr	an(B)
4.00	8.00	46,321.76	–13,000.00

Table 7.3.11 Step 2. Type I, Class A.4 financial problem.
P/Yr = 1, C/Yr = 12.

per	I/Yr	pr	fu
9.00	3.00	–46,321.76	60,659.42

Table 7.3.12 Step 3. Type II, Class C.4 financial problem.
P/Yr = C/Yr = 12.

per	I/Yr	pr	fu	an(B)
9 x 12	8.00	–4,500.00	60,659.42	–324.56

If the education fund is delayed by 5 years, with all other parameters the same: Step 1 is the same as above.

Table 7.3.13 Step 2. Type I, Class A.4 financial problem.
P/Yr = 1, C/Yr = 12.

per	I/Yr	pr	fu
4.00	3.00	–46,321.76	52,219.82

Table 7.3.14 Step 3. Type II, Class C.4 financial problem.
P/Yr = C/Yr = 12.

per	I/Yr	pr	fu	an(B)
4 x 12	8.00	–4,500.00	52,219.82	–811.44

Thus, the new monthly savings amount is $811.44.

32. False. TVM and DCF analysis methods can only provide estimates to your personal finance problems — for two basic reasons. First, in TVM and DCF methods, interest rates are assumed over the entire period. However, we all know that interest rates vary daily. This is why, to get the most out of TVM and DCF analyses, you need to revisit the calculations. Secondly, rounding off TVM parameter values can result in calculating very different values for, say, the amortization examples. As explained in Chapter 3, not all financial calculators provide identical calculated values, because they use different rounding-off procedures. Financial institutions will also have different procedures so that what you calculate on a financial calculator may not be the same as calculated by the bank. You should look at TVM and DCF methods as estimation tools that can help you make intelligent personal finance decisions.

33. By redoing the calculations at least once a year.

The St. Louis-based X Prize Foundation is offering a $10 million US prize for the first space vehicle that can transport three adults 62 miles above the earth, make two flights in two weeks, and land intact. There are currently 16 groups trying for the prize.

7.4 NOMENCLATURE

an	Annuity payment
an(B)	Annuity payment made at beginning of each period
an(E)	Annuity payment made at end of each period
APR	Annual Percentage Rate or nominal interest rate
2nd, APR	Annual Percentage Rate calculator keys for TI BA–35
2nd F, APR	Annual Percentage Rate calculator keys for Sharp EL–733A and EL–735
SHIFT **, APR**	Annual Percentage Rate calculator keys for Casio FC–100
B	Beginning–of–period annuity payment
C/Yr	Interest Compounding per year
C/Y	Interest Compounding per year calculator key label for TI BA II Plus
CF0	Initial Cash flow for DCF analysis
CFi	i^{th} Cash flow for DCF analysis
COMP	Sharp EL–733A and EL–735, and Casio FC–100 first calculator key to press to calculate a TVM parameter (second calculator key)
CPT	TI BA II Plus and TI BA–35 first calculator key to press to calculate a TVM parameter (second calculator key)
DCF	Discounted Cash Flow

E	End-of-period annuity payment (ordinary annuity)
EFF	Effective interest rate; Effective interest rate calculator key label for Casio FC-100
■, EFF%	Effective interest rate calculator keys for HP 10B
2nd, EFF	Effective interest rate calculator keys for TI BA-35
2nd F, EFF	Effective interest rate calculator keys for Sharp EL-733A and EL-735
Eff/Yr	Effective interest per year
fu	Future value
FV	Future value calculator key label for TI BA II Plus, TI BA-35, HP 10B, Sharp EL-733A, Sharp EL-735, and Casio FC-100
i	Periodic interest rate calculator key label for Sharp EL-733A and EL-735
i%	Periodic interest rate calculator key label for Casio FC-100
%i	Periodic interest rate calculator key label for TI BA-35
in	Periodic interest
in%	Periodic interest in percent
IRR	Internal Rate of Return
I/Y	Interest per year calculator key label for TI BA II Plus
I/Yr	Nominal Interest per year in percent; Interest per year calculator key label for HP 10B
$(I/Yr)_{adj}$	Adjusted Nominal Interest per year in percent
n	used in cash flow diagrams to denote period; also Period calculator key label for Sharp EL-733A, Sharp EL-735, and Casio FC-100
N	Period calculator key label for TI BA II Plus, TI BA-35 and HP 10B
Ni	Frequency of ith Cash flow group for DCF analysis

■, NOM%	Annual Percentage Rate calculator keys for HP 10B
NPV	Net Present Value
PMT	Annuity payment value calculator key label for TI BA II Plus, TI BA–35, HP 10B, Sharp EL–733A, Sharp EL–735, and Casio FC–100
PV	Present value calculator key label for TI BA II Plus, TI BA–35, HP 10B, Sharp EL–733A, Sharp EL–735, and Casio FC–100
P/Yr	Payment per year; Payment per year calculator key label for HP 10B
P/Y	Payment per year calculator key label for TI BA II Plus
per	Period
PRIN	Principal
pr	Present value
TVM	Time Value of Money
Yr	Year
+/–	change sign of value in the calculator display
x	multiplication symbol
÷	division symbol
+	addition symbol
–	subtraction symbol
*	Display symbol used by TI BA II Plus to indicate valid calculated value in a worksheet

Only about 2,000 women in the world buy haute couture — made–to–measure clothes using the most expensive fabrics by designers such as Yves Saint Laurent, Chanel, Givenchy and Versace. In 1998, starting prices are about $10,000 US for a suit and up to $100,000 for an evening gown.

8

INDEX

A

B

C

D

E

Reader's Response Form

Please complete this form and return to **Personal Finance Solutions** to help us improve on the book. Your comments and suggestions are appreciated.

Rate the book in regards to its informational content *(5 is the best)*:

Completeness	1	2	3	4	5	Ease of understanding	1	2	3	4	5
Accuracy	1	2	3	4	5	Useful examples	1	2	3	4	5
Systematic	1	2	3	4	5	Useful procedures	1	2	3	4	5
Ease of reading	1	2	3	4	5	Overall rating	1	2	3	4	5
Ease of finding	1	2	3	4	5						

1. Did you find the information you were looking for? If not, what is missing?
   ____

2. Do we need to add more examples? If so, in which chapter or section?
   ____

3. Did you have difficulty understanding the discussions and examples? If so, where?
   ____

4. Which was the most helpful section? The most important section?
   ____

5. Which features of the book did you find excellent?
   ____

6. If you found any errors in the book, please provide relevant information.
   ____

7. Which areas in the book can we still improve upon?
   ____

Have you ever used a financial calculator?

____________ Never
____________ Occasionally
____________ Always

What is your background in personal finance?

____________ Beginner
____________ Intermediate
____________ Advanced

Name: ______________________________________

Company Name: ______________________________

Address: ____________________________________

City: ____________________ State/Province ____________________

Zip/Postal: ______________ Country: ____________________

Telephone (______) ______________

If this is a library copy, please photocopy this Reader Response Form.

Book Order Form

Price: $29.95 Canadian ($19.95 US)

Please send ______ copy(ies) of *Control Your Personal Finances*
Plus shipping: $9.50 Canadian or $7.50 US for orders of 5 books or less (free shipping for orders of 6 or more books)
Canadian Orders, please add 7% GST

Work on one column only, *$Canadian* or *$US* column.

	Item	$ Canadian	$US
Book Price	A	$29.95	$19.95
Subtotal = No. of copies x Item A	B		
Shipping Price: (select one only) ▸ 1–5 books ($9.50 Cdn, $7.50 US) ▸ 6 or more books (free, $0)	C		
Subtotal = Item B + Item C	D		
Orders in Canada; add 7% GST Item D x 0.07	E		$0.00
Total: Item D + Item E	F		

Company Name: ______________________________

Name: ______________________________

Address: ______________________________

City: ____________________ State/Province: ____________________

Zip/Postal: ______________ Country: ____________________

Telephone: (______) ______________

Payment: Money Order enclosed ☐ Total Amount, from Item F above.

or VISA Number: ____________________ Expiry Date: ____________

Name on Card: ______________________________

Signature: ______________________________

Send Postal Orders to:

Personal Finance Solutions
2025 Guelph Line, Suite 236
Burlington, Ontario L7P 4X4
Canada

Phone No. (905) 331-0200
Fax No. (905) 331-0244

If this is a library copy, please photocopy this Book Order Form.

Seminar Manual Order Form

Price: $19.95 Canadian ($12.95 US)

Please send ______ copy(ies) of *Applications of Personal Finance*
Plus shipping: $9.00 Canadian or $7.00 US for orders of 5 manuals or less (free shipping for orders of 6 or more manuals)
Canadian Orders, please add 7% GST

Work on one column only, *$Canadian* or *$US* column.

	Item	$ Canadian	$US
Manual Price	A	$19.95	$12.95
Subtotal = No. of copies x Item A	B		
Shipping Price: (select one only) ▸ 1–5 manuals ($9.00 Cdn, $7.00 US) ▸ 6 or more manuals (free, $0)	C		
Subtotal = Item B + Item C	D		
Orders in Canada; add 7% GST Item D x 0.07	E		$0.00
Total: Item D + Item E	F		

Company Name: ______________________________

Name: ______________________________

Address: ______________________________

City: ____________________ State/Province: ____________________

Zip/Postal: ______________ Country: ____________________

Telephone: (______) ______________

Payment: Money Order enclosed ☐ Total Amount, from Item F above.

or VISA Number: ____________________ Expiry Date: ______________

Name on Card: ______________________________

Signature: ______________________________

Send Postal Orders to:

Personal Finance Solutions
2025 Guelph Line, Suite 236
Burlington, Ontario L7P 4X4
Canada

Phone No. (905) 331-0200
Fax No. (905) 331-0244

If this is a library copy, please photocopy this Seminar Manual Order Form.

Seminar/Presentation

Personal Finance Solutions presents the one-day seminar, *Applications of Personal Finance*, based on this book, *Control Your Personal Finances.*

Each attendee will be provided with a copy of *Control Your Personal Finances;* the seminar manual, *Applications of Personal Finance;* copies of the overheads used, *Summary Notes for Applications of Personal Finance;* and a financial calculator.

In addition to greatly simplifying the concepts being taught in this book, the seminar leader will be available to answer all your important questions.

The author is also available for one-hour or half-hour speaking engagements.

For inquiries:

Write to: **Personal Finance Solutions**
2025 Guelph Line, Suite 236
Burlington, Ontario L7P 4X4
Canada

Phone No. (905) 331-0200
Fax No. (905) 331-0244

PFS

Your key to financial success.

PFS Mission Statement

Realizing that the very first and most important step to taking control of your financial future is to understand the basics of personal finance,

PFS therefore commits to:

- Deliver products that will raise the public's awareness of the basics of personal finance.
- Work with technical and professional associations, educational, public, and private institutions, and the general public to teach the basics of personal finance.
- Market PFS products on a global basis.

ABOUT THE AUTHOR

Elindoro Suarez Rodriguez II — Bob, for short — is a presenter and a seminar leader whose goal is to empower people to make informed financial decisions. A chemical engineer by education, he received a B.S. CHE degree from De La Salle University in Manila, Philippines and an M.S. CHE degree from the University of Notre Dame in Indiana, USA. By experience, he is an applications engineer in the field of computer process control. When he started to focus on his own financial future, he realized that his analytical and presentation skills could be put to good use to help people grasp the fundamentals of personal finance.

PFS

Your key to financial success.